D0411600

frenemies

t 8
x

ALSO BY KEN AULETTA

frenemies

The Epic Disruption of the Advertising Industry (and Why This Matters)

KEN AULETTA

HarperCollins*Publishers*

HarperCollins*Publishers*
1 London Bridge Street
London SE1 9GF

www.harpercollins.co.uk

First published in the US by Penguin Press 2018
This UK edition published by HarperCollins*Publishers* 2018

1 3 5 7 9 10 8 6 4 2

© Ken Auletta 2018

© Ken Auletta asserts the moral right to be
identified as the author of this work

A catalogue record of this book is
available from the British Library

HB ISBN 978-0-00-829698-8
TPB ISBN 978-0-00-829699-5

Printed and bound in Great Britain by
CPI Group (UK) Ltd, Croydon, CR0 4YY

All rights reserved. No part of this publication may be
reproduced, stored in a retrieval system, or transmitted,
in any form or by any means, electronic, mechanical,
photocopying, recording or otherwise, without the prior
written permission of the publishers.

MIX
Paper from
responsible sources
FSC
www.fsc.org FSC™ C007454

This book is produced from independently certified FSC™ paper
to ensure responsible forest management.

For more information visit: www.harpercollins.co.uk/green

For Matt and Sam

CONTENTS

INTRODUCTION

n a 1970 TV commercial, a group of child actors portraying Louis Armstrong, Fiorello La Guardia, and Barney Pressman as kids are sitting on a New York City stoop and asking each other what they hope to be one day. Armstrong says he wants to be a musician. La Guardia says he wants to be mayor of New York. The bespectacled Barney Pressman is quiet, so they prod him: "Whaddaya gonna be when you grow up, Barney?" Pausing to adjust his glasses, the future founder of Barneys clothing store says, "I don't know. But you'll all need clothing."

For more than three decades, in books and in my Annals of Communications pieces and profiles for *The New Yorker,* I have reported on the digital hurricane that has swept across the media industry. I have tried to "follow the money," to understand the source of the economic harm that has struck newspapers, magazines, television, and radio, all reeling from shrinking advertising revenue—revenue now fueling Google, Facebook, and a myriad of other new digital enterprises. You can almost hear the young Barney Pressman trilling the world, "You'll all need advertising and marketing."

Worldwide, advertising and marketing is variously said to be a $1 trillion to $2 trillion industry. Of that astronomical sum, roughly three quarters is categorized as marketing dollars. Often, rather than joining together the words *advertising* and *marketing*, we employ the shorthand, advertising. We do so because advertising is a more familiar term, and to utter both terms together is a mouthful. In fact, advertising and marketing are interchangeable. They take different forms, but each involves a sales pitch. A thirty-second TV ad or a full-page ad in a newspaper seeks to sell something, which is also a marketing pitch. A direct mail or newly designed brand name or email solicitation or giveaway coupon is listed as a marketing expenditure, but it's also an advertising sales pitch. So the two categories are really one.

Yet advertising and marketing, like the media industry it has long subsidized, is convulsed by change, struggling itself to figure out how to sell products on mobile devices without harassing consumers, how to reach a younger generation accustomed to dodging ads, how to capture consumer attention in an age where choices proliferate and a mass audience is rare.

In the course of my work as a journalist, I have tended to shift back and forth between the disrupters and the disrupted. My first book, *The Streets Were Paved with Gold*, published in 1978, chronicled how New York City had been hit by a Category 5 economic and social storm that shattered its manufacturing base and spurred the flight of its middle class. My focus on the people on the wrong end of change continued in 1981, in a three-part series in *The New Yorker* that grew into a book, *The Underclass*. A reporting sojourn to Wall Street in the mid-1980s resulted in *Greed and Glory on Wall Street*, a battlefield account of the corrosive greed that brought low Lehman Brothers, the oldest partnership on Wall Street, and signaled the Wall Street gluttony that produced insider trading scandals and would bear such disastrous fruit in 2008.

It's fair to say that at this point I was a naïf about the advertising industry's true economic power. That began to change in 1985, when I embarked on a nearly six-year odyssey through the world of network television while reporting my book *Three Blind Mice*, a report on how the three dominant television networks—CBS, NBC, and ABC—were being disrupted by a new technology, cable. Advertising was central to that story, for unlike cable, the networks were 100 percent reliant on advertising. And so when the estimable Tina Brown, the new editor of *The New Yorker*, offered a regular platform in the magazine, which she called the Annals of Entertainment, I demurred. I told her that in reporting *Three Blind Mice* I glimpsed how the world of media was being transformed, and so we needed a broader rubric—the Annals of Communications—because studios and publishers and television and digital companies were increasingly invading each other's turf.

Over the next quarter century, unsettling change was the subject of much of my work for the magazine and for my books, and the advertising industry was often a backdrop for the stories, and usually an underexplored one. I witnessed the flight of advertisers from old to new media with my reporting for *The New Yorker* about Google, which led to the book *Googled: The End of the World as We Know It*. The flight of advertisers from old to new media started in the late 1990s and accelerated in the new century, and its impact was hard to miss. Less obvious was the impact on the ad industry itself. In the public imagination, we were still in the age of Don Draper, but I began to see more and more clearly how this industry that had been intrinsic to the disruption of old media was itself facing fundamental challenges to its existence.

Trying to understand the media without understanding advertising and marketing, its fuel supply, is like trying to understand the auto industry without regard to fuel costs. A war correspondent would be derelict not to try to calculate whether General Patton had enough gas in his Third Army tanks to race across France in 1944 (he did not). But it's not merely that a reporter covering the communications business would be remiss not to follow the up to $2 trillion advertising and marketing sector; anyone who takes a moment to ponder this pool of money can't avoid the inescapable truth that capitalism could not exist without marketing. True, the force of marketing is often malign, seeking to manipulate the emotions of consumers. Readers of this book will, hopefully, share my rage at the many tricks marketers practice. But marketing has a purpose in a free society, and intellectual honesty compels us to recognize that those who sell products need a way to share information about them with consumers. In a non-state-dominated economy, advertising is the bridge between seller and buyer. It would seem an obvious statement, but I've found it bears repeating. And that bridge is teetering, jolted by consumers annoyed by intrusive ads yet dependent on them for "free" or subsidized media. In this sense, consumers are frenemies.

To dig deeper into this world is to realize that more is being disrupted here than the flow of marketing dollars. The agency edifice itself is being assaulted, as new rivals surface—tech and consulting and public relations and media platform companies—many of whom have long been allied with the agencies and claim still to be. A once comfortable agency business is now assailed by frenemies, companies that both compete and cooperate with them.

For many years, I examined advertising as an aspect of some other story I was telling. It crept up on me that there was much to be learned by turning that around and looking deeply into the advertising industry itself, and through it out onto the wider world—a world of artificial intelligence (AI) and algorithms and big data that raises fundamental issues, including issues of privacy, issues of whether the science of advertising can replace the art, whether relationships still matter, and where—and whether—citizens get their news.

This book is populated by characters who represent the points of tension within this world. You will meet artists like Bob Greenberg, founder of the R/GA agency, who rail at consummate executives like Martin Sorrell, CEO of WPP, the world's largest advertising and marketing holding company; the scientists, including the engineers at Facebook and IBM, who fervently believe in their machines; the clients, like Unilever's Keith Weed and GE's Beth Comstock and Linda Boff, who must wrestle with trust issues between clients and their agencies; and you will meet Michael Kassan, a charming man who relies on relationships to link the artists and managers and clients and scientists.

This book attempts to peer deeply into this world. I sought to step into the shoes of many important actors and frenemies in the marketing world, old and new, disrupters and disrupted alike. It is a world stocked with passionate and creative people, but it is also a world roiled by anxiety. Ultimately, this is a story of a world whose fate is imperiled, and why that fate matters to us all.

1.

THE "PERFECT STORM"

Characterizing the rebates as "criminal extortion," he said of the giant advertising holding companies, "At least four of them, maybe five, are doing this."

—Jon Mandel, March 2015 speech to the Association of National Advertisers

ormer advertising colleagues were shocked when Jon Mandel morphed into a whistle-blower. Mandel had been a member in good standing of the advertising establishment for nearly four decades, a former chief executive officer of media agency power-house MediaCom, a reasonably popular joke-cracking executive with a chubby, beardless face and a full head of dark hair. But he seemed a different person on March 4, 2015, when he stepped onstage before his former clients, the Association of National Advertisers, or ANA, at their annual Media Leadership Conference in Florida. He looked different to old colleagues. He was rail thin and almost completely bald, with a trim grey beard that gave him a severe, almost Mephistophelian look. Before the very advertisers that fund his former agency, Mandel trembled, knowing that former coworkers would "try to kill me professionally" when he accused them of corruption. Agencies, he declared, engaged in a "pervasive" practice of demanding "kickbacks" from media companies and platforms like magazines, newspapers, TV, radio, and Web sites in exchange for their ad dollars. "There are cases where there are rebates that should be going to clients that are instead going to agencies."

The assertion was atomic to this audience: the ANA represents about seven hundred companies, including Coca-Cola and Procter & Gamble, which spend more than $250 billion annually in the United States to advertise over ten thousand brands. Moreover, Mandel was placing a cloud over the many billions spent worldwide on marketing as well as advertising. Coupled with the ongoing disruption of the industry by Facebook and Google and the Internet, the controversy threatened to upend the flow of monies that finance the public's news and entertainment.

* * *

Wearing a dark suit and open-necked grey shirt, with tiny eyeglasses perched on his bald dome, Mandel spoke out against what he depicted as the rot in the agency world, the world in which he'd spent his entire career. Now, he and his marketing consulting firm, Dogsled Enterprises, were paid by the ANA to prosecute the case against agencies. Most of Mandel's career had been spent at Grey Advertising, and when WPP, the giant marketing holding company, acquired Grey in 2004 they retained MediaCom and he had served as CEO of this media-buying unit, reporting to GroupM global CEO Irwin Gotlieb.

The practice Mandel accused agencies of is common, and legal, in countries like Brazil and China. It once was common in France and Western Europe, before being declared illegal. Speaking in a high-pitched nasal voice, Mandel claimed that the practice had spread to the United States. The "kickbacks" or rebates, he said, come in several forms: in cash; in a gift of additional ad space that giant advertising holding companies hold on to and resell to other clients; in the form of promises of a larger future media buy in exchange for an ownership stake in the vendor by the agency; or "in the worst case," the agency resells the purchased ad time to the client and makes money on it. "Have you ever wondered why fees to agencies have gone down and yet the declared profits to these agencies are up?" Mandel asked the audience. He estimated that media and digital companies kick back 18 to 20 percent of the media buy to the agencies, and that the agencies hide kickbacks that total "well into nine figures across agencies."

Mandel's blast helped stoke "a perfect storm," in the words of Andrew Robertson, the CEO of the BBDO agency. Advertising clients were already uneasy with their advertising agencies. They had long complained about steep agency costs and a lack of transparency about how agencies made money. Clients were pleased that the agencies that dominated media buying had leverage over media platforms and could demand better terms, but they worried that agencies kept secrets from them. The trust issue was even more acute because advertising clients were under greater pressure to curb costs and were insecure about the digital disruption that shook the very foundations of their business— from smartphones that turned their banner and pop-up ads into annoyances; to ad-blocking software consumers were embracing to repel ads; to a younger generation grown accustomed to ad-free YouTube and Netflix, and to ad-skipping digital video recorders (DVRs). Mandel's allegations reinforced these anxieties.

His assertions were damning, but Mandel did not cite a single agency by name. In a presentation sweeping in its condemnation of agencies for their lack of transparency, he was hardly transparent himself. Not about the 18 to 20 percent kickbacks. Not about the figure of at least $100 million in kickbacks he said were collected by agencies. His clear implication was that most agencies were guilty.

When Mandel concluded his remarks, ANA CEO Bob Liodice came onstage and energetically shook his hand. "That was fascinating and frightening," he said, and was "very courageous." So, Liodice asked, "What should clients do to gain greater transparency?"

"You've got to go in somewhat doubtful."

"You're saying a prenup is not enough!" Liodice said.

"Yes, and beware: you've got to audit not just the agency but the holding company," Mandel declared.

The stakes are huge, for advertising and marketing dollars subsidize most media and Internet companies. Today, the amount of money spent on advertising and marketing is up to $2 trillion worldwide, says Pivotal Research Group senior analyst Brian Wieser, perhaps the industry's most widely respected marketing analyst. Based on a Publicis Groupe study, this estimate was backed by Maurice Levy, the CEO of Publicis, and separately by Adam Smith, GroupM's futures director, who says the estimate "is in the ballpark." WPP CEO Martin Sorrell insists the true number is close to $1 trillion. Irwin Gotlieb cautions that the figure could be higher, or lower, because these were "soft numbers," guestimates. For example, Sorrell's guess does not include marketing awards programs, free coupons, or marketing messages in McDonald's food tray liners; Wieser's guess does.

Over lunch some months later, Mandel sipped from a glass of Pellegrino and calmly described the changes in the business that had led to what he considers kickbacks. Agencies, he said, were once "a trusted adviser, just like your lawyer," and were paid a handsome 15 percent commission. But agencies became part of today's dominant advertising holding companies—UK-based WPP, U.S.-based Omnicom Group and the Interpublic Group (IPG), France-based Publicis and Havas, and Japan-based Dentsu. Two thirds of global ad expenditures flow through these six companies and through privately held Horizon Media. "What has happened is there is a certain need to grow to show increased profit year to year. At some point the agency business model changed because of the financial pressures. It wasn't just no more commissions. It was, 'I don't care how you make your money. You just better show me ten percent year to year.' They were incented financially to worry more about themselves." Over time, clients began to ask, "Is what you're recommending to me good because it will be great for my business? Or is it because you will be making more money?"

He characterized the rebates as "criminal extortion," and said of the major holding companies, "At least four of them, maybe five, are doing this." At lunch Mandel changed his estimate of the unit of money involved from millions to "billions," which did not inspire confidence. The one company he identified by name as guilty was WPP, for whom he worked before moving in 2006 to take a new job at Nielsen. WPP, he continued, "wanted me to actually set up the thing, ironically, that years later I'm now known for condemning: all those kickbacks. I said to Irwin [Gotlieb], who's a personal friend—though since March 'personal friend' is on the back burner . . . He wanted me to set this up, to basically take what was going on in Europe and bring it to the U.S. I said, 'That's not right.' He said, 'We need it to compete.'" His accusations, he admits, are "hard to prove. It's like sex crimes: 'He says, she says.'" Gotlieb flatly denies that he had ever encouraged Mandel to set up a rebate system at GroupM's MediaCom: "Not true. Find one person or one company who would support that statement!"

■ ■ ■

Michael Kassan was not in the audience when Mandel delivered his broadside, but when he saw the March 6 headline in *Advertising Age*—FORMER MEDIACOM CEO ALLEGES WIDESPREAD

U.S. AGENCY "KICKBACKS"—he knew it would ignite a wildfire. Kassan was troubled. "I felt like the ANA had endorsed his position without evidence," he says. But Kassan knew Mandel's assertions would "light a fuse," and the resulting blaze would produce new business firefighting opportunities for his company, MediaLink, for which he was grateful.

As the CEO of MediaLink, the company he founded in 2003, Kassan is arguably the supreme power broker in the advertising and marketing industry. With a staff of 120, MediaLink serves as a hub, linking clients like publishers who seek ad dollars with the agencies and brands that dispense them, and linking brand advertisers to new agencies. MediaLink's blue-chip client list includes Unilever, AT&T, L'Oréal, Bank of America, Colgate-Palmolive, American Express, NBCUniversal, the *New York Times*, the Walt Disney Company, Viacom, 21st Century Fox, Verizon, Condé Nast, Hearst, the newspapers of News Corp., including the *Wall Street Journal* and the *New York Post*, the *Washington Post*, Gannett, iHeartMedia, Turner Broadcasting, Bloomberg, Flipboard, and Vox Media, among others.

Anything that provokes clients to seek a new agency is good for Michael Kassan's business, for MediaLink conducts agency reviews, orchestrating the entire process from helping choose the competing agencies, defining what the client seeks, helping judge the agency's creative and strategic pitches, to participating as the client reaches a decision. MediaLink also performs a headhunter role, linking executives to vacant agency and client positions. It also introduces start-ups to investor capital, performing as an investment banker. It serves as a sherpa, making introductions between agencies and Silicon Valley and Hollywood, taking clients on tours of Google, Facebook, Twitter, and Microsoft, all companies it has represented. MediaLink also represents agencies, arranging speakers for various advertising conferences, where

Kassan induces them to cosponsor MediaLink parties and arranges for their executives to appear on panels. Agency and client executives are regularly invited to record one of Kassan's one-minute daily radio interviews syndicated on iHeartMedia, which he tapes in bulk once or twice a month.

The ever-affable Kassan, then sixty-four, is a pear-shaped teddy bear of a man with a soft, round, tanned face, the sunny smile of a practiced politician, and the jokey shtick of a stand-up comedian. In an increasingly insecure business assaulted by change and rife with mistrust, "they are a bridge company," Charlotte Beers, former CEO of Ogilvy & Mather, says of Kassan and MediaLink. "The way we used to talk to each other now needs an interpreter, and that's MediaLink." Baffled by the digital revolution, clients seek guidance from what they think of as "a neutral corner."

If one thought of concentric circles of power within the marketing and advertising world, Michael Kassan belongs in the center, alongside a few others like Martin Sorrell, CEO of WPP, the world's largest advertising and marketing holding company. Kassan's influence would place him ahead of most of the CEOs of the other five major holding companies and ahead of their clients. Yet outside of advertising and media industry enclaves, Kassan is virtually unknown. Create a Google Alert for WPP's Martin Sorrell and up to a dozen stories appear daily; a Google Alert for stories about Kassan generates maybe one mention per month.

After Mandel's ANA speech, MediaLink's neutral corner became a destination for the world's biggest brand advertisers. It was nothing short of a stampede. Starting in the spring of 2015 and running through 2016, advertising clients announced they were putting up for review a total of $50 billion of advertising business, and clients knocked on Kassan's door asking him to organize agency reviews. In all, MediaLink was hired to orchestrate two thirds of these reviews. Unilever, Procter & Gamble, Coca-Cola, L'Oréal, Kraft Foods, Mondelēz International, Bank of America, General Mills, Sony, 21st Century Fox, Johnson & Johnson, and CVS were just some of the advertisers who put their agency business up for review.

Mandel's kickbacks speech was a spur for the reviews, but it was hardly the only one. Indeed, its timing was exquisitely awful because advertisers were already being buffeted by change, facing disruptive forces in practically every sector of their business. As Alvin Toffler wrote in *Future Shock*, any industry bombarded by menacing changes endures "the dizzying disorientation brought on by the premature arrival of the future."

MediaLink brands itself as a neutral Switzerland, positioned comfortably in the middle, which is an odd definition of neutrality since MediaLink often represents all sides at a negotiating table. Kassan has been strategically shrewd. "He doesn't do agency reviews because they are wildly profitable," his friend Irwin Gotlieb says. "He does reviews to gain information and because it gives him influence in the business. He has a small headhunting operation. That makes money. But it also gives him influence because key people in the business know that if they're going to make a career move they should talk to him. The reason he is able to galvanize people in the industry is that everybody knows he is going to be conducting a review, so they don't want to piss him off."

❋ ❋ ❋

The agencies were indeed pissed off about Mandel's speech and agonized about the subsequent tsunami of reviews, which were akin to an audition to keep your job, knowing that your competition would be auditioning to take it from you. Clients putting individual agencies up for review was common; the torrent of reviews was not. The "pitchapapalooza" reviews meant a cruel summer of long hours and canceled vacations in order to create new pitches to clients. Top agency executives frantically tried to reassure and soothe clients. Laura Desmond, then the global CEO of Starcom MediaVest, the media agency arm of Publicis, estimated that over the summer of 2015 the reviews consumed eighteen thousand hours of her agency employees' time. Agencies had to prepare creative and strategic presentations for current as well as prospective clients. Presentations are time consuming and expensive—about $1.5 million for each, Bob Greenberg, the founder and CEO of R/GA says—and the expense is shouldered by the agencies, not the clients.

The advertising agency community reacted angrily to Mandel's speech, no one more so than Irwin Gotlieb. He had had a paternal relationship with Mandel, once recommending him as his successor as chairman of a prestigious industry committee. He denied Mandel's assertions, saying that he had removed Mandel from a trading role at the firm because they had a trading head and "you can only have one head of trading." So, he continued, "Why would I have a conversation about rebates with someone not involved in trading?"

The day after Mandel's speech, Gotlieb had GroupM's lawyers deliver a letter to Mandel accusing him of violating his separation agreement and the "significant compensation" received in return for agreeing not to disparage GroupM. The law firm warned that it was "considering its options," and urged him to keep his mouth shut. Martin Sorrell suggests that when Mandel left WPP's employ he did not do so voluntarily; instead of saying he was terminated, Sorrell said, "He was exited."

The near universal complaint from agencies was that in his speech Mandel named not a single transgressor, and thus was making a blanket condemnation of all agencies. It was not uncommon to hear agency executives accuse Mandel of McCarthyism. "It was irresponsible," charged Bill Koenigsberg, founder and CEO of Horizon Media, the largest privately held advertising and marketing agency, and the chairman of the American Association of Advertising Agencies (the 4A's). "It should not have been allowed in a public forum to paint an entire industry with a broad brush without any evidence."

Yet there is certainly smoke here, if not fire. Rebates are common outside the United States, and media buying is an increasingly global process. And as more and more advertising is being done by machines (called programmatic advertising) across a large number of media platforms, the opportunities to conduct speculative price arbitrage to bank lower prices for ads for later use arguably becomes reasonable business practice. The clients want to share the rewards. The agencies say clients are unwilling to share the risks, so why shouldn't agencies be rewarded for taking risks?

Of course, the issues raised by this controversy were broader than just rebates. Is advertising a relationship business, where accounts are won and lost on the golf course and over three-martini lunches, as had been caricatured for decades? Or is it a creative business, where consumers' hearts and minds are captured by big, original ideas articulated with aesthetic brilliance, as the doyens of the Creative Revolution claimed? Or is it, increasingly, a science, in which leadership will gravitate to those who can capture and analyze the most data, as Silicon Valley and its digital gurus claim?

Did Gotlieb's WPP, which is headquartered in the UK, hide U.S. rebates?

"We don't do rebates in the U.S.," Gotlieb firmly answered, leaving no doubt that it was not a practice with which he or WPP were involved. But he left a clear impression that maybe others partook in the United States. Dave Morgan, the CEO of Simulmedia, a marketing technology company that uses data to target TV ad buys, believes most do it. "Mandel is telling the absolute truth," he says.

"Kickbacks are massive in the U.S. I've been shaken down constantly. They tell us that if I get fifty million dollars, I have to pay them five million."

In a public conversation with Liodice weeks after Mandel's speech, Gotlieb made a larger point, one that illustrates how the relationship between agencies and clients has changed. He challenged the ancient assumption that agencies had an obligation to "put your clients' interests before your own." The client is under increased pressure to produce profits, and so are the agency's public holding companies, he said. Clients insist that the agency be paid based on the clients' sales performance. "I don't control the result, so I'm taking a business risk. It renders the term 'agent' redundant. You cease to be an 'agent' the moment someone puts a gun to your head and says, 'These are the CPMs [cost per thousand viewers] you need to deliver over X period of time.'" If GroupM's contracts with clients specify that its costs or the amount of rebates received overseas are to be disclosed, GroupM complies. But if the contract is silent, so is GroupM.

* * *

On whichever side of the argument one falls, it is inarguable that Mandel's assault came at a fraught moment and struck a raw nerve. Taken aback by the irate agency reactions, the ANA quickly did damage control, issuing this statement: "We regret any impression that agencies in general are engaged in questionable activities and apologize to those who were offended." A few days later it appointed a joint task force with the 4A's to study the issue.

The ANA issued an open, competitive RFP (request for proposal) to locate a firm to conduct the study, ultimately choosing K2 Intelligence, an investigative cyber defense and compliance firm owned by Jules B. Kroll and his son, Jeremy, which employs former prosecutors and law enforcement professionals like former New York City police commissioner Ray Kelly. The ANA also chose Ebiquity, an auditing firm that has a history of challenging agency spending practices on behalf of brand clients. Seething that the ANA made this decision on its own and chose a prosecutorial firm and, in Ebiquity, what he perceived as a business adversary, Martin Sorrell declared, "They went unilateral." Koenigsberg was equally livid, saying of K2 Intelligence and cofounder Jules Kroll, who helped build his estimable reputation by tracking down the illicit activities of dictators: "Bringing in a spy agency didn't send the right message. It kind of sounds like a witch hunt." The rupture between the ANA and the 4A's ended their joint task force. By the winter of 2016, K2 and Ebiquity were deep into interviews and jittery agencies feared the worst.

※ ※ ※

Michael Kassan was not nervous; he comfortably settled into his friend-of-all-sides stance. On the one hand, he said, Mandel "painted the industry with too broad a brush. . . . I'm a firm believer that this industry is made up of good people." The ANA wrongly "staked out a position" they should not have by embracing Mandel, Kassan says he told Bob Liodice. On the other hand, "If you're a CMO and your CEO sees an allegation in the press that agencies are getting rebates and undisclosed kickbacks, you're going to insist on knowing whether your agencies are doing this." He encouraged clients to do so. Agencies, he agreed, were not sufficiently transparent, particularly about digital ad purchases. "Media agencies began to create trading desks for online purchases of media. And they were doing it without fully disclosing the amount of online media they bought. They did this because they were buying in bulk and reselling and taking a principal position. They were not wrong. If I'm an agency and I say to you, 'This particular inventory is being bought on a nondisclosed basis, meaning I am not going to tell you what I paid but I am telling you I will get you a really good price, and I'm telling you I will make money on the spread but I'm not going to tell you how much'"—as long as this was stipulated in the agency contract, he thought it was OK. It would fail the transparency test, he says, if it was not part of the contract.

To conduct MediaLink's agency reviews, Kassan leaned on Bernhard Glock, who for twenty-five years as a senior executive at Procter & Gamble orchestrated more than one hundred agency reviews, and fellow senior vice president Lesley Klein. The process they shaped began with an in-depth discussion with the client as to what was expected of an agency, after which MediaLink would help narrow the choices of prospective agencies to a handful, who were invited to meet with the client for what MediaLink vice chairman Wenda Millard calls "a chemistry meeting. It's like a first date. If I don't like you, no second date."

MediaLink then prepared a dozen-or-so-page single-spaced RFP to send to the contending agencies. The RFP took time to answer, for it sketched a timeline for the review process and imposed upon the agencies a number of key requirements: specify who would staff the account; specify the fee structure the agency would employ and the methodology to be followed to arrive at a fee; delineate the proposed marketing strategy; sketch the agency's digital, technology, and e-commerce prowess; share the agency's media-buying capabilities and data strategy; specify the transparency guidelines to be followed to assure, for instance, that the client shares in any rebates; give a detailed account of the agency's work on other accounts and its approach to innovation; and it stipulates the return on investment, or ROI, targets the agency expects in return for a bonus and, if the target was not met, the size of the agency penalty. After the client digested these answers, agencies were then invited to offer their proposed creative presentations and marketing plans. The RFP always specified that the agency alone is totally responsible for any costs they incurred during this process.

The process MediaLink followed was explored in the fall of 2015 during the weekly Monday afternoon staff meeting at their 1155 Avenue of the Americas office, with employees from the Los Angeles and Chicago offices joining via videoconference. On this Monday, Wenda Millard devoted the meeting to a presentation by Bernhard Glock of the agency reviews MediaLink was coordinating. Standing in the middle of an eighth-floor conference room crowded with staffers, Glock spoke of what the process taught about the changing dynamics between client and agencies. "There are six key components we hear every time from advertisers," he said. "The first question the advertiser asks is, What are the cost savings the agency promises? Increasingly, they ask a fresh question: Will the agency agree to peg its pay to how the marketing campaign performs? More and more I see performance sneak in as part of the compensation." Why? "Because there are more and more procurement people in the reviews." The difference between the chief marketing officer and the procurement people, he said, is that the CMO tends to focus on building the brand and the procurement officer on cost savings.

The agency's marketing strategy is a second key component; increasingly, he observed, the client is mistrustful of agencies, and he no doubt exaggerated when he added, "They rely on us" to help shape the strategy.

Operations and efficiencies are a third client concern. Clients ask: How fast can we move? How do we communicate with each other? How do we integrate the planning and buying and creative realms?

Partly because of the Mandel speech and the ANA inquiry, transparency became a fourth component, he said. Our clients "want to know: Can I still trust my agency? Do I get to know of kickbacks or rebates?" Are these shared with the client? Inevitably, the increased wariness of clients "leads to tighter contracts."

The fifth component is the agency's use of data and analytics and how it measures performance. Clients commonly ask, "Who owns my data?" They want to know the competence of the agency in new machine tools like programmatic advertising. And they want to know if they are paying for fraudulent clicks.

Finally, and as central to the client as are costs, they want to know about what talent will be assigned to their account. "What I see happening more and more is advertisers want guarantees on key people," Glock said. They worry whether the agency has enough scale to service the client. And the client defines talent more broadly. "It used to be a given that only the creative agency sat at the table. Now that has changed. Public relations agencies sit at the table. Media agencies sit at the table. Digital agencies sit at the table."

"The problem agencies have," Millard interjected, is that cost pressures from clients "is causing agencies to pay less to their employees. Because of that, they're not as attractive. Why would I go to an agency that looks like a dinosauric entity rather than go to Google, or Facebook, or LinkedIn? Why would I do that, and be paid what I would be paid to work in a sweatshop around lots of unhappy people?" Contradicting Mandel's thesis that agency margins swell, Millard said, "It's a real problem for agencies because they can't make any money. Their margins are getting squeezed. This is a very bad scenario for everyone, including the clients who are not getting the best work out of agencies because they are not getting the best talent."

"I remember," she explained over a cup of tea in her office after the meeting concluded, "when I was growing up in this business the pride General Foods and Young and Rubicam would have when they'd say, 'We've been in business twenty-five years with Jell-O. We built this business together. This is a partnership, a great cause for celebration.' That's gone. Agencies live in great fear that they're going to go into review at any moment. Agencies are now treated as vendors."

Millard described a meeting she had that morning with one of her clients, Time Inc. Executives there complained of not being able to "have a strategic discussion with an agency. It's all about pricing." She says the same is true of MediaLink's other media clients who want to sell space to media-buying agencies. She offered this example: "If Time devises an elaborate $3.5 million sale of space for its multiple magazines, the agency says, 'I need $1 million.' You're having a price conversation before you even finish telling them what the idea is. All they know is that they have to skinny you down because they're being skinnied down. They're being judged by how well they're doing on pricing."

Little wonder clients turn to MediaLink, Millard said. "We don't have a dog in this race because we love each agency equally. And we're going to help the brands through some of this decision making because we don't care if they choose Omnicom or Publicis. But they can't go to Omnicom and ask, 'Am I in the right place?' They are more likely to come to us and ask, 'Should we be working differently with our agency? Or should we put our account up for review?'"

■ ■ ■

The tidal wave of accounts up for review swept through the agency business. Agencies lost part or all of the business of longtime clients. Publicis, for instance, lost Procter & Gamble and General Mills, as well as Coca-Cola, Mondelēz, and Delta; it gained Visa, Bank of America, and Taco Bell. Omnicom lost Johnson & Johnson, Bud Light, and Adidas; it gained Procter & Gamble, Delta, and Subway. WPP lost AT&T, as well as Bank of America and Coors; it gained General Mills and Coca-Cola. IPG lost American Airlines and Kmart; it gained Johnson & Johnson, Bank of America, and Chrysler; Havas and Dentsu gained slightly more client dollars than they lost.

Publicis lost more accounts than its rivals, but the loss that especially rankled Maurice Levy of Publicis was an Omnicom win. The company he had embraced as an equal merger partner in 2013, only to watch the merger collapse the following year, took what a senior Publicis executive described as "a $100 million haircut" to snatch the P&G business away from Publicis. On the other hand, Levy was overjoyed to best the man he regularly trades public insults with, WPP's Martin Sorrell, by winning part of the Bank of America account.

More was at stake, of course, than relations between advertisers and agencies. "Advertising works as a value exchange," Andrew Robertson of BBDO, says. "In exchange for advertising, consumers get free or reduced content costs." Or needed information. It is easy to be cynical or dismissive about the role of advertising in a consumer economy, but its role can hardly be overstated. Commerce and most forms of communication would shrivel without it. Many retail stores would shutter, the number of new products would dwindle, financial service companies would sputter, consumers would complain they are shopping blindfolded. Google, with 87 percent of its $79.4 billion in 2016 revenues supported by advertising, Facebook with over 95 percent ($26.9 billion out of $27.6 billion) in 2016, and Snapchat with 96 percent from advertising, would—like the TV networks and most radio—cease to be "free." A prime reason U.S. newspaper employment plunged from 412,000 in 2001 to 174,000 in 2016 is that advertising dollars—which account for more than half of all newspaper revenues—dropped from $63.5 billion in 2000 to $23.6 billion in 2014, the last year the Newspaper Association of America released newspaper revenues. Facebook's advertising revenues alone exceeded the combined ad dollars of all U.S. newspapers. Overseas, in that same span, newspaper ad revenues sank from $80 billion to $52.6 billion.

Advertising and marketing "provides the oil for the economy's energy," Martin Sorrell says. Princeton professor Paul Starr, whose authoritative history of the media, *The Creation of the Media*, credited advertising with assuring journalism's independence: "American journalism became more of an independent and innovative source of information just as it became more of a means of advertising and publicity."

A 2015 study on the impact of advertising by IHS Markit, a London-based financial services company, concluded that in the United States each dollar spent on advertising alone spawned nineteen dollars in sales and supported sixty-seven jobs across many industries; they predicted that by 2019 advertising would kindle 16 percent of all economic output. A 2016 study of Western Europe for the World Federation of Advertisers, based in Brussels, concluded that each euro spent on advertising equates to seven euros of economic value. Predicting the exact impact of advertising on consumer behavior is not an exact science—though this book will demonstrate that going forward data will yield better evidence—but by anyone's measure, advertising and marketing packs a mighty economic wallop.

Naomi Klein chose to measure the impact of advertising in a very different way. In her book *No Logo*,[*] first published in 2000, she portrayed advertising "as the most public face of a deeply faulty economic system" that promoted sweatshops to produce their often unhealthy products, and that propped up global companies that held sway over politicians to advance globalism, which exported jobs. Her harsh critique of advertising as addictively manipulative was echoed sixteen years later by Tim Wu, whose book *The Attention Merchants*[†] argues that by demanding their content be "free" and refusing to pay subscriptions or micropayments, consumers invite intrusive ads and receive inferior journalism and content.

No question: without advertising many citizens would feel liber-

---

[*] Naomi Klein, *No Logo* (New York: Picador, 2000).
[†] Tim Wu, *The Attention Merchants: The Epic Scramble to Get Inside Our Heads* (New York: Alfred A. Knopf, 2016).

ated from annoying and often misleading interruptions. But what's indisputable is that advertising and marketing dollars serve as an underlying subsidy for much of the media and the Internet—in other words, for our information ecosystem and, often, for the architecture of our everyday lives. Without this free ATM machine, many companies would be doomed. But as any good advertiser knows, asking someone to sit through all the ads in the TV show they've recorded because those ads fund the channel the show is on is just about as thankless as asking people to pay more for a product because it's good for the environment. Some percentage of consumers may make that choice for the greater good; many more will not. Today, the consumer is in control, and increasingly the challenge for advertisers is to create experiences that people will *want* to have because they will no longer *have* to have them. That is a tectonic shift for a once comfortable industry, and it is worth a look back at how this economically essential industry got here.

2.

"CHANGE SUCKS"

"I'm prepared to eat our children, because if I don't somebody else will!"

—Martin Sorrell, WPP CEO

The word *advertising* derives from the verb *advert*, which means "to give attention to." All markets or competitive economies rely on advertising. Thousands of years ago, advertising consisted of Egyptian, Greek, and Roman wall paintings or rock scrawls. Five centuries ago, farmers selling produce relied on word of mouth; villagers selling a service put up signs like TAILOR or BLACKSMITH. With villages transformed into cities as the Industrial Revolution swept across the nineteenth century, sellers of products turned to a better means of communicating with potential buyers. Thus advertising agencies were born.

The first full-service modern advertising agency, N. W. Ayer & Son, emerged just after the Civil War. What would become the primary means of compensating agencies, the 15 percent commission on all advertising, was also introduced in 1905 by N. W. Ayer & Son. The introduction of the automobile early in the twentieth century became an advertising catalyst. As auto companies proliferated, their reliance on ads to distinguish themselves grew, as did the use of billboards to catch the attention of drivers. Radio in the 1920s and television after World War II became inflection points for new waves of advertising. The burgeoning Internet at the dawn of the twenty-first century became another inflection point.

As population and products mushroomed, advertising made it possible for consumers to discover things they needed, or thought they needed. Advertising seduced consumers and created familiar brands. Initially, the ads for those brands were informational, often dull and dutiful. Nineteenth-century newspapers were festooned with dense rows of classified ads, occupying the entire front page of many papers. Increasingly, ads began to flirt with consumers' emotions. In the 1920s, Edward Bernays, nephew of Sigmund Freud, became the father of the public relations industry. A hundred years after Shelley declared poets the unacknowledged legislators of the world, Bernays announced in his 1928 book *Propaganda*—a word he used with none of the pejorative connotations it would later acquire—that now this was true of marketers: "The conscious and intelligent manipulation of the organized habits and opinions of the masses is an important element in democratic society. Those who manipulate this unseen mechanism of society constitute an invisible government which is the true ruling power of our country." As one might expect of one of Freud's kin, Bernays's mission was to discover the hidden motives for human behavior and learn how to tickle them. "Men are rarely aware of the real reasons which motivate their actions," he wrote. "A man may believe that he buys a motor car because, after careful study of the technical features of all makes on the market, he has concluded that this is the best. He is almost certainly fooling himself."

Today the definition of marketing extends from the damage control of public relations firms summoned when a company like Volkswagen is embroiled in scandal; to survey research before a new product is introduced; to the targeting that data companies like Oracle sell to agencies and brands; to designing corporate logos or rebranding companies, as was done when Time Warner Cable was renamed Spectrum; to corporate positioning advice McKinsey & Company offers CEOs; to direct mail, blogs, podcasts, coupons, sponsorships, naming rights, purchased shelf space, corporate Web sites, in-store promotions, membership rewards programs, exhibitions, and young influencers like the Betches, who are paid to extol products on sites like YouTube.

The tentacles of this industry reach wide and deep. It employs an estimated one million people worldwide. One hundred thousand are said to congregate in New York each September alone for the annual Advertising Week in the Times Square area. Then there are the one hundred seventy thousand or so who attend the Consumer Electronics Show, or CES, in Las Vegas in January, the hundred thousand who attend the Mobile World Congress in Barcelona in February, the armies who attend the Association of National Advertisers in different locales, the South by Southwest (SXSW) in Austin in March, the American Association of Advertising Agencies Transformation in Miami or Los Angeles in April, the Cannes Lions International Festival of Creativity in June, and the conferences that Advertising Week's impresario Matt Scheckner has introduced to London, Tokyo, Mexico City, Shanghai, and Sydney.

It is an industry that has never lacked the capacity to take itself seriously. Jeremy Bullmore, the former J. Walter Thompson chairman, whose company was acquired by Martin Sorrell's WPP in 1987, today sits in a small, cluttered office at WPP's London headquarters on Farm Street, where Sorrell relies on him to write sparkling essays about the industry and to help produce a robust annual company report. "Of all the models for successful economies," Bullmore says, looking out from under bushy white eyebrows that give him an almost cherubic appearance, "nothing yet has been able to compete with a liberal, open market. Which is not to say it's without flaws. If you go back five hundred years to a village, there were people who have milk and carrots and there were other people in the village who want them." Only some form of communication can close the distance between "those who want and those who have." He thinks most of the gap is filled by advertising. "Edison didn't actually say, 'Who makes the best mousetrap, the world will beat a path to his door.' If he had said it, it would have been absurd. If you build a better mousetrap and you're in the woods, until somebody knows you've got the better mousetrap, there's no point in building it." He cites the former Soviet Union and its satellites: "Look at Communist countries. No advertising. None of the consumer goods companies thought it necessary or worthwhile to innovate because if you do something that's quite interesting but you can't tell anyone about it, and your competition are not doing it, why bother?"

As First Lady, Michelle Obama championed learning how to "use the power of advertising to our favor" by promoting exercise and eating healthy foods like fruits and vegetables. "We all know that advertising works, so we figured why shouldn't fruits and vegetables get in on the action?" she said. Advertising also works in negative ways, witness the Camel ads that once successfully touted cigarettes as a health product, proclaiming, "More doctors smoke Camels than any other cigarette." Or mentholated cigarettes were pitched as assuring improved health.

But neither advertising nor the industry that produces it works the way it once did. The industry is being disrupted by frenemies advancing from the north, south, east, and west. Martin Sorrell impersonates an alarmed Paul Revere, seeking to rally the traditional ad industry, summoning his WPP troops to meet the "continuous disruption threat" from various competitors. While pacing his all-white, bare-walled London townhouse office, he says, "You've got layers. You've got our direct competitors, like Omnicom. You've got the frenemies, let's call them Facebook and Google principally. You've got the consulting companies, like Deloitte, McKinsey, et cetera. And then you've got the software companies, like Salesforce.com and Oracle and Infosys, and Indian software companies." He combats new threats by aggressively investing in digital upstarts and jettisoning companies whose economic performance lags. "We've invested in Vice. We've invested in Fullscreen. We've invested in Refinery29," each a digital company. And, he adds, "I'm prepared to eat our children, because if I don't somebody else will!"

* * *

It does not please Sorrell that one clear beneficiary of this tumult and fear—and the client backlash triggered by Jon Mandel's speech—is Michael Kassan's MediaLink. Publically, Sorrell may mute his criticism of Kassan, but he dislikes third parties getting between his agencies and his clients. It annoys him that Kassan's varied clients flock to MediaLink—not WPP—because they seek a reassuring neutral voice and are distressed by the speed and enormity of change. Sorrell has a broader range of knowledge and business acumen than Kassan—and most contemporaries, for that matter. But Kassan is comforting, providing for his clients what he describes as a cushion, a "membrane between" the cartilage and the bone. Martin Sorrell would never describe himself as a cushion.

Like a doctor with a good bedside manner, Kassan knows his clients have reason to be insecure, and he seeks to address their fears. His clients discuss the accelerated spread of mobile phones, whose approximately six billion global users have replaced the desktop and the television as the dominant platform. They marvel at its awesome power:

today's iPhone 8 has more computing power, says Rishad Tobaccowala of Publicis, than was used for the first space shuttle. They enthuse that a smartphone platform and its embedded GPS open opportunities to track and engage personally with users. They are awed by China's Tencent, a corporate giant focused on mobile services that connect people, providing access to WeChat. In mid-2016, Tencent had almost 800 million users, 80 percent of whom spend more than an hour a day on one of its sites, especially WeChat, to communicate with family and friends and strangers. They use simple bar codes to partake in 500 million daily transactions, employing 300 million credit cards that link to 300,000 stores, all without switching to another app. If the client does not know, Kassan can explain that WeChat is a one-stop service that combines the varied functions of PayPal, Facebook, Uber, Amazon, Netflix, banks, Expedia, and countless apps. It is clear to Kassan: the mobile future is being shaped in China, not Silicon Valley.

But this frightens his clients, because they know China is a hard market to crack, and they know the U.S. companies that control mobile will drive hard bargains with agencies and advertisers. They also know the limitations of mobile. Ads on mobile phones soak up battery life, are constricted by small screens, and are so intrusive and irksome to consumers that about one quarter of Americans and one third of Western Europeans sign up for ad blockers to prevent the interruptions. How, clients anxiously want to know, do they reach the mass audience so essential to introducing new products and to building brand identity when ads on mobile phones are not as effective and consumers are dispersed among many new channel choices and social networks? And what the hell do they do to reach the next generation—including the digitally savvy millennials age twenty-one to thirty-four, and the even younger Generation Z born after 1997, who detest being hawked to? A reason people might be annoyed by ads is because, on average, citizens are bombarded daily by an astonishing five thousand marketing messages.

Kassan's clients and agencies do marvel at new data mining tools that offer advertising and marketing companies more weapons to target consumers. But they're also frightened by some of Kassan's digital clients—Facebook and Google in particular—who cooperate with advertisers but also compete by collecting massive amounts of data, which they do not fully share. These digital frenemies use this data and the marketing services they've acquired—like Google's DoubleClick and Facebook's Atlas—to become agency and platform rivals. More and more of his clients are terrified of Amazon, for Amazon has even better data than Facebook or Google, because it tells when a consumer made an actual purchase decision, and like Facebook and Google it walls off its data. Particularly worrisome to brand clients, Amazon promotes its own products, as Google is accused by the European Union of using search to steer users to its own products. For example, if you ask Alexa, Amazon's digital assistant, to choose a battery, it will choose an Amazon battery, the reason Amazon batteries dominate battery sales on Amazon.

Kassan's clients and agencies also worry about something else: the data that will yield rich targeting information could trigger a backlash if citizens come to believe their privacy is violated and clamor for government protection. While more data fortifies agencies with better tools to target consumers, it also unnerves them because it arms clients with information about which of their ads sell and which don't. And technology does something else: it democratizes information, giving citizens more choices, more ability to skip ads, to voice their opinions, to vote with their fingers and flee traditional media platforms.

Everyone in the advertising and marketing business marvels at the platform choices technology enables. Consumers can be reached via an ever-expanding number of TV channels, social networks, apps, blogs, podcasts, and e-mail alerts. But they fear the miniaturization of the mass audience and wonder how to introduce a new product so that it captures people's attention in this new world.

The advertising industry collectively worries that what they think of as their art—big creative ideas—will be replaced by machines weaponized with data and algorithms and artificial intelligence. The primary machine we increasingly rely on is the smartphone, and many in the industry would not be comforted to listen to Tim Armstrong, the CEO of AOL and before that Google's senior vice president of advertising for the United States and Latin America. In 2015, Armstrong sketched a future in which marketers will have to talk to a consumer via their mobile machine: "And the machine is going to highly disrupt what kind of advantage and what kind of messaging and what kind of interaction you have with a consumer." Within five years, he continued, six billion people will be connected to the Internet, meaning marketers "are going to have to interact with their machine, which we refer to around here as 'the second brain.' You're going to have an advertising model that works fluidly for the consumer but also works fluidly for what that machine is." He illustrates the machine's power by telling of a visit he made that week to a Mastercard board reception where they displayed future products. One was a gas station pump that recognized your Mastercard and regulated the price at the pump based on whether you were a regular customer or not. "In the future, the pump pricing may change based on what type of customer you are and whether you're in a points program. But also, the company will have a lot more information on you." And the smartphone will "keep track of all your relationships with all the companies you deal with. The exponential power of using that data will change consumer behavior. It will shift more power into the consumers' hands. And it will shift more power to companies that move faster into this world."

Marketers will have to befriend the machine, he continued. "The phone or machine will be as powerful as a second you, with a lot more ability to use software to simplify things for you. Today, the consumer does all the work. You have to get in your car and drive to the store. You have to go online to Amazon and figure out what you want to buy. But in the future if you have this machine that has a deep understanding of what you do, when and how you do it, the things that may be helpful for you, it's likely that the onus on the consumer to do all the shopping will shift to the corporation." Information for the consumer will be screened and presented by your smartphone's digital assistant, which will be more sophisticated versions of Amazon's Alexa, Apple's Siri and its HomePod speaker, Google Home, and Microsoft's Cortana. "It may watch how you behave over the course of a year and say, 'Here are all the things you're doing and here are three or four products that may help you live a longer life, may help you save twenty percent of your income.'" The digital assistant becomes your agent, potentially supplanting the middleman, including the agency middleman.

Agency employers stewed over all this. And as they also stewed over Jon Mandel's claims in 2015, Michael Kassan heard a new drumbeat from various clients: trust. Or mistrust. Kassan was all too aware of the views of a frequent client, Beth Comstock, who was promoted to vice chair of General Electric after the innovations she instigated as their CMO. "You hear this time and time again, a lot of people are frustrated that there's a disconnect between their agency and what they want," she says. "I think we want more media properties to come to us," to bypass the agency and collaborate directly on creating an ad campaign, as the *New York Times* did in creating an award-winning virtual reality campaign for GE. Over the years, she says, the mistrust between client and agency intensified because the media-buying agencies came to see themselves as the customer. "They gathered all the clients together. They negotiated the sales." They, not the client, directly paid for the ads. They didn't always assign their best people to a client's account. They were sometimes opaque about rebates or why they placed bets on different media platforms. To Comstock the trust issue boils down to this: "Are you working for me or for the media company? I'm paying you!"

Agencies are naturally anxious not to become superfluous middlemen, supplanted by clients who seek lower costs by building their own in-house marketing departments, or by turning to advertising platforms that retain MediaLink—like the *New York Times*, the *Wall Street Journal*, or Vox, which double as ad agencies, going directly to brands and offering to craft their ads. Agencies worry that as consumers shift to the convenience of online buying and do it on their iPhones, reliable advertising clients like department stores and retail outlets will do more than contract—they will perish. Big agency holding companies "are dinosaurs," thinks Bob Greenberg of R/GA, a thriving digital agency, because they grow by buying companies and become hobbled by an inability to harmonize disparate cultures, while at the same time being challenged by formidable consulting companies with deeper pockets and intimate relationships with the CEOs of major brands. They are collapsing, he says, because "everything is run by accountants and bean counters." Greenberg obviously makes an exception for IPG, the holding company which acquired his R/GA.

"Change sucks," sighs Rishad Tobaccowala, the resident futurist for Publicis. "I hate change. I work for the same company I joined thirty-four years ago. I live in the same area of Chicago for thirty-six years. I met my wife in India when I was twelve. I hate change. The reason why change sucks is if you do something different, you don't know what you're doing. Therefore you make mistakes. You make a fool of yourself." Senior executives don't want to look foolish, or admit they don't have answers. "So what people do is they put out press releases pretending they know what they're doing. And they hope this will go away before they retire. But it is happening faster."

In human terms, what marketing execs like Tobaccowala, Sorrell, and Kassan know all too well is that many of the jobs held by their employees are threatened by technology. They know that new technologies like programmatic or computerized buying of advertising eliminate jobs. They know personalized ads dispatched by Instant Messages (IMs) or e-mails can be created by machines. They know algorithms and machines powered by AI increasingly decide what we see or read. They know, as Kassan says, "Technology is the number one threat to agencies. Technology allows for a more direct relationship between a buyer and a seller, with less need for an intermediary."

Deep down, Kassan, like most media executives he advises, fears that marketing dollars will not just be redirected, they will actually shrivel. Their fear calls to mind this brief exchange between two friends in Hemingway's *The Sun Also Rises*:

Bill Gorton: "How did you go bankrupt?"

Mike Campbell: "Two ways. Gradually and then suddenly."

3.

GOOD-BYE, DON DRAPER

"Today clients are not married to an agency. They are only dating."

—Michael Kassan

Mad Men's Don Draper was a fictional stand-in for midcentury advertising executives like David Ogilvy, Bill Bernbach, and George Lois, who reigned at a time when the creative departments ruled agencies, when a single street—Madison Avenue—was synonymous with advertising. In those days, there was no need for a company like Michael Kassan's MediaLink. In fact, Kassan and MediaLink would have been treated as an interloper, for the ad agency, as Jon Mandel and clients like GE's Beth Comstock claimed, was the agent of the client.

Newspapers starting in the late nineteenth century began to compensate agencies with a fixed 15 percent commission on all advertising placed in their pages. Magazines followed, then radio and television. It was an unusual compensation system—the ad was paid for by the advertiser, but it was the seller of the advertising, not the buyer, that paid a percentage of the fee to the agency. In addition, agencies were paid a 17.65 percent commission on all ads created, and were separately reimbursed for production costs. The arrangement "was pretty lush," concedes Miles Young, the CEO of Ogilvy & Mather until 2016.

Randall Rothenberg has been immersed in the industry for more than a quarter century. He wrote one of the most instructive and entertaining books about advertising, *Where the Suckers Moon: An Advertising Story*,* and today serves as the spokesman for digital companies as president and CEO of the Interactive Advertising Bureau. He believes the commission system fortified the agency business, boosting their profit margins. "There was collusion between the agencies and the publishers to keep prices high. The myth was that the client was the marketer. In fact, the client was the publisher. The ad agency acted as a broker for the publisher." Ad agencies did not often haggle with publishers on price. The more ad dollars publishers received, the more the agency got paid.

Doyle Dane Bernbach's Bill Bernbach—the creative decision-maker behind such iconic ad campaigns as Volkswagen's "Think Small," and "You Don't Have to Be Jewish to Love Levy's"—reigned at a time when ad agency execs and their place in the world was secure. When the CEO of fledging Avis offered his account to Bernbach, he qualified his acceptance by telling him, "But you must do exactly what we recommend."† The campaign Bernbach crafted—"When You're Only No. 2, You Try Harder. Or Else"—changed Avis's fortunes. George Lois, like Bernbach a Bronx-born maverick, had won a basketball scholarship to Syracuse, and his hulking physicality and booming voice could be menacing. More than once, Jerry Della Femina, a creative colleague, recalls Lois screaming at clients, "I'll jump out this window if you don't approve this ad!"

---

* Randall Rothenberg, *Where the Suckers Moon: An Advertising Story* (New York: Alfred A. Knopf, 1994).
† Bob Levenson, *Bill Bernbach's Book: A History of the Advertising That Changed the History of Advertising* (New York: Villard Books, 1987).

"In the old days, creative guys were the only ones in the room to pitch clients," recalls Michael Kassan, whose advertising career started in media buying. "They never met Harry"—Harry Crane, media buyer and head of Sterling Cooper's TV department—"who was treated as a nerd in *Mad Men*. But in the late 1970s, independent media buyers spun off as companies, and in the '90s they gained respect. The suede-shoes guys challenged the power of the white-shoes guys."

A recurring debate within agencies in the *Mad Men* era was over what constituted a great ad campaign. In the 1950s, Rosser Reeves, the chairman and creative head of Ted Bates & Co., argued that advertising was a quasi science. He promoted what he called a "Unique Selling Proposition," claiming that one idea that consumers could latch on to foretold whether an ad campaign would succeed. It had to be unique, but it also had to win the approval of survey research predicting it would sell. Colgate ads for toothpaste that "comes out like a ribbon and lies flat on your brush" was unique, but it wouldn't sell, he said. Colgate ads for toothpaste that "cleans your breath while it cleans your teeth" was both unique and successful. Recruited to pioneer thirty-second TV ads for Dwight Eisenhower's 1952 presidential campaign, Reeves ordered a Gallup poll that identified three issues on which the Democrats were vulnerable: corruption, the economy, and the Korean War. Reeves coined the phrase "Eisenhower, Man of Peace," and portrayed Ike as a war hero returned to America to bring about domestic and international peace. His opponent, Adlai Stevenson, who didn't own a television and thought TV ads talked to citizens as if they were second graders, countered by spending 95 percent of his TV ad budget on a half-hour telecast of his speeches. He reached a minuscule audience.*

---

* An account of the 1952 TV campaign is offered in David Greenberg's *Republic of Spin: An Inside History of the American Presidency* (New York: W. W. Norton & Company, 2016).

Reeves's peer Bill Bernbach had a very different view. He was not a slave to research, relying instead on gut instinct. Research, he told Martin Mayer,* "can tell you what people want, and you can give it back to them. It's a nice, safe way to do business." But it usually produced pedestrian ads. "Advertising isn't a science, it's persuasion. And persuasion is an art." Another legend, David Ogilvy, was both Reeves's protégé and at one point his brother-in-law, but their philosophical differences grew so intense that they stopped speaking to one another. Ogilvy extolled the value of a consistent brand personality shaped by what he called "trivial product differences." In many an Ogilvy print ad, the headline and graphics were followed by short essays touting the brand. In one famous ad, after the bold headline—"At 60 miles an hour the loudest noise in this new Rolls-Royce comes from the electric clock"—the text enumerated thirteen reasons to buy the luxurious car. In the consumer's mind, he believed, the brand stood for something.

Ogilvy broke with Bernbach as well, albeit less vociferously, asserting that Bernbach's "art" got the better of his content. "What you say in advertising is more important than how you say it," Ogilvy declared.

Bernbach firmly disagreed. "Execution can become content," he replied. "It can be just as important as what you say."[†] It was an argument without end.

Whatever differences divided the industry's titans, however, they were united in the belief that it was the companies doing the buying— the advertisers—that ultimately wielded the power. Fearful of offending white viewers, initially advertisers vetoed the idea of an all-black variety show starring Sammy Davis, Jr. With tobacco ads making up

---

* Martin Mayer's *Madison Avenue, U.S.A.* (Lincolnwood, IL: NTC Business Books, 1991).
† See Mayer's *Madison Avenue, U.S.A.* and Randall Rothenberg's *Where the Suckers Moon* for a cogent exegesis on the differences between Reeves, Bernbach, and Ogilvy.

almost 10 percent of their ad revenue, network newscasts rarely reported on smoking's health risks. Over the years, when program schedules were decided, the head of network sales was always in the room, for no network wanted an ad to appear in what was deemed an unfriendly environment. A medium dependent on advertising for its revenue knows that its primary business obligation is to corral an audience for its ads. Bill O'Reilly seemed to be surviving his sexual harassment scandal at Fox, until a group launched a successful boycott campaign against his show's advertisers. When advertisers fled *The O'Reilly Factor* in April 2017, Fox News quickly pulled the plug on cable TV's top-rated anchor.

* * *

Over time, for industry-specific reasons and also due to a larger shift in American business culture, ad agency clients began to bring more and more scrutiny to bear on the whole cost structure. Jon Mandel's *j'accuse* moment did not come out of a clear blue sky. After the 2008 economic crisis in particular, CEOs increasingly turned to their chief financial officers or chief procurement officers to more closely monitor marketing spending. Inevitably, the power of CMOs, who hired the agencies, eroded. "In Don Draper's days there was never a procurement department," says Wendy Clark, who has been a CMO of Coca-Cola and AT&T and is today the North American CEO of Bill Bernbach's former agency, DDB Worldwide. "In new business briefs," she says, in addition to the CMO "we have two procurement officers in meetings."

Irwin Gotlieb saw this beginning to happen in the early 1990s, when procurement officers would hire auditing firms like Accenture and Ebiquity to monitor agencies. They became the agency's adversary, he explains. "They got compensated for generating savings," and they had a built-in "conflict of interest. They ran around saying, 'The sky is falling!' And then they sold you umbrellas." By slicing marketing costs, they boosted short-term company earnings at the expense of the long-term health of companies, he argues, correlating marketing dollars with growth. An inevitable consequence, he says, was a loosening of the bond of trust between client and agency.

"Today clients are not married to an agency. They are only dating," observes Kassan. Clients who previously conducted agency reviews every ten years now accelerated their review cycles, sometimes dramatically. Keith Reinhard, the chairman emeritus of DDB Worldwide, retained Anheuser-Busch as a client for thirty-three years, and he dealt directly with the family patriarch, August Busch. "We had a top-to-top relationship," he says. "But when product managers came in under CMOs, that diminished, and in some cases eliminated, top-to-top relationships." Today, many CMOs are not members of their CEO's C-suite or top executive team—CEOs, COOs (Chief Operating Officers), CTOs (Chief Technology Officers), and CFOs (Chief Financial Officers)—and their tenure is often just a few years. David Sable, the CEO of Young & Rubicam, laments, "The biggest difference between our day and Don Draper's is the relationship between agencies and clients. In those days, you had a problem and you called your agency. You were partners."

Connected to the rise of procurement officers was the end of the 15 percent commission to compensate agencies. "The agency did not have to put forward a proposal for agency compensation, justifying how many people worked on the account or what they did. Compensation was worked out by how much money the client was prepared to spend on media," Michael Farmer writes in his book, *Madison Avenue Manslaughter.**

---

* Michael Farmer, *Madison Avenue Manslaughter: An Inside View of Fee-Cutting Clients, Profit-Hungry Owners and Declining Ad Agencies* (New York: LID Publishing Ltd., 2015).

※ ※ ※

The first major client to rebel was Shell, which in 1960 decided to abandon its agency, J. Walter Thompson, and replace the commission system with a fee system. The new agency was Ogilvy, whose head, David Ogilvy, claimed credit for the new form of compensation, which would over the next three decades spread almost everywhere. "Experience has taught me that advertisers get the best results when they pay their agency a flat fee," Ogilvy explained in his memoir. An agency is "expected to give objective advice," and may not be able to when its compensation is based on how much the client spends on advertising. "I prefer to be in a position to advise my clients to spend more without their suspecting my motive. And I like to be in a position to advise clients to spend *less*—without incurring the odium of my own stockholders."*

Ogilvy was correct about aligning the interests of the agency and the advertiser, but he was unmindful of the consequences for agencies. The 15 percent commission system plus a commission on all production costs did undermine trust; but the fee system undermined the creative agencies. "The commission system was an absurd system," admits Jeremy Bullmore. "But it worked. What it did was make agencies compete on services, not price." A fee-based system invited CFOs and their procurement officers to drill down on costs, to question why a high-priced copywriter could not be replaced by a junior copywriter. Over time, says Miles Young, it slashed the earnings of agencies "by maybe one third or half."

Of course, no change was more disruptive to the advertising community than the proliferation of consumer choices brought about by new technologies. "In Don Draper's days you had probably six media

---

* David Ogilvy, *Confessions of an Advertising Man* (New York: Atheneum, 1986).

channels to engage with the consumer," Bill Koenigsberg of Horizon Media says. "You had television. You had print. You had radio. You had newspapers. And you had out-of-home"—outdoor advertising, for example. There was also, he said, "below-the-line direct marketing," including direct mail. "Today the ability to engage with consumers lives in hundreds of different media channels. That channel explosion is a huge difference." It lives, as well, in billions of smartphones, personal devices with our own apps that we carry everywhere, sometimes to bed, and that allows advertisers to reach, and often to annoy, consumers. People spend more time on their mobile phone than watching television, says Carolyn Everson, Facebook's vice president of global marketing solutions. Armed with more data that yields more information about each consumer, instead of spraying the audience with a TV shotgun ad and not being sure who has been hit, digital companies like Facebook say they let advertisers aim a rifle at individual consumers. This innovation is promised by every digital platform. "As opposed to marketing at people, it is marketing for people," she says. "The biggest difference from Don Draper days is data," says Keith Weed, a three-decade Unilever veteran who oversees marketing and communications for the world's second largest advertiser. "Data has always been there. The difference is the ability of the computer to analyze the data."

But even with the data, the marketers are not in control. "The single biggest difference between today and Don Draper days," thinks Rishad Tobaccowala of Publicis, "is that consumers are increasingly determining what they want to interact with, and when." Today, the consumer is the real king. Tobaccowala dates the empowerment of consumers to 2007, the year Apple introduced the iPhone, the first smartphone, the same year Facebook shifted its audience focus from college students to everyone, and the same year Amazon's Kindle was introduced. In years past, advertising was based on a premise that information was scarce. Advertising informed us of products. We traded our attention for information, industry observer Gord Hotchkiss has written on *MediaPost*, an online marketing publication. Today we are glutted with information and have "too little attention to allocate to it. . . . This has allowed participatory information marketplaces such as Uber, Airbnb, and Google to flourish. In these markets, where information flows freely, advertising that attempts to influence feels awkward, forced and disingenuous. Rather than building trust, advertising erodes it." Evidence of advertising fatigue is found in ad blockers and in Nielsen data that says half of those who watch TV shows they have recorded on their DVR devices skip past the ads.

The anxiety of the advertising community is revealed in the gibberish or verbal smokescreens they now employ. Just before the millennium, advertisers began to refer to themselves as "brand stewards," as if the brand had a soul. Nike, as an amused Naomi Klein observed, announced that its mission was to "enhance people's lives through sports and fitness"; Polaroid said it was selling "a social lubricant," not a camera; IBM was promoting "business solutions, not computers."

All this begs a fundamental question that comes up often in the advertising and marketing community: Are they sufficiently alarmed about the menace they face? There is a lot of brave talk, but it's reasonable to wonder to what extent much of the community is simply kidding itself, living, as Robert Louis Stevenson once wrote, not "in the external truth among salts and acids, but in the warm, phantasmagoric chamber of his brain, with the painted windows and storied wall."

■ ■ ■

At advertising confabs like Cannes, Unilever's Keith Weed will often wear ostentatious chartreuse sports jackets. He is less the showman when seated in his London office in jeans and a long-sleeved grey button-down shirt. "There's been more change in the last five years than in the previous twenty-five," he says. In his early days, a media plan consisted of a couple of pages. Today it is as thick as a book. "The complexity of choice is brilliant, but equally challenging."

The challenges of the advertising and marketing world and the erosion of trust between agencies and clients are often the subjects discussed at MediaLink's weekly staff meetings. President Wenda Millard sits at the head of a long, rectangular, reddish-stained white oak table facing two large wall screens, one of MediaLink employees in Los Angeles and one in Chicago; in New York, MediaLink staffers occupy black leather swivel chairs and stand along every inch of wall space. At sixty-two, Millard is the elder in this room, but her dark, pixieish pageboy and exuberance are that of a much younger person. JC Uva, a MediaLink managing director, thinks of Wenda as Felix to Michael's Oscar. "Felix was the neat one. That's Wenda. You can literally tell time by Wenda's schedule. Michael is a moving target."

Millard called this February 2016 staff meeting to order at precisely 2:30 P.M. About four dozen MediaLink execs gathered in the glassed conference room. Michael Kassan was to be present via video feed from Los Angeles. After attending the Mobile World Congress in Barcelona, he had slipped away with his wife to a spa in Germany. Not seeing him on the screen, Millard said, "We'll wait for Michael."

"The spa did me good because you don't see me!" Kassan announced. He was smiling from the Los Angeles table, casually attired in a grey crew-neck sweater over a pale blue shirt.

Millard asked him to share his interpretation of the bad blood that Jon Mandel's 2015 speech had inspired.

"It reminds me of the gallows humor of being at a spa in Germany and of how the world has changed," Kassan said. "Now Jews are paying Germans to put them in rooms and not feed them!" Kassan's humor does not bat one thousand, but it is always enthusiastic. He went on to explain the unease MediaLink's ad clients were feeling about what they believed to be a lack of agency transparency. "More of our clients are saying, 'I'm getting screwed by my agency. At the end of the day I might want to deal directly with publishers.'" He cited how programmatic ad buying, run by machine algorithms that target desired audiences, "may be able to cut out the agency. The agency/client/marketing model is being challenged now the way it has never been challenged before, based not only on technology potentially disintermediating . . . but when you break down the trust barrier," because the client doesn't know how its money is being spent, the disintermediation accelerates.

So what stance, an executive asked, should we take with clients?

"I harken back to my baseball days: get a cup," Kassan answered. To protect MediaLink, their task is to serve as "a bridge between the buyer and the seller. We shouldn't harbor any side here. We're on all sides. We are also very close to all of the agencies."

"I get calls every day," interjected another executive, "from people at agencies saying they want to leave the agency."

"They're all running for the exits," Millard observed. "It's extraordinary how many people want out. Their margins are all getting squeezed. One of the big issues we have is, if I can make forty thousand dollars at an agency as a media planner but I can make sixty thousand at Facebook, what am I thinking? This is not a happy industry."

Millard could have cited results of a 2016 survey by *Campaign US*, a global business magazine focused on the marketing world, that found that 47 percent of those who've worked in advertising and marketing more than five years say their morale is low, the primary reasons being "inadequate" leadership, "lack of advancement" opportunities, and "dissatisfaction with work." A LinkedIn survey the same year, with a vast sample size of three hundred thousand, found that when nine industries were ranked by ten questions, advertising came in last in "work/life balance" and "long-term strategic visions," and next to last in "comp & benefits," "strong career path," "job security," and "values employee contributions." Advertising had mediocre rankings in each of the four remaining questions.

Dark clouds may hover over agencies, but Kassan saw only azure sky for MediaLink. "I would hope you all see," he concluded, "why that continued chaos and disruption is kind of a blessing in disguise for us. Actually, I don't think it's in disguise. It's a blessing."

What Kassan saw as bright sky, others would describe as the eye of the storm, but that didn't faze him. The current turbulence was nothing compared to some of the ordeals he'd endured in the past, which on some days seemed like another lifetime and on others, he would admit, seemed like a shadow still chasing him in his rearview mirror.

4.

THE MATCHMAKER

Michael Kassan is advertising's Dolly Levi, the match-making lead character in the musical Hello, Dolly!, *whose score he loves to hum.*

Wenda Millard likes to say of her partner that he believes that everything is a yes, symbolized by the two-word sign above his desk: ALL GOOD. Millard has more shoes than Imelda Marcos, she says, "but my shoes have dents in the toe from shoving my foot into his shoe because I know he's going to say yes." An oft-told MediaLink story illustrates Kassan's skill at pleasing others. He carries in his black Tumi backpack multiple portable devices—a Samsung Galaxy, two iPhones, a BlackBerry, an iPad, along with phone chargers and connector wires. Several years ago, the brand stamped on the back of his cell phones was either Verizon or AT&T. The latter was a client, and he had flown to Dallas for a dinner meeting with an imposing AT&T senior female executive he barely knew. After dinner, as they stepped outside the restaurant his phone rang. Reaching into his bag, he pulled out the Verizon phone.

"Michael, you didn't just take a Verizon phone out of your pocket, did you?" she exclaimed.

"I think to myself, 'You fucking idiot, Michael Kassan!'" Instantly, he flung the Verizon phone to the pavement, smashing it into pieces with his heel. Turning to her, he exclaimed, "Excuse me, was there a question?"

She smiled. He smiled. He explained that he needed a Verizon phone in Los Angeles because AT&T service there was patchy. "It was a bonding moment," he recalls.

It is also a moment shared by more than one MediaLink executive as emblematic of their boss. "He has this perpetual smile on his face," says Robert Salter, who was Kassan's second chief of stuff, as he calls his chief of staff. "When he does something that is so clearly wrong, he does it with a smile and in a way that somehow earns the affection of the person on the other end. He manages to charm them. He's able to make awkward conversations very easy."

He gets the charm from his father, Michael's wife, Ronnie Kassan, observes. "The teller of jokes. His mother was very tough, and had a very shrewd business sense. Michael has that too." He was raised in a modest two-family home in East Flatbush, Brooklyn, that they shared with his mom's dad and aunts and uncles. "It was basically a shtetl," Michael recalls. He had two older sisters, and his mom focused on raising the three children while helping his dad run several dry cleaning stores. "My dad was a stand-up comic in the Catskills. It was a very, very, very sad thing that he did not follow that." Asked what he sees in himself of his parents, Michael says, "I have a million jokes in the file cabinet of my brain. My dad had an extraordinary quick wit and humor. That's the strongest gene I have from my father." When the kids were older, his mother became a successful real estate broker. "My mother refined the use of Jewish guilt to an art form," Kassan jokes. She played on the insecurities of potential customers.

His dad sold the dry cleaning business and relocated the family to Los Angeles when Michael was three, and started a thriving new chain of dry cleaning stores. Michael was gregarious and a good student, but never terribly tractable; the only bad marks he remembers receiving were in classroom cooperation. "I was a wiseass," he says. "I would never raise my hand in class if I wanted to speak. I was a showman."

His sister's husband told him that the University of Miami had the best parties, so he enrolled there, but at the end of his freshman year he transferred home to USC for a year, then to UCLA, where he graduated as an English major. He stayed in California to get a law degree at Southwestern Law School.

In his second year of law school, Kassan met the Bronx-born Ronnie Klein, who had moved to Los Angeles after receiving a psychology degree from the University of Miami and an MA in counseling from New York University. She took a job as a school counselor in Los Angeles. They met when Michael had to fly to New York for a February wedding but didn't have a winter coat. He remembered that a friend who lived in San Diego owned a really nice camel hair coat and he asked to borrow it. The friend happened to be coming to Los Angeles and was happy to drop it off. When Michael returned from the wedding, the friend told him that another friend was driving south to San Diego the next weekend; could Michael call her and drop off the coat? That friend was Ronnie Klein.

When Kassan called Ronnie she said she'd be at her apartment in the early afternoon. He didn't ring the bell until 6 P.M. Annoyed, she took the coat from him and hurriedly shut the door in his face.

"I felt he was a little difficult. I was doing him a favor, and he was a pain in the ass," Ronnie says.

"She had the most beautiful blue eyes," he says. "I saw those eyes and went, Whoa!"

Michael phoned and asked her out the next weekend. Ronnie brushed him off by saying she couldn't plan anything because she might be going to Palm Springs that weekend. She would let him know. "I never heard from her," Michael says.

On Friday afternoon he was crossing Beverly Drive and Wilshire Boulevard on his way to lunch and they almost collided on the crosswalk. "Well, I guess you didn't go to Palm Springs," he said.

She was speechless. "I didn't have an excuse. I was so embarrassed," she recalls.

"I guess we're going out then," he said, shaming her into saying yes.

In early February 1974 they went to the theater and dinner. "It was a really nice evening, much to my surprise," she remembers. He kept calling. They started going out twice a week. She'd kiss him goodnight, but made excuses why he couldn't come in. They dated other people, and while not yet lovers they were becoming close friends. He brought her to Passover dinner with his parents in April.

"At dinner in early May, he told me he was in love with me," she says. "I told him I appreciated it, but I wasn't there." By mid-May, "I slept with him for the first time." In late May, they spent a weekend together and "I realized I had feelings for him." She had another date the next night but phoned Michael and asked if he could stop by her apartment because "I want to talk to you."

"I just want to tell you I think I'm in love with you," she announced.

They kissed and embraced. She mentioned that she was flying to New York in June to be matron of honor at her friend Randi's wedding. "I should go to New York with you," he told her.

He wasn't invited, she said. Besides, Randi didn't know him or even know she was dating him.

"Tell her you're bringing someone," he persisted.

She dialed Randi. Cupping the phone as it rang, she asked him, "Who do I tell her I'm bringing?"

"Tell her you're bringing your fiancé."

"Randi," she blurted, "I have to call you back. I think I just got engaged!"

They married in December 1974 and moved to New York. He enrolled in NYU law school's Master of Law (LLM) program in tax law; Ronnie supported them by working various jobs. They went back to Los Angeles in 1976. With his mother orchestrating the search, they tried to buy a house, but lacked the money to get what they wanted, so they rented an apartment. The next day "Michael went out and bought a Porsche, which was a little irresponsible," Ronnie says. Then his mother discovered a great house in Sherman Oaks, which they were able to purchase with a helpful loan from his cousin, major Disney shareholder Stanley Gold, and from their parents.

Ronnie might have been exasperated by the Porsche, but by now she understood her husband. "Michael feels that everything will work out all the time," she says. There is a reason the epigram at the end of each e-mail he sends reads ALL GOOD.

Michael was doing tax law for a firm; Ronnie was pregnant with the first of their three children. His salary was $1,500 per month, plus a percentage of any new business he brought in. He recruited twelve new clients the first month. "Being a rainmaker was easy for me," he says. In 1977 he joined another firm, and a year later he and some friends opened their own law offices. Michael was restless. "He always wanted to be in business," Ronnie says. "I think he felt that through some client somewhere something would happen. And it did."

He became counsel to his law firm in 1986 when one of his clients, International Video Entertainment, at the time the largest independent home video company, distributor of such popular fare as *G.I. Joe* and *The Transformers*, enticed him to become president and COO. The company was run by Jose Menendez, one of the few individuals Kassan will not volunteer a kind word about. "He was very tough," he says. "He had a chip on his shoulder the size of Cuba. And he used it always. 'Good morning' to him was adversarial." Kassan helped engineer the sale of the company and left in 1987, two years before Menendez and his wife were famously murdered by their two aggrieved sons. He returned to his law firm, but still yearned to be a businessman.

Some years before, while attending a children's birthday party at Harry's Open Pit, the owner asked if he knew anything about franchise law because he wanted to franchise his rib restaurant. Michael said he did, and told him a first step with a franchise was to hire an accountant to prepare an audited financial statement for the state Division of Corporations. He put him in touch with an accountant, and some months later the accountant called Michael and said he was working with the owner of a Mexican chicken restaurant, El Pollo Loco, who wanted to franchise. Michael became both their lawyer and a believer. "I tasted the chicken in the guy's garage and said, 'This is unbelievable.' It was healthy, nonfried fast food." He recruited some of his law partners as fellow investors. He went to the American Heart Association and persuaded them, he says, "to put the heart-healthy logo on a fast-food restaurant. It had never been done." The healthful and delicious Mexican chicken franchise would take off. Over the next fifteen years El Pollo Loco opened forty franchises, and Michael branched out by investing in Rally's Hamburgers. He also continued as a law partner at his firm.

But he made a classic business mistake. The chicken franchise expanded too rapidly. "We took the concept to Las Vegas and we got our clock cleaned," he says. They poured money into Vegas, and soon the business plunged from profit to loss. In California, the vast Hispanic population might eat at El Pollo Loco three times per week; in Vegas, with a relatively minuscule Hispanic population, one visit per month was more common. To shore up the franchises in Vegas and prevent its bankruptcy, Kassan became more engaged. They borrowed more money from the banks, and without seeking board approval transferred monies from El Pollo Loco franchises in California, weakening them. He had shifted monies from healthy California chicken franchises, albeit not to enrich himself, but to fortify cash-starved Las Vegas franchises. On the books, Kassan did not camouflage this act, recording these as loans. Soon the business could not meet the bank loan payments. Kassan drained $150,000 from his own pocket to help make the payments. In January 1994, investor Joel Ladin, one of the four partners in the law firm and the best man at Michael and Ronnie's wedding, confronted Kassan with evidence of the unauthorized withdrawals. After Kassan admitted that he withdrew the funds, he was terminated. The next month Ladin filed a formal complaint against Kassan to the police, charging him with embezzlement. Kassan quickly repaid the entire $240,000 he had borrowed from the healthy El Pollo Locos, plus interest. "There were nights," Kassan says, "Ronnie would say to me, 'I just want to keep the house.' It was Armageddon."

In June 1995, a Superior Court judge found him guilty of "grand theft by embezzlement," but ruled that his motive in taking the money was not personal greed but a desire to keep El Pollo Loco alive. Kassan won a measure of leniency when he reached an agreement with prosecutors to withdraw a planned not guilty plea. He says he did not know that a guilty plea resulted in automatic legal suspension in California, and he would not have pled guilty if he knew this. He received a suspended sentence, was placed on probation for three years, and ordered to perform five hundred hours of community service. He knew that if he successfully completed the terms of his probation, California law allowed him to change his plea to not guilty, and his felony conviction was reduced to a misdemeanor and eventually expunged. The State Bar of California, however, offered no leniency; he was formally suspended. In June 1996, after completing a year of probation, Kassan's felony conviction was reduced to a misdemeanor and erased from his record. But the shame continued to haunt him.

Kassan was despondent. He poured out his hurt to a psychiatrist—four times each week, he says. He was determined to appeal the State Bar ruling, not because he cared to practice law again—he says he did not want to—but because he couldn't bear the thought of his Jewish mother knowing her son could not practice law. "My mother always said, 'You need something to fall back on.'" He appealed to the Supreme Court of California, challenging his suspension from the State Bar. "The one and only chance to tell my story was by challenging the California State Bar," he says. After hearing the case, in April 1999 the state's highest court ruled in his favor, finding:

> In the matter before us the record is clear that respondent's primary motivation was to save the various El Pollo Loco operations. . . . In respondent's case there was no attempt to hide this conduct, and when confronted he immediately acknowledged his actions and made immediate arrangements to make good his theft. . . . We make no effort to minimize the seriousness of respondent's criminal misconduct. He fraudulently converted a large amount of money to his own use in violation of a most fundamental rule of honesty. Nevertheless, considering the circumstances surrounding the criminal conduct, twenty years of blemish-free practice prior to the misconduct, respondent's immediate restitution, recognition of wrongdoing

and genuine remorse we believe the record demonstrates that disbarment is not required to achieve the goals of attorney discipline.

A Google search for Michael Kassan finds mention of his felony conviction and near disbarment only if one is willing to scroll through many pages; his Wikipedia profile is silent about it. Understandably, it is something he would prefer not to dwell on, and yet it's never entirely gone from his thoughts. For much of his adult life since, he says, he has glanced up at the rearview mirror, fearing that he was being chased. His shame has remained dormant, but ever since there have been two Michael Kassans—the cheerful charmer and the sinner. Most see Michael Kassan the successful optimist; few see the self-conscious man fearful that his humiliating past could somehow come back to haunt him.

Dennis Holt, who had been a law client of Kassan's, knew of his legal tribulations and in 1994 offered him an outstretched hand. Holt had founded Western International Media in 1970. At a time when agencies sold themselves as one-stop shopping places, offering clients a full range of creative, strategic, and media-buying services, Western successfully unbundled media buying. With thirty-seven offices and a thousand employees, Western became the world's foremost buyer of local TV, radio, and out-of-home advertising like billboards or supermarket promotions. "He was the equivalent of what Irwin Gotlieb is today," standing atop the most powerful media agency, Kassan says. "He was the largest independent media agency in the world." Holt says he chose to ignore Kassan's prior felony conviction. "I was the one who restored him," Holt says. The business had outgrown Holt's managerial style, which was to personally sign every check. "We had gotten so big and did so many different things that I wasn't having fun anymore," Holt says. He was determined to hire Kassan. At Nate'n Al's in Beverly Hills, Holt looked him in the eye and said, "I'm not offering you a job. I'm offering you a life." He was offering a way to regain his self-confidence, his swagger. Kassan's prime mission would be to sell Western. Within six months, Kassan succeeded, consummating a sale to the Interpublic Group, then the world's largest advertising holding company.

Kassan remained as president of the company for five years. By 1999, he was clashing with Holt, who had stayed on as chairman, as well as with senior executives at the parent company. Asked if Kassan did a good job, Holt did not answer for several seconds, then said "No," adding, "he did a good job with the process of selling the company." The clash with IPG became ugly. In August 1999, the firm locked Kassan out of his office and Kassan filed a $63.5 million lawsuit against them, alleging that IPG defamed him by claiming financial misconduct, and also breached his five-year employment contract. Days later the company announced that Kassan was "terminated." IPG executives won't discuss the matter. Kassan will only say, "What I am allowed to say is we amicably resolved our differences." Dennis Holt, who remained with the company until 2000, says, "IPG wanted to fire him many times, but I defended him," a claim that causes Ronnie Kassan to roll her eyes. IPG was offended by Kassan's steep expenses, Holt says, including massages and charges on the New York City suite he maintained at the St. Regis hotel. Baloney, says Kassan's friend Irwin Gotlieb, who first got to know him as a Western competitor. Because Michael was paid a handsome annual bonus from IPG as part of his five-year payout from the sale of Western, his jealous IPG boss "wasn't the kind of guy who could watch someone else make a lot of money."

The lawsuit was settled out of court, with IPG stating that it had conducted an audit and was satisfied there were no irregularities. But for the second time in less than a decade, it wasn't "ALL GOOD" for Michael Kassan. "He was depressed," Ronnie Kassan remembers. "We have a very close friend"—now Cerberus Capital Management vice chair, Lenard B. Tessler—"who called Michael every day and said, 'I'm calling you because I don't want you to think no one calls you.' Michael didn't want to go back to law. He just didn't know what he wanted to do."

Another close friend, prominent attorney Howard Weitzman, who is known in Los Angeles as an attorney for Hollywood celebrities, had participated in the launch of a software digital rights business, Massive Media, and in late 1999 Kassan was recruited. Kassan was enthused about the media and marketing business and intrigued because he saw Massive Media as a vehicle to broaden his expertise. "It gave me exposure to what was happening in the digital sphere," Kassan says. His task, Weitzman says, was to boost sales and help shape business strategy.

One of the other partners in the company, former Viacom CEO Frank Biondi, who had never met Kassan before, was impressed by him; Kassan struck him as "a huge personality." Biondi was shaken when a lawyer friend phoned to say he was representing a potential investor that Kassan had approached, and when the lawyer did his due diligence he discovered that Kassan had been convicted of fraud and almost disbarred. Weitzman assured Biondi that Kassan was of good character. And Biondi says that for the first year Kassan did a good job. "But the firm needed to raise more money, and Michael volunteered to lead the raise. The Internet bubble had begun to burst." The money dried up. "In the end, Michael was totally unsuccessful in raising funds. In fairness to him, I'm not sure God could have raised money at that point."

"He was home a lot," Ronnie Kassan says, and people would call seeking his advice. "Michael, why don't you charge them?" she asked him.

■ ■ ■

He listened to her. Over the next three years he performed a variety of consulting jobs for companies in the U.S. and Europe, mostly smaller companies asking him to help them strategize and to connect them to other companies.

Kassan saw a void he could fill. The advertising and marketing world was in turmoil, soon to be disrupted by the Internet and digital upstarts like Google and Yahoo. Clients who paid for and media platforms that sold advertising sought guidance, but couldn't turn to agencies for neutral advice. Sellers wanted to be introduced to buyers, digital companies to brands. His experience with brands and media companies at Western and with digital companies at Massive Media—plus the insecurities of an industry seeking a life raft, plus his charm and connections and the three years he spent as a consultant—convinced Kassan he could build a unique service company. He and MediaLink would serve as both a connector and a hand-holder.

He set out to recruit a financial partner to help him quickly scale the business, and thought the Hollywood talent agencies would be a natural fit. "I walked up Wilshire where the talent agencies were located with my hat in my hand," he recalls. "I didn't need a job. My consulting business was doing well. But I wanted to do it with a team. The agencies gave me a lot of 'Ya, ya. No, no.'"

Undaunted, he launched MediaLink himself in 2003, expanding over time to perform an array of related functions. MediaLink's purpose, Kassan said, "was to provide adult supervision in the midst of chaos." His friend Irwin Gotlieb sees a perfect match between a warm, capable personality and a frightened industry. "He knows everybody. My special talent is, you show me a number and I'll remember it forever. Introduce me to three people, and I will have forgotten their names in five seconds. Michael will remember their names forever. He would be a natural politician."

This time, Kassan monitored his appetite, growing MediaLink slowly. The fifth employee, Karl Spangenberg, was not hired until 2007. An experienced ad sales executive with a wide range of media and digital companies, Spangenberg says that when he was a senior marketing executive at AT&T he "hired Kassan and MediaLink to open doors for me."

A New York office with a creaky freight elevator and little furniture was opened in 2008. Kassan gained a measure of fame when he was hired by Microsoft in 2008 to galvanize the digital community in opposition to Google making a search deal with Yahoo, and succeeded.

"When Wenda joined in 2009, the business exploded," Spangenberg says. Wenda Millard's résumé displays the laurels of thirty-five years of traditional publishing and digital media jobs, including publisher of *Family Circle* and group publisher of *Adweek*, *Mediaweek*, and *Brandweek* magazines; chief sales officer for six years at Yahoo when that company was an Internet darling; and chief Internet officer at Ziff Davis Media and executive vice president of DoubleClick. She had also chaired the Interactive Advertising Bureau and was former president of the Advertising Club of New York. Millard and Kassan had known each other for years. When he approached her she was president and co-CEO of Martha Stewart Living Omnimedia, a company whose mercurial owner could be unsettling. Like Kassan, Millard knew most people in the business. Unlike him, she was fastidiously well organized. She mentioned that she was about to leave as co-CEO of Martha Stewart and was thinking of setting up her own marketing consultancy.

"Don't do that," he exclaimed. "We might end up as competitors. Let's do this together and have some fun." He then owned 100 percent of MediaLink, and offered her one-third ownership and the title of president and COO. He gave her the pitch: "MediaLink lives where Madison Avenue meets Silicon Valley, meets Hollywood, meets Wall Street. We live at that nexus." She was intrigued, though some of her friends were not. One close friend says she told Millard she thought his slickness didn't mesh with her sincerity, and mentioned a vague recollection of a rumor that some people in the industry whispered: Wasn't he once convicted of something?

Millard signed on. Their sail has not always been smooth—they are indeed opposites in many ways, but measured by growth and reach, their partnership has been a success. Together, by the spring of 2017 they supervised 120 or so employees; most work with assigned clients in several divisions. Data & Technology Solutions under managing director Matt Spiegel, a digital entrepreneur who was Omnicom Media Group's global digital CEO, advises companies on a range of technological solutions they might pursue, from programmatic advertising to AI to cybersecurity. If clients want to meet key people at Google, Kassan will help introduce them. When Unilever, one of MediaLink's initial clients, was their first client to ask, seven years ago, for a tour of Silicon Valley, Kassan arranged it, including visits with Google, Facebook, and Twitter. "We were keen to understand what was going on," Unilever's Keith Weed says. "I'm a great believer in what Woody Allen once said: 'Eighty percent of success is just showing up.'" Unilever, the world's second largest advertiser, is today one of Google and Facebook's biggest advertisers.

Marketing Optimization under managing director Lesley Klein, a former account director at Deutsch, offers consultation to companies on an ongoing basis; it is an influential part of MediaLink's business, for it provides a client base. Potential start-up clients usually are courted by Kassan. Once signed on, they pay a monthly retainer that can range from $35,000 to several hundred thousand dollars per month; more established companies spend more time with Kassan and pay per project or place MediaLink on an ongoing retainer. The ninety-one clients serviced at the Cannes Lions Festival in 2016, for example, may already have been on retainer, or may have been billed just for this service. The Marketing Optimization division offers strategic or organizational advice, introduces them to people or ideas that might transform their business, and helps negotiate agency contracts. Lesley Klein and senior vice president Bernhard Glock also orchestrate the agency reviews for brand companies. The initial sales pitch is usually made by Kassan.

Business Acceleration, which each division has a hand in, services a bevy of traditional media clients like Hearst, the *New York Times*, the *Wall Street Journal*, Condé Nast, Time Inc., Comcast, and NBCUniversal. They turn to MediaLink to help devise a corporate growth strategy and to make them more visible by arranging meetings, or to consult by coming in and doing what a McKinsey would and help devise a corporate reorganization, as MediaLink did for Condé Nast. "We advise these companies on chaos," Kassan says. Like many traditional print companies, "they need to reimagine themselves as a media and not a print company. We try to help them reimagine their business." Meredith Levien, executive vice president and chief revenue officer of the New York Times Company, says, "The landscape is complicated, and MediaLink helps us get in front of the right people." Senior vice president Howard Homonoff, a former PricewaterhouseCoopers and NBCU executive who is part of this division, says their work can get pretty granular. Clients naturally fret about the speed of change and say to him, "'Help me look at the next three to five years and help me define what it will look like and what are the best ways for me to succeed and grow in new areas. What are the new forms of advertising? And help me think through who my acquisition targets or partners might be.'"

A similar function is performed for digital publishing companies grouped in the Emerging Media division, which advises clients like

Twitter or Refinery29 on strategic and marketing issues. This division is overseen by managing director Sunil Kapadia, a former Silicon Valley software engineer and Boston Consulting Group executive. Philippe von Borries, the cofounder of Refinery29, described what Kassan does for a smaller company like his that hopes to bust out: "Michael is the great connector. We think of Michael as an adviser, someone who has the ear of everyone in this space, connecting us to brands, media companies, platforms."

A fifth division, the Investor Strategy group, is supervised by managing director JC Uva, a former investment banker. It serves clients who want to explore an acquisition or investment, including corporations, private equity firms, hedge funds, and venture capitalists, as Disney asked MediaLink how it would affect their family-friendly brand if they invested in Vice Media. Without identifying Disney, MediaLink called twenty-five of their clients and asked if an established media company partnered with "an edgy" company like Vice, would it help or harm the established brand? MediaLink is often asked by clients whether to buy a company outright; whether MediaLink should act like a venture capital firm and invest its own money in emerging companies; or whether MediaLink should accept stock in a start-up in exchange for its services. In performing these roles, JC Uva says MediaLink competes with consultants like McKinsey, and sometimes investment bankers or venture capitalists. Because of their breadth of experience and contacts in advertising, marketing, and the tech space, "our advantage is that we have more detailed information."

Sometimes MediaLink, or just Kassan and Millard, have invested their own money and made a financial killing. Kassan as a personal investor and MediaLink in its role as strategic adviser were paid a bounty for steering the sale of two longtime clients—Maker Studios, a producer of digital video content, to Disney for $700 million, and Buddy Media, a company that creates an advertising infrastructure across social media platforms, to Salesforce.com for $850 million. "Our role in that space," Kassan explains, "has been enhanced because we are, fortunately, a very credible resource for people who have businesses that are premised on advertising as one of the primary revenue sources. It is good to have someone who is not just a banker but who can validate the business opportunities."

A sixth division, the Talent@MediaLink group, performs a headhunting function for clients looking to fill positions, be they brands, publishing platforms, digital and traditional companies, or agencies. "We started seven years ago for GE," Kassan recalls. They had advised the company on how to reorganize its global branding and marketing division, and the CMO, Beth Comstock, deputized MediaLink to lead the search to fill two new jobs. The next year, he says, "They wanted to build a Digital Centers of Excellence. What would it look like? Who would they hire? They wanted to ask Spencer Stuart. We said, 'No, we'll do it.' Now executive search is almost fifteen percent of our business." MediaLink has several advantages, he says. One, because his company is enmeshed in the industry, they offer "a scouting report from someone who has played shortstop while the other guy was at second base. We've done double plays together." Two, because they often do strategic work for the same company, MediaLink has a leg up on their strategy and what best fits their corporate culture. And third, they earn gratitude. "It gives us an unfair advantage because often we're placing someone who becomes our client."

By early 2017, managing director Laurie Rosenfield, an experienced recruiter who has held executive positions at CBS, TiVo, and 20th Century Fox and who reported to Wenda Millard, says that she and her ten-member team were engaged in fifty executive searches. When the 4A's on behalf of ad agencies in late 2016 sought a replacement for President and CEO Nancy Hill, who chose to retire from her $700,000-a-year job, they retained MediaLink. Jack Haber, longtime Colgate marketing chief who retired in 2016, was startled that MediaLink's intelligence network provided an early warning system that reached into his organization. "One day," he says, "my global VP of Marketing resigned. MediaLink already knew. They said, 'We have a list.'"

Another division, Market Visibility, is overseen by managing directors Brett Kassan Smith, Michael's daughter, an experienced marketing and public relations executive, and Lena Petersen, who hails from the advertising agency world. Many of these divisions overlap at various points, but this one takes the lead in the promotional or connector role, including getting iHeartMedia or GroupM to invest in MediaLink events at Cannes or the CES, recruiting speakers for ad agency panels at conferences, making sure that the clients who come to Cannes or CES have scheduled meetings with agencies and brands. When Michael Kassan got Universal Music to gift Lady Gaga to perform at Media-Link's CES party in 2016, it was Brett Kassan who had to intervene to halt her father from violating the fire code by inviting more guests. Her group, more than the others, performs the convener function.

* * *

Kassan himself is, of course, the ultimate convener at MediaLink.

Michael Roth, CEO of IPG, starts laughing when he describes Kassan as a "matchmaker," and offers this example: "We hire him on a consulting basis. Or sometimes he wants us to sponsor one of his events, and he'll call me up and tell me, 'John [Wren, CEO of Omnicom] and Martin [Sorrell] are going to do it. Are you going to?' Then he calls John and Martin and says 'Roth is going to do it.' Then we'll all meet at the event and say, 'Why the fuck are we doing this?'"

One gets a sense of Michael Kassan, connector, watching him confer with his chief of stuff, Martin Rothman, on the leased six-seat NetJet as it leaves Miami after a 4A's conference in April 2016. They review a draft presentation he had dictated and the staff honed, which he's to present to a client the next day, suggesting how the client should market itself and what new media efforts it should undertake. "One of the questions the client asked," Kassan says, "is how do we benchmark against what our competitors are doing?" He smiles. Of course, he doesn't say that "some of the competitors are also our clients." Nor, he adds, do they share information with any of them. They review a list of potential speakers he will recruit to attend client Alan Patricof's Greycroft Partners annual June conference in Montauk. They review a staff-drafted memo to a bevy of clients for his signature. They review and he prioritizes from a long list of phone calls he needs to make, and breakfast, lunch, cocktails, and dinners he needs to schedule. Although Rothman lives in New York, when Kassan is in Los Angeles or traveling elsewhere, he is usually at his side, taking notes at his meetings, briefing Kassan before his hundred or so daily phone calls, listening in on them and taking notes, and being copied on what he describes as up to five hundred "actionable e-mails" Kassan receives daily.

Kassan's day is usually broken up into somewhere between five- and twenty-minute increments, and it begins around 7:40 A.M. and ends every day before or after dinner. Every meeting has a purpose, an action. "The only thing Michael has is his time," says Grant Gittlin, his first chief of stuff and today MediaLink's chief execution officer. Kassan is overwhelmed by a torrent of e-mails, calls, meetings, he says. "You get to a point where you're so busy it's hard to actually delegate. Having someone who can listen in lets him play jazz" while the chief of stuff takes notes and follows up. "My job was to be the steady rhythm man." Of course, playing jazz is instinctual, improvisational. Kassan often drives his coworkers mad as he flits from meeting to meeting, subject to subject, unable to sit down for a meeting or to allow them to pry a definitive answer from him. "Michael invented ADD," Millard says. "It is very difficult for him to focus on any one issue"—until he has to, she adds. Even his beloved Ronnie remembers how angry she was with him in August 2015, when they rented a home in the Hamptons. "The first two weeks in August he left me in the Hamptons and worked in New York." When they rented a house in the Hamptons the following summer, she issued an ultimatum: "I made a deal with him. If he went to New York City I would fly back to LA."

Kassan's network of relationships grants him immense power. He is advertising's Dolly Levi, the matchmaking lead character in the musical *Hello, Dolly!*, whose score he loves to hum. When Wendy Clark was being wooed by Omnicom to leave Coca-Cola and become North American CEO of DDB, she says he negotiated her contract, serving as "my attorney, my counsel," and would take not a penny. "I have only paid MediaLink one time, when I was at Coca-Cola and he arranged an executive tour at CES," she says. Facebook's Carolyn Everson says of him, "He's kind of like the Godfather of this industry. When Michael likes you and respects you, you become part of his family. He treats me like his niece. He invited me to his first grandson's bris." Dana Anderson, former senior vice president and CMO of Mondelēz, who joined MediaLink as its CMO in mid-2017, still marvels how with just two days' notice he was able to deliver Kim Kardashian to a Mondelēz gathering.

While few fail to mention Kassan's charm and intelligence as reasons for his success, Rishad Tobaccowala of Publicis has known Kassan for many years and offers this explanation of his power: "What he has managed to do is to play on all sides of the party. I don't know how he did it, but hats off. I would feel somewhat squirrelly because I wouldn't know whether I could trust you. But what he has basically done is become a sort of synapse of the industry. And so now people are very scared that if they don't pay him they will lose something. No one opposes him, and the reason no one opposes him is because he runs pitches like the Bank of America agency pitch." This feeds into Tobaccowala's underlying explanation for Kassan and MediaLink's power: "This industry is full of deeply insecure people who don't know what is happening and are buying hedges." Over the years, when agencies discussed with Kassan the possibility of acquiring MediaLink and mentioned that under them it would be a conflict for MediaLink to conduct agency reviews, Kassan knew that would neuter Media-Link, because agencies would no longer fear what he whispered in the ear of advertisers. Often, he is retained by agencies as well as advertisers and platforms that sell ad space. Tim Andree, executive chairman and executive vice president of Dentsu's operations outside Japan, said his agency retained MediaLink for certain projects. So too, chimes Havas CEO Yannick Bolloré, does his agency.

Veteran advertising observer Jack Myers, chairman of MyersBizNet, which provides a steady stream of marketing and other data to companies, says of Kassan, "Michael is a maestro at convincing people they can't do business without him. He is the most powerful of the power brokers in that business. No one comes close." Bob Pittman, chairman and CEO of iHeartMedia, the largest radio company in the U.S., likens him to nineteenth-century Chinese compradors, who built trading bridges to the West. Les Moonves, chairman and CEO of CBS, describes him as "a wheeler-dealer" who "represents everybody. He was always a player, but in the last six, seven, eight years he's definitely become a power broker." Kassan regularly solicits CBS executives under Moonves, suggesting they meet one of his clients. "He's a little slick. But he gets stuff done," Moonves says.

What surprises people is how little muscular competition Media-Link confronts. Beth Comstock of GE says, "I am shocked that MediaLink doesn't have more competition." Yes, there are individuals like Shelly Palmer, whose Strategic Advisors serves advertising clients, distributes a regular and smart blog post, and arranges tours and meetings at confabs like CES. But he lacks size. "No one else has scaled it," Irwin Gotlieb says. "You can't scale if you're just an individual. What Michael did most successfully was he expanded from a one-man operation." There are consultancies that headhunt or advise on management, but these are siloed efforts. After operating largely uncontested since 2003, MediaLink benefits from network effects.

Michael Kassan has his critics, though the fiercest criticism is usually volunteered only after the critic is guaranteed anonymity. "Media-Link is like the Mafia. You pay them for protection," the CEO of one tech firm who retained them says. "I used to pay them twenty thousand dollars per month during year one. Year two went up to twenty-five thousand per month. At first I'd meet with Michael and Wenda. Then you're dealing with a kid. . . . You pay them money so you can go to their CES party. I no longer pay so I'm no longer invited." Kassan counters, "Only clients are invited." Aghast at what he sees as the contradiction between where advertising is heading and the P. T. Barnum character that Michael Kassan represents, one digital executive fumes, "We have an industry that says we are moving from art to science, away from the hucksterism and legerdemain of the last two centuries and into the era of definable return on investment that can identify who watched an ad and whether it registered a sale. And who is the character that is the connective tissue for the entire industry? It's a guy who is all legerdemain and hucksterism."

This harsh critique dovetails with another criticism sometimes lodged against Kassan: that he blows smoke at people, too eager to be everybody's friend. When he conducts interviews onstage, as he does at confabs like Advertising Week, CES, and Cannes, he asks knowledgeable questions but only after unashamedly lacquering his guests with praise, telling the audience that Bob Pittman's rebranding of iHeartMedia, which, he fails to mention, has to pay down huge debts and through the end of 2016 lost money over twenty-seven consecutive quarters, is "a great story." He usually spares his real or potential clients uncomfortable but essential questions, as when he interviewed Les Moonves in Cannes and did not ask if he would support a merger of CBS and Viacom and whether he yearned to become CEO of the new entity, as the controlling shareholder, the Redstone family, desired.

There are several ways to look at Kassan's ingratiating manner. One, as the critic who compared him to P. T. Barnum does, is to label him a bullshit artist. Two, as his friend Howard Weitzman does, who when told that Kassan reached out and recently invited to dinner his nemesis, Dennis Holt, said, "I'm not sure I would have done that. Michael sees the good in people, and sometimes ignores the bad. He's a generous person." Like Weitzman, Ronnie Kassan would not have gone to dinner with Dennis Holt. She agrees that her husband is a generous soul. But she adds this twist, which she means as a loving observation that others may interpret differently: "Michael has got some insecurities. He really wants to be liked."

The other criticism aimed at Kassan centers on MediaLink's perceived conflicts of interest. How, critics wonder, can Kassan represent companies that are rivals—Facebook, Google, and Microsoft, or Disney, 21st Century Fox, and NBCU, or both buyer and seller—and wall off information from each side? How can Kassan personally invest in companies—Maker Studios, or marketing companies like Buddy Media—without being tempted to urge his brand clients to divert ad dollars to them? How can he represent all sides in a negotiation—the buyer of ads (the client and the agency) and the seller (the publisher or platform)?

Those who deal with Michael Kassan acknowledge his charm. Armies of friends attest to his capacity for friendship and loyalty. And as to his alleged conflicts of interest, Kassan likes to say, "No conflict, no interest." Even when he represents clients on opposite sides of the same table, he says, "our special sauce" is that they trust MediaLink not to betray them or their information. Although his is an unusual definition of neutrality, he insists he is "transparent" because everyone at the table knows he represents both parties. "We really do represent everyone. We're so conflicted that we're not conflicted anymore. There's an old joke about the lawyer who used to say, 'Two clients in a category is a conflict, three is a specialty.'" He laughs, charmingly.

5.

ANXIOUS CLIENTS

"If you want a good kisser, we're your date!"

—Michael Kassan

A t dinner at one of Michael Kassan's favorite Italian restaurants, Scalinatella on East Sixty-first Street, a darkened, downstairs cave where waiters greet him by name and he hugs Johnnie, the majordomo, and everyone knows he prefers his vodka martinis dry without olives and straight up, Kassan ordered a tomato-and-onion salad followed by a generous veal chop with a side of broccoli rabe. Tucking into his meal, attired casually in the California style he prefers of a sweater over an open-necked shirt, dark khakis, and soft, black shoes, he recounted a pitch he'd made to the CEO of a major advertiser. "You talk to all my competitors," the worried CEO told him. "How can I feel comfortable opening my kimono to you?"

"Look at it this way: we're fortunate that we get to kiss lots of girls," Kassan told him. "We never kiss and tell. It just informs our ability as kissers. So if you want a good kisser, we're your date!" Kassan likened his mix of powerful clients to the Hollywood law firm of Ziffren Brittenham or New York entertainment lawyer Allen Grubman: "You go to them because they represent everybody and know everything."

Spurred, in part, by Jon Mandel's assault on agency holding companies, throughout 2015 and into 2016, brand clients reviewing whether to kiss their agencies good-bye—Unilever, Bank of America, 21st Century Fox, among others—turned to Kassan for guidance. The trust issue went far deeper than a matter of hidden kickbacks, as Bank of America's longtime CMO and now vice chair, Anne Finucane, would explain. Finucane believes that financial transparency can be codified in agency contracts, and she has done so, but a larger issue is that the agencies are now parts of bigger marketing Goliaths offering a range of services, which pull agencies away from "thinking like a client." It bugs her when agencies bombard her with "hard sell" proposals for new services from their sister divisions.

Jack Haber of Colgate makes a similar point about how agencies sabotage trust by constantly peddling a variety of services. Once, the relationship between client and agency was simple, he says. Instead of a lucrative 15 percent commission, agencies now negotiate a fee. And they are part of giant holding companies seeking more and more fees. "When I worked at an agency, I wanted to sell ads. Now our agency, WPP, wants to sell other services. Their strategy is to get more money out of clients." In earlier days, "the focus was on the work. Now the conversation has shifted." Agencies talk more about data, and spending more money to target audiences, and bringing in public relations and social network experts. He says he keeps asking, "Where are the creative people?" The biggest change in his own behavior as CMO, he says, was that "we had to be more demanding."

There are, of course, other logical reasons for tensions between clients and agencies. Step into the shoes of the client: new technologies and a multiplicity of digital platforms offer baffling and expensive choices.

No secret drawer contains a checklist of the correct answers to the dizzying array of new choices clients face. No agency or McKinsey adviser who is not insufferably arrogant would declare they know the answers. The CEOs of the brands badger their team about company profit margins, as if marketing costs were an extravagance. The agencies complain they are being choked by low fees, but the CEO knows that agency holding company profit margins are still a relatively robust 15 or so percent. So the company CEO demands to know the return on investment of what is spent on marketing, and the honest answer is at best a guess. Corporate raiders are circling, pressing companies to manufacture short-term gains. The average CMO holds office for only about two years before being replaced by a new CMO. The new CMO is probably inclined to bring in a new agency and to insist that the agency reduce its costs.

What does the CMO do about the digital fraud issue? A 2015 study by Distil Networks concluded that one of every three digital ad dollars is wasted by ad fraud, meaning ads are clicked and paid for but are not viewed by desired consumers. Often, the culprits are computer programs or bots. The CMOs' official spokesman, Bob Liodice of the ANA, said in late 2015, "Roughly at least twelve percent of digital ads are going to nonhumans, and twenty-three percent of digital ads are going to criminals." He pegged the cost to his advertiser constituents at $6.5 billion, and bluntly blamed clients for being "negligent. We spend nothing on cybersecurity." The Distil study totaled the loss to clients in 2015 at a much higher $18.5 billion. Liodice's global counterpart, the World Federation of Advertisers, estimated that if fraud continued unpoliced, by 2025 global marketers would be robbed of $50 billion annually.

The CMOs feel trapped. Their CFO or procurement officer demands that the company stop wasting money on false clicks and ads that were paid for but never delivered to an audience. But how? Can the CMO fully trust social networks like Facebook, given that the more reported viewers of an ad, the more Facebook gets paid? The CMO doesn't completely trust the ad agency, for they are compensated for placing the digital ads. The CMO is wary of Nielsen or other measurement agencies, for they still have a primitive way to gauge the size of the digital audience and whether an ad was actually viewed.

Not all clients are dissatisfied with their agencies. Keith Weed of Unilever, for example, has four hundred brands served by multiple agencies, foremost among them the agencies of WPP. Weed flatly says, "I don't trust my agencies less." And as for the cost cutters, he says, "Procurement works for me at Unilever." It would have pleased advertising agency executives to attend a crowded panel discussion among CMOs on the beach at the 2016 Cannes festival. Marc Pritchard, the chief brand officer of Procter & Gamble, the world's largest advertiser, surprised members of the audience by expressing sympathy for agencies and criticism of many clients: "When we treat our agencies as partners, we get great work. When we treat them as suppliers, we get crap work." He heaped blame on procurement officers: "The single biggest complaint agencies have is that this relationship is managed by procurement. The problem is we are thinking of marketing as a cost rather than a value."

Brad Jakeman, then president of the Global Beverage Group at PepsiCo, jumped in, noting that his company eliminated the procurement function earlier that year in order "to focus on marketing." By moving procurement "out of a control function," Michael Kassan would later say, PepsiCo had boldly relegated them "from first string violin to the orchestra." Jakeman went on to express sympathy for beleaguered agencies: "They knew we respected that they had to make money. They're a public company, like we are. They have margin commitments to hit, just like we do. They have revenue targets to hit, just like we do. And the only variable they have to play with to hit these margins is the quality of the people they put on your business. So if we pay them less, they're going to put more junior people on the business. Probably not as talented people. And that's going to show up in the quality of the work."

* * *

The agency reviews of 2015 engendered some bitter feelings. Maurice Levy of Publicis, as we've seen, was angry that Omnicom bested Publicis to snatch the P&G account from them, and he was ecstatic to pluck the Bank of America strategic planning business from WPP's Martin Sorrell. Levy was on his game for that pitch, exuding Gallic charm, and in control of the message from the broad strokes down to a granular level. He promised that his respected chief strategist, Rishad Tobaccowala, would be directly involved with BofA in planning and executing its annual $2 billion marketing spend. By contrast, BofA executives grumble that they were offended by WPP's performance: Martin Sorrell brought in a truckload of different CEOs, many of whom did not seem to know one another, and their presentation was disjointed. Bank executives felt Sorrell and Irwin Gotlieb lectured them. "Martin spoke for a half hour," a senior executive says, "and Irwin for one hour. That only left a half hour for discussion."

There was nothing new about nailing a pitch in an agency review, or blowing it, for that matter, but the wave of agency reviews that started post-Mandel's 2015 speech felt different. For the first time ever to this degree, efforts were intensifying to discard the middleman. Increasingly, clients were taking work away from agencies to do it in-house. Procter & Gamble has created its own proprietary programmatic ad buying system, taking some—not all—of programmatic buying away from its agencies. The ANA reported in 2016 that 31 percent of advertisers responding to one of their surveys said they had brought elements of programmatic ad buying in-house. Obstacles remain, particularly for smaller companies, because programmatic buying rewards scale, but for agencies the trends are ominous.

Even more worrisome, clients are also doing more creative work in-house. Unilever outsourced Unilever Studio to a company to perform tasks once outsourced to agencies. Airbnb CMO Jonathan Mildenhall, who left a top marketing job at Coca-Cola to join this digital upstart in 2014, says half his marketing department "are creative. They're writers and art directors and photographers and videographers." A major reason, he says, is that agencies don't move fast enough. A client performing more of its own creative work was a practice he followed when he was at Coca-Cola, and it's practiced at companies like Apple. It's true as well in the world of fashion, where the designers' vision is central, and where internal marketing departments are usually entrusted to create marketing campaigns.

More nimble public relations firms now commonly supplant ad agencies to tweet, blog, and podcast for advertisers. Edelman is the largest privately owned public relations firm in the world. For clients like Samsung or Taco Bell they engage in online discussions with consumers on social networks or on the client's Web site, or recruit influencers to engage consumers on various digital platforms. For the Dove Hair team, for example, CEO Richard Edelman says they created a variety of colorful, curly-haired Love Your Curls emojis, generating 414 million impressions on sites like Fashionista.com, HypeHair.com, MarieClaire.com, and SheSpeaks.com. With newspapers contracting or closing, he says, "We're trying to find other channels because we can't pitch to reporters anymore. We're now dealing with Buzzfeed and Vice and Business Insider. They want sponsored or branded content. They want something funny, clever" to sneak past the defenses of millennials on guard against interruptive ads. To millennials, he is selling advertising, not news.

But even with more work migrating to PR agencies or in-house for the creation and execution of big brand ideas, clients are still usually reliant on their agencies. While Mildenhall says "eighty percent of my content needs I do in-house," he also says that his agency, TBWA\ Chiat\Day, "gets eighty percent of my media budget." His in-house creative revolves mostly around promotional materials and activities like designing corporate Web sites. Because speed counts, clients increasingly take in-house their blogging and tweeting and social network posts. What retards a client's ability to do more of its own creative work is that creative executives don't clamor to work for a single brand, as ad agency executives proclaim, because abundantly talented creatives don't want to devote themselves to only one client. "The best people want to feel free to work for many clients and across many sectors," Sorrell's éminence grise Jeremy Bullmore says. Nevertheless, clients moving more work in-house poses an ongoing challenge to agencies.

Another assault on agencies comes from publishing platforms performing the creative functions of ad agencies. This effort is fueled by native ads which can take the form of stories about a brand that appear in newspapers, magazines, or online and look like news stories; or compelling human interest stories in which the brand is barely mentioned. An impetus for these native ads came from the introduction of ad blockers, which imposed a nearly impregnable wall to block clearly labeled ads. Because they don't appear to be ads, native tricks the ad-blocking software and, often, the consumer. Vice was a native pioneer when it went to Intel in 2013 and created an online Intel art exhibition that encouraged residents of certain areas to communicate with each other by joining, say, the Brooklyn Art Project. Publishing platforms sell the storytelling ability of the journalists they hire to craft native ads, and bypass the agency to pitch clients directly. The *New York Times* may be shedding older journalists, but it had hired 110 copywriters and art directors (almost one third of its ad sales department) to create native ads for brands. Agencies desperate not to offend clients have little leverage to counter this new threat.

To discuss the various threats to his agencies, Martin Sorrell leans forward on the wooden chair facing the small conference table cluttered with papers in his second-floor London office. He is not blind to these threats, and often speaks of the competition from digital and consulting and PR and publishing platforms. If anything, his constant travels and attendance at conferences and meetings with an array of frenemies make him unusually aware of potential threats to his business. Of the threat posed by platforms serving as agencies, he notes that WPP has partial ownership stakes in some of these potential competitors, including Vice. "Just think about our strategy: It's to get the Don Draper companies—the traditional companies—to move quickly into digital. It's to get the digital companies to go even faster," and he cites the aggressive move to beef up the digital operations of such WPP companies as Wunderman, Ogilvy, and AKQA. He dismisses the notion that the *New York Times* poses an advertising threat. "I don't worry about them. The *Times* should be worried, because 110 people creating native content are not going to put off the evil day, the continued decline of print."

* * *

Bill Bernbach and David Ogilvy would be horrified by the behavior of today's restive advertising clients. Those, of course, were simpler times. Ad agencies were once mom and pop businesses that oversaw everything, from devising the strategy to creating the ads to buying ad space. But when the founders of these agencies sold to emerging holding companies, these giants consolidated strategy and media buying under separate media agencies whose size granted leverage over the TV and media platforms who were selling ads. And as the profitability of creative agencies contracted and marketing functions expanded, holding companies purchased direct mail and public relations and polling and design and other marketing agencies. In place of a single 15 percent agency fee, each agency charged a separate fee for their services.

The media landscape changed just as fundamentally. "Back in Don Draper's day you had three major networks," says GE's Beth Comstock. "You had people's attention. People had fewer choices." Today, she continued, "digital changes the definition of what advertising is. A well-done thirty-second spot in the right form is really very good. But luckily it's not my only option anymore."

Comstock's early career did not herald that she would be an innovator. She joined NBC as publicity coordinator for NBC News in 1986, worked in publicity for CNN and CBS News, returned to NBC in 1994, and became chief of all NBC communications in 1996. GE was the parent company of NBC, and when its top communications job opened in 1998, CEO Jack Welch plucked her for the job. She made it her business to become expert on an array of subjects, from the digital upheaval to social networks and new ways of marketing. After CEO Jeff Immelt elevated her to CMO, she took it upon herself to become GE's digital point person, constantly exploring how digital would change not just marketing but all of GE. Then as vice chair heading Business Innovations, Comstock became the company's chief futurist, attending digital confabs, planting herself in Silicon Valley, scouting and making it her business to know cutting-edge agencies and entrepreneurs, seeking out partners for unusual ways to market. A marketing challenge for GE, enunciated at every monthly marketing meeting chaired by CMO Linda Boff, with their agencies in attendance, is to shift the brand ID of GE from an old industrial to a cool digital company. Cool digital companies are more attractive to Wall

Street because they are perceived as growth stocks, and are seen as welcoming to the young engineers that shape digital companies.

A way to advance this goal was for GE to establish under the auspices of the CMO a four-person office, the Disruption Lab, directed by Sam Olstein, thirty-three, who comes to work with his hair spiked and wearing jeans and sneakers. His foremost task, he says, is to "have a good perspective of trends and technology; of where we see activity of new start-ups forming around, say, messaging, around content creation." He says they search "for what people think is cool and interesting and primed for growth." He scans Apple's App Store to check on new apps that break into the top 100. Encouraged by Comstock and Boff, he pushed, he says, to make GE "a publisher, a content creator. What our brand represents is science and technology and the awe around science and technology, and that's a very focused perspective. It's the same focused perspective that HBO has, that Discovery channels have, that the Walt Disney Company has. We want to build a platform with the reach of any other media and entertainment platform out there." It need not be branded like Disney, but he believes GE can create content and distribute it over its own Web site, over Facebook, Instagram, Twitter, Snapchat, National Geographic channels, or online publications like *Slate*.

As a content creator, GE formed a partnership with the National Geographic Channel "to bring to life great stories" for a six-part series called *Breakthrough*. It was directed by Ron Howard and shaped by Howard and his Imagine Entertainment partner, Brian Grazer. (WPP owns 10 percent of Imagine.) Each one-hour segment covered scientific topics like robotics, the brain, and energy. GE did not suffocate the drama with advertising. Instead, each hour opened by saying it was codeveloped by GE, and Boff says the episodes featured "our scientists or technologies or customers, but in an organic way."

GE has worked hard to create an image as a "cool" company, a company welcoming to young engineers. One of their notable marketing campaigns was "What's the Matter with Owen?" A college graduate, Owen decides to go to work for GE, to the disappointment of his friends and family, who grouse that 138-year-old GE is not an innovative company. Owen is a bit of a nerd, but he has a sense of humor. We follow his journey over the course of the marketing campaign, as he—and thus GE—becomes cool. The Owen campaign brings to mind Apple's funny but potent "I'm a Mac" campaign a decade earlier, in which the cool Mac guy in a T-shirt makes fun of the uncool Microsoft "I'm a PC" guy in a suit and tie. GE boasts that its Owen videos were viewed fifty million times on WeChat in China.

A more offbeat marketing campaign materialized when GE stretched to try to make, in Boff's words, "GE more relatable" to young people, especially aspiring engineers. The idea they settled on was to produce a trendy hot sauce that would be packaged in a ceramic container composed of such advanced materials as silicone carbide and a nickel-based superalloy used in making GE's jet engines. These materials are able to withstand temperatures of 2,400 degrees Fahrenheit. Using two of the world's hottest peppers, GE manufactured a limited supply of the hot sauce and sold and promoted it on Thrillist, a popular men's shopping site. When it sold out, the news went viral. Message: GE is *cool*. GE's Podcast Theater produced ten- to fifteen-minute science fiction stories that over eight weeks, according to Andy Goldberg, Boff's deputy and chief creative officer, were the most downloaded "podcast on iTunes seventeen straight days, generating four million downloads." The only advertisement was "Brought to you by GE" at the start of the podcast. At the end of the podcast, Goldberg says, "The consumer says, 'GE gave me a great piece of content.' They don't say, 'GE makes great engines.'"

For almost a century, GE has relied on the same lead ad agency, BBDO. Reflecting another change in the agency business, GE now farms their work out to a half dozen agencies and to many outside project partners, like the *New York Times*. Once a month, Boff chairs a meeting of all the agencies. "The belief is that you have to have different points of view in the room," says Goldberg. "Not every agency is good at everything." VaynerMedia, for instance, is expert at social media marketing, a reason they're invited along with a couple dozen attendees. "I don't know who half these people are," Alan Cohen, a cofounder of Giant Spoon, said after one meeting. But, he adds, "The GE model is to pick people they like. So we feel like we're employees of the company." David Lubars, the creative director of BBDO, says he welcomes "other partners" and that "healthy paranoia" drives all agencies to better performance. Linda Boff insists that the agencies are not competitive with each other, that they collaborate because they want "to be their best selves." Perhaps. It's a noble sentiment. But the Buddha is not often among us, particularly in times of wrenching change, when much of what is solid melts.

But there is no question that GE's marketing efforts are widely and justly admired. For a relatively puny annual marketing budget of $100 million, because GE has been innovative its footprint is much larger. Lou Paskalis, an experienced marketing executive who today is a senior vice president of marketing at Bank of America, praises the team culture GE and Linda Boff have forged among agencies to deliver amazing work. "Linda is so far ahead in what she is doing in content marketing. She is the gold standard of turning jet engines and trains into iconography that people love and that speaks volumes about the commitment to the environment, as well as trains and jet engines! Actually, they're performing alchemy over there. I envy that." The alchemy, however, has not impacted GE's stock price, which fell 27 percent between September 7, 2001, when Jeff Immelt was anointed CEO, and June 13, 2017, when it was announced that he was stepping down.

■ ■ ■

The marketing team effort can fall short of Boff's teamwork ideal because talented people do not easily restrain the ambition that accompanies talent. Take Gary Vaynerchuk, who admires how GE "tries different things," yet makes it clear that the agency he founded, VaynerMedia, is competitive and will not be content just doing social network marketing. "I know we'll get a bigger piece and one day take over the TV ads that BBDO does," he says. More than once, Vaynerchuk, who bristles with ideas, has phoned Boff with creative ideas for TV spots.

VaynerMedia is emblematic of the type of digital-first independent agency that aims to disrupt both advertising and its big agencies. Presided over by forty-one-year-old Vaynerchuk, the eight-year-old company had revenue of $100 million, the bulk of it from Facebook marketing campaigns. He delights in sticking his fingers in the eyes of the advertising establishment. "You're going to die," he declared when invited to address the ANA's Masters of Marketing Conference in October 2016. "It's an amazing time to be in this industry if you're on the offense. It's the worst time if you're on the defense, and ninety-five percent of you are on the defense."

In a pitch to a prospective client, Chase Bank, that wanted to hire an additional agency to do their social media and digital marketing, Vaynerchuk took a seat in the middle of a crowded white Formica conference table wearing jeans and a crew-neck sweater. After his business affairs executive described how VaynerMedia had grown, Vaynerchuk shared a partial account of his own life.

Born in the Soviet Union, he immigrated to the United States with his family in 1978, when he was three. They moved from a studio apartment in Queens to Edison, New Jersey, where his father would eventually open two liquor stores. Cursed with dyslexia, Gary was a poor student who didn't play sports or date girls. His dream was to be an entrepreneur, and starting in elementary school he sold baseball cards and comic books, opened a lemonade stand, and arranged garage sales. After graduating from Mount Ida College in Massachusetts, Gary took over his father's Springfield, New Jersey, store in 1999. He learned everything he could about wine, became known as an expert, and launched a transformative online sales Web site and a daily wine Webcast. A year after YouTube surfaced, he inaugurated his own YouTube wine show channel. Soon after Google's AdWords advertising platform went up in late 2001, he invested the wine store's ad dollars. When new digital companies appeared—Twitter, Pinterest, Snapchat— he was an early adapter, posting wine news. His WineLibrary.com became the country's largest online retailer of wine, outselling such familiar names as Sherry-Lehmann and Zachys.

He and a younger brother started VaynerMedia in 2009. A couple of years later, with the wine business having expanded from $3 million to $65 million, Gary stepped aside to work full time at VaynerMedia. Convinced that the big ad agencies were ignoring social media, he shaped his agency's identity around social media marketing. His first client was the New York Jets football team, and eventually other clients—PepsiCo, Anheuser-Busch, Mondelēz, Unilever, Toyota, and GE—followed. With money he and his parents made in the wine business, he invested in start-ups like Facebook, Twitter, Uber, and Tumblr. Appearing regularly on YouTube, his fast-talking, clever rants went viral, leading to a multibook contract. The first of these, a Web marketing book, *Crush IT!: Why Now Is the Time to Cash In on Your Passion*, became a national best seller.

By 2016 he had produced four best sellers, had a YouTube channel, served as a Miss America pageant judge, and became a regular panelist, along with Gwyneth Paltrow and will.i.am, on Apple's *Planet of* *the Apps*, a reality TV series that evaluates pitches by app developers seeking funding. Today he will announce to strangers that he has watched every play of every Jets game since he was in sixth grade, when he says he told a friend, "I am going to own the Jets one day." He is neither modest nor demure. "If you've never seen me onstage," he writes in his fourth book,* "I model my performance after the comedians I idolized in my youth, like Eddie Murphy, Chris Rock, and Richard Pryor."

"Our religion is attention," he told the Chase marketing executives, explaining that what he loved about constructing marketing campaigns on social media is that they were "underpriced." There was little "ad waste" because he could try out so many alternative messages, and because in the digital realm results were often measurable. And unlike agency holding companies, which peddle expensive and unmeasurable broadcast television ads, he assured them that Vayner "sold on depth, not width." He showed several Vayner online campaigns. Soon after the pitch meeting ended, Vayner won the Chase account, including its new upscale Sapphire Reserve credit card.

In a creative brainstorming meeting about Chase's new travel credit card with six members of his team some weeks later, Vaynerchuk stabbed with his fingers at pieces of sushi from a take-out order and tried to frame Vayner's purpose and the business opening that yawned: "Vayner-Media was built on 'We're going to do a deal with apps and start-ups that nobody else is doing because we come from that world.' We did. It helped us grow." But now they've grown and proven they can craft video and TV pitches. They no longer have to sell themselves as just a digital agency. Vayner can siphon business from traditional agencies. "We've established traditional chops as believers in storytelling," he

---

* Gary Vaynerchuk, *#AskGaryVee: One Entrepreneur's Take on Leadership, Social Media & Self-Awareness* (New York: HarperCollins, 2016).

continued. "Now we can walk in and say, 'We can make video for you. We can make TV.'"

Imagine, he said, rapidly throwing out an idea that just came to him and was unrelated to the banks' credit card business but was related to the way he approached social media: "What if the retweet button on Twitter was brought to you by Xerox, because it's a copy!" On second thought, he added, "Twitter will never do that." On third thought, "People don't aim high enough. They say no. I just said no."

Members of his staff gently steer the discussion back to the subject of the meeting. One of the challenges with travel, a member of his team interjects, is that people don't want to cart heavy luggage. They can pack lighter by shipping their clothes ahead. We have to think of the customer and what they can afford, Vaynerchuk said. "Are you guys familiar with a start-up called Affirm? It's a financial company that makes consumer credit more accessible. It was started by Max Levchin, a cofounder of PayPal." And, he adds, if you go online to the Casper mattress company to buy a mattress, "when you go to the shopping cart and put the credit card in you'll see the confirm button. You know what this is? It's making three equal payments. It's allowing you not to pay at once."

What would be "amazing," he says, is if Vayner could lock up customers for their credit card client by signing exclusive deals with retail companies to use a button on their Web site for the Sapphire Reserve credit card. "We could find out if the ability to create a Sapphire card button that triples the points can be integrated into their Web site." Customers could pay in installments without being hit by steep interest charges. "If we quietly made deals with fifteen companies" we thought would be major businesses in the future, he said, we could "do what Walt Disney did with Orlando. Nobody knew he was buying all the property" that would turn into Disney World. "If you bet on companies early enough," Vaynerchuk later says, no doubt thinking of his early relationships with Twitter and Facebook, "you create a disproportionate emotional relationship." With this front-row seat, Vayner would be serving their Chase client. They would also be serving Vayner by building relationships with, and collecting data on, these consumers. "We would lock in a new generation of shoppers," he said.

If Gary Vaynerchuk is one day to own the New York Jets, which remains an obsession, he knows he needs to branch out and be more than a digital ad agency; in fact, more than just an agency.

※ ※ ※

One gets a sense of the changed dynamics between client and agency by attending the marketing meetings of Bank of America, a Michael Kassan client. They are presided over by Anne Finucane. Her pedigree is not that of a typical banking executive. One of six children, she was raised in Boston by a mother who was a distant cousin of Democratic House Speaker Tip O'Neill, and a father who was a prominent lawyer whose clients included the New England Patriots, back when they were known as the Boston Patriots. Soon after college graduation, she joined the staff of Boston mayor Kevin White, where she would meet and later marry prominent *Boston Globe* columnist Mike Barnicle. They were close to the Kennedys and other Massachusetts Democrats. She became a senior executive at Hill Holliday, a Boston advertising agency, and in 1995 was appointed vice president of marketing and corporate affairs for Fleet Financial, a troubled bank that in 1993 paid $100 million to settle claims that it was guilty of predatory lending practices. Her main task over the next several years was to dig Fleet out of this mess by making acquisitions and assuaging elected officials and local regulators intent on protecting consumers and jobs. She became a confidante of two Fleet CEOs. By 2004, Fleet was itself an attractive acquisition target, and Bank of America bought it. With her deft political and interpersonal skills, she became a confidante of CEO Kenneth D. Lewis, and then of his successor, Brian T. Moynihan.

The secret to her relationship with four different bank CEOs? "I think it's because I am not a banker. My expertise is in the world of marketing, communications, public policy, data analytics, research. If you have somebody who has neither the interest nor background to want your job, and you believe the individual is good at their job, then you're set up to be a trusted adviser."

No bank came out of the financial crisis of 2008 in more parlous shape than BofA. That year they further burdened themselves with the acquisition of the collapsing Countrywide Financial for $4.1 billion, and troubled Merrill Lynch for $50 billion. Like most of the nation's largest banks, BofA was on federal life support. Unlike most banks, its stock price and profits took longer to rebound, not regaining profitability and stock price growth until 2015. When Finucane put up for review the varied agencies who serviced BofA in 2015, she turned to Michael Kassan. "He knows how other pitches go," she explained. "He knows who's hot and who isn't. He knows who won business and who didn't. He knows who lost creative people or account people. He knows what's happening in the media and what the freshest pitches are."

With 50 million banking and brokerage customers, 4,689 financial centers, 16,000 automated teller machines, 13 percent of all U.S. banking deposits, and a political climate in which big banks make for an inviting piñata, marketing BofA is not simple. Bank of America operates a retail bank, an investment and corporate bank and trading company, and an investment services wing. For their quarterly marketing meetings chaired by Finucane, two dozen or more agency and BofA executives congregate on the Fifty-first floor of the Bank of

America building that looms over Bryant Park on West Forty-second Street. For the June 2016 meeting, in addition to senior BofA communications, marketing, consumer, government, data, and enterprise executives, in attendance were two WPP executives, Donald Baer, chairman and CEO of Burson-Marsteller and former communications director for President Clinton, and Joel Benenson, CEO of the Benenson Strategy Group, who served as President Obama's and in 2016 as Hillary Clinton's principal pollster; Rishad Tobaccowala from the Publicis Group; several executives from the primary creative agency, Hill Holliday, an IPG agency; Stephanie Cutter, partner in Precision Strategies, who was Obama's deputy campaign manager in 2012; and John Marshall, senior partner and chief strategy and innovation officer of the corporate identity firm of Lippincott. Each had assigned seats around a vast table formed into a square and draped with a white cloth.

This June meeting demonstrated how dependent the bank was on forces it could not control, and how advertising often takes a backseat at a marketing meeting and why more money is spent on marketing— media strategy, public relations, polling, lobbying, consulting, research, design, direct mail—than on advertising. This meeting commenced with a report on BofA's finances. Bank profits rose from $4 billion in 2014 to $16 billion; the bank's liquidity was four times as large as in 2008. But this good news was drowned out by the background noise of an angry presidential campaign where expected Democratic nominee Hillary Clinton and her challenger, Bernie Sanders, and likely Republican nominee Donald Trump, vied to criticize big banks.

Surveys reveal that support for banks dropped five points, Finucane said. "My concern is Bank of America should not be a focus of the conversation when the talk is about Dodd-Frank."

Pollster Joel Benenson said Sanders enjoyed broad support when he declared, "We have a rigged economic system." That issue won't disappear after the election, in part because "corporate profits are at record highs and yet wages are largely frozen."

Repeating her caution, Finucane said, "We don't want to be the tip of the spear." How does BofA mitigate the issue?

Despite the strides BofA has made by improving mobile banking and home mortgages, global corporate communications and public policy executive Jim Mahoney answered, "Candidates screaming makes it difficult to communicate effectively."

They discussed the positive steps BofA has taken to demonstrate its good citizenship, including the support the bank provides for reducing carbon emissions and for what's known as "sustainable growth"—BofA is the number one underwriter for green bonds. "Right now we're better than the rest of the financial service industry, but what kind of a goal is that?" Finucane asked.

The conversation veered to how the bank could better engage with its customers by serving as a "curator," or helper. Already, their user-friendly mobile banking app has more than 22 million customers. The bank is aided by the data it collects on its customers. A potential consumer who downloads their Zillow app offers "a clear indication" of whether they seek a new home loan. BofA doesn't have access to the names, nor do they share or sell customer data with anyone outside the bank. But in addition to the information gathered by their apps, the bank often knows of other online customer behavior and can tailor their messages accordingly. "We don't just need to run ads" at them, Lou Paskalis, who oversees their marketing investments, says. "We need to engage with them. We don't say, 'Click here to get that loan.'" They take it slow, banking the consumers' cookies so they can track them on ad-supported sites. Maybe, the BofA document that was distributed before the meeting says, they "insert a Home Ownership thought leadership content piece" when the consumer is reading the

New York Times online. Or serve them a "Best Rates" message when they're on their ESPN mobile app.

This, Paskalis said, is "one-to-one marketing"—what he identifies as "the deterministic model." It occurs when Amazon offers recommendations to customers: people who purchased this book or music also purchased these. Increasingly, it is invading television advertising, especially OTT (Over The Top) or television streamed over the Internet. One to one marketing where advertisers can tailor different individual messages to each household in an anonymized way, sheltering their privacy, will be a game-changer, he believes.

As is often the case in these meetings, Finucane is eager to hear the thoughts of soft-spoken Rishad Tobaccowala, their principal outside strategist, who she privately describes as "the smartest guy in the room." They appear to have very different personalities. She wears oversized eyeglasses and is capable of commanding a conversation. He wears round, frameless eyeglasses and his slight frame conveys an almost professorial air, which is enhanced because he sits, Buddha-like, and does not rush to speak. In a voice so soft people craned forward or sideways, as if it would help them hear, he cautioned: "We are at the beginning of this journey." When the bank talks about its environmental deeds, for example, it is not "a targeted, one-on-one message. It is a narrative, and it relies on emotion. Lou is right: We will know, increasingly, what people want because of their behavior. But the struggle is what does the consumer want from Bank of America. Successful companies realize we outsource the work to the customer. We do the listening and the responding. The reason Amazon in its deterministic form—or Facebook—can tell you everything is because you are creating your own bundle of what you want." But don't confuse a single product or purchase with what consumers want from a brand. "What Americans are asking for is, 'Who is on my side?' Sanders and Trump built surprising support because the message sent is: 'They are on my side.' If you think about a bank's purposes, no one is as close to aligning with them as you are."

In concluding, he tried to bring the discussion back to how the bank tried to rebrand itself in 2013 by adopting this slogan: "We know we're not the center of your life, but we'll do our best to help you connect to what is." BofA can help them achieve a better financial life, Tobaccowala said, evoking the one word—empathy—he believed was essential. "If they know they can trust a company, then when they see a particular offer it is no longer a creepy offer. The big word, which I haven't heard, is empathy."

Clients like Bank of America know they must fashion marketing messages in a very different way, a way often labeled branded content. These paid messages can arouse empathy, and don't beat the consumer over the head with a sales pitch; they often tell a story about something noble the brand is associated with, arouse emotion, and are most successful when the consumer doesn't realize the advertisement is an ad because it tells a compelling story or provides valuable information. This is why BofA partnered with the nonprofit online education Khan Academy in 2013, offering videos that explain complicated financial topics—like their series "Better Money Habits," elucidating compound interest—on sites like Pinterest.

The ideal for a subtle ad pitch is the two-minute television narrative that BBDO's Indian agency created for Procter & Gamble's local detergent, Ariel. It opens with the young wife racing about to calm her children, make tea for her oblivious husband, who is watching television, answer the phone, cook dinner, lay out the dishes, and load the laundry in the washing machine. While she services everyone's needs, her father is in the apartment and viewers hear his voice describing what he is seeing, seemingly for the first time. In a sorrowful voice, he says, "Sorry for every dad who set a wrong example," sorry that his daughter is just doing what he compelled her mother to do, that "your husband must have learned this from his dad." He leaves a note for his daughter, gets up, hugs her, and you hear him say as he leaves the apartment, "Sorry on behalf of every dad." He then appears at home with his wife, whom he hugs and startles by stopping her from doing the laundry. He takes the laundry basket, stuffs the garments into the washing machine, and pours from a box of Ariel as these bold white letters fill the screen: "Why is laundry only a mother's job?"

Ariel launched a national "Share the Load" campaign, blanketing India with promotional messages and labels asking, "Is laundry only a woman's job?" Doing social good was good for Ariel's business; they claimed sales jumped by 60 percent.

Can a marketing campaign, any marketing campaign, warm the cockles of a consumer's heart toward a bank in the same way? Anne Finucane understands the nature of the challenge. She closed BofA's monthly marketing meeting by stressing her biggest single takeaway: it is mission critical for the bank to gain the trust of more consumers. Their surveys tell them that only 28 percent of the American public trusts the banking industry. Over eight years out from the global financial crisis, banks were still climbing out of the wreckage of their reputations. "We can't lose our ability to sell our strategic message," she told her marketing team. But for Finucane and BofA, broad brand and product advertising is a relatively small piece of their marketing pie—a $100 million slice out of $2 billion. Even if it were much bigger, no one thinks there's a single magic spell that can be cast to win back all of the trust that has been lost.

6.

"SAME HEIGHT AS NAPOLEON"

"Seventy-five percent of our revenues comes from things—$15 billion of nearly $20 billion—Don Draper wouldn't recognize."

—Martin Sorrell

I n another restaurant where he's well known, Milos on West Fifty-fifth Street, where the chef emerges from the kitchen to recommend dishes and the maître d' automatically delivers a dry martini, Michael Kassan slipped into his seat on this May night fresh from having seen *Hamilton* a third time. Sipping his martini, Kassan came down from the up the musical inspired as he spoke of the difficult challenges confronting the agency world and its four largest holding companies in mid-2016: the lack of a rising new generation of leadership. "John Wren [CEO] of Omnicom is the youngest at sixty-four or sixty-five, Martin Sorrell of WPP is seventy-one, Maurice Levy of Publicis is going to be seventy-five, and Michael Roth of IPG just turned seventy. There's no clear successor for any of them. You've got no identified next generation of leadership in this business." He saw agencies as imperiled. "How does a traditional holding company deal with disruption? I'm not sure. The answer is that they're at real risk. They're not going out of business. But clients are chipping away." And the more they chip away, he tells his staff, it is unavoidably true that "for MediaLink this is really good news. The opportunities for MediaLink become really robust as people come to rely on their agencies less." And Jon Mandel's speech, he knows, hurt agencies and helped MediaLink.

One can appreciate why what Kassan considers good news for MediaLink would anger the leaders of these holding companies. In this regard, the agencies are as one. Otherwise, there are certainly plenty of differences among the large agencies. WPP is the Goliath, ranked number one ($18.7 billion) among all world agencies in 2015 revenues, followed, in order, by Omnicom ($15.1 billion), Publicis ($10.6 billion), IPG ($7.6 billion), Horizon ($6.5 billion), Dentsu ($6.3 billion), and Havas ($2.4 billion). Each claims to have a distinct brand identity. Omnicom does not advertise that its CEO, John Wren, spends much of the year at his home in Palm Beach, but it does tout its award-winning creative work, and that by reorganizing its media agency endeavors under a new entity, Hearts & Science, they captured more new business in 2016 than any other holding company. Publicis lost more accounts than its competitors in 2016, but Maurice Levy says that his company is truly global and unlike most competitors, including WPP, doesn't view the world through "Anglo-Saxon eyes." Publicis was, he says, first to create a beachhead in China. Michael Roth, CEO of IPG, says, "The DNA of our company is entrepreneurial rather than command and control." He touts the unusual digital work of one of its agencies, Bob Greenberg's R/GA. Roth sees his role as an "allocator of capital," and as the public face of IPG.

The other companies, though large, do not offer the same full range of services. Japanese-based Dentsu offers strong media agency services, but outside of Japan they usually partner with outside creative agencies. Bill Koenigsberg, the CEO of Horizon Media, also is focused on media services and partners with outside creative agencies. He says, "We don't try to sell various services," and because they are "privately held," they are not preoccupied "with quarterly earnings," leaving him to be concerned with "only two constituencies, employees and clients." While France-based Havas is the smallest by revenue of the big marketing companies, Yannick Bolloré, the CEO, matches Koenigsberg's claim that because his firm is family owned "we are not dependent on the market," and he adds something that is easier to assert than prove: their culture "is more collaborative."

No one is more vocal about the swarm of new competitors all of these players are combating than Martin Sorrell. Sorrell is less diplomatic and more nakedly competitive than Levy, Wren, or Roth. While the others express warm feelings for Kassan, Sorrell openly looks upon Kassan and MediaLink as a frenemy, as he does Facebook and Google.

This bristly, on-guard stance is part of Sorrell's DNA. His Jewish grandparents immigrated to London from Ukraine, Poland, and Romania. In the poorer East End of London, his grandparents and parents felt the lash of anti-Semitism, a reason they changed the family name from Spitzberg to Sorrell. To help support his family, his father, Jack, dropped out of school at thirteen, abandoned his violin and the scholarship offered by the Royal College of Music, and went to work as a salesman for Max and Francis Stone, Russian Jews who owned appliance stores. By the time Martin was born in February 1945, Jack was the general manager of their 750 stores and the Sorrells enjoyed a measure of affluence. They lived first in a comfortable flat in northwest London, then upgraded to a bigger detached house in Mill Hill, a leafy suburb. After a brother died in childbirth, Martin remained an only child and the recipient of the full attention of his parents. His mother, Sally, devoted herself to being a housewife and caring for her son, carefully wrapping his school lunch sandwiches in plastic. His father was an amateur Shakespeare scholar and could recite entire passages from the Bard's plays.

Jack Sorrell is still a presence in his son's cluttered second-floor London townhouse office, located in a residential mews at 27 Farm Street in Mayfair. The largest photograph in the room, dwarfing all the small framed photographs on the credenza leaning against the bare white wall facing his desk, is of Jack Sorrell. It is unframed and slightly faded. The picture portrays a man of regal mien, his dark, full mustache trimmed, his eyes dark, his black hair combed straight back, his formal dark suit accompanied by a black tie with white polka dots and a white pocket square. There is a hint of a smile on Jack Sorrell's closed mouth, as if he is suppressing it. There is little physical resemblance between father and son. Martin's hair is greyer and shorter, he wears unframed eyeglasses, and he is mustache free. Unlike his father, he thinks of himself as an entrepreneur who is unabashedly proud to say he personally built the WPP from a wire basket company to the world's largest advertising and marketing entity. Like his father, Martin does not suffer fools and carries a chip on his shoulder. "My father," his son says, "never felt he had the advantages—because he had to leave school at thirteen, he couldn't take the scholarship. He had a very good brain but he was probably upset that he worked like a slave but was not an owner. . . . We were so close because he wanted to give me the advantages he didn't have."

His dad pushed Martin to go to the right schools, and Martin pushed to make his dad proud. He also relied on his father as his consigliere. Jack Sorrell, he once told a *Forbes* magazine reporter, was "somebody you could talk to who doesn't have an agenda but your interests at heart." Apart from his wife, Martin said, no one filled that role today.

Esteemed historian Simon Schama, who met Martin when they were eleven-year-old students at the elite Haberdashers' Aske's Boys'

School in northwest London, describes Martin as "exuberantly tough" and "full of a kind of cuddly warmth" that is often camouflaged. They were "brotherly close," he says, with sterling grades when together they entered Christ's College, Cambridge, in 1962. On Fridays Martin's mother would wrap a roast chicken in silver foil and plastic and put it on the train to Cambridge. "I would pick it up," recalls Martin. "The chicken was still warm." Schama would make risotto to accompany the chicken. The chicken was kosher, as was all their food. "We were slightly left-wing Zionists" living a semibohemian lifestyle, Schama says. Together, they edited and published a glossy magazine, *Cambridge Opinion*, which appeared six times a year, each edition devoted to a single subject. In 1964 the subject was America. With the assistance of a professor who was a friend of Daniel Patrick Moynihan, Schama wrote the New York Democrat and arranged to visit when he and Sorrell went to America that summer. Moynihan wangled press credentials for them to attend the Democratic National Convention in Atlantic City. The two nineteen-year-olds fervently supported Lyndon Johnson over Barry Goldwater. The next summer, after their junior year, they traveled together to Vienna, Berlin, and Eastern Europe, seeking to better understand what Schama describes as "the ghosts" of anti-Semitism; their eyes flooded with tears visiting former concentration camps.

Among Cambridge classmates, it was common to aspire to be a writer, professor, or lawyer. Martin was different. An economics major, he had "a steely" determination to be a businessman, Schama says. "Martin always felt that Jack had been mistreated, he had been disadvantaged" by the Stone brothers and by early poverty. "Martin certainly wanted to vindicate his father by succeeding." He graduated from Harvard Business School with an MBA; he often says the case-study approach taught him to think like a CEO. After working for a consulting firm in Connecticut, he reintroduced himself to Mark

McCormack, founder and chairman of IMG, an international agent for sports figures and celebrities, whom he had met when McCormack spoke at Harvard. McCormack remembered Martin as the brash young man who made it his business to converse after class, and offered him a job opening at an IMG office in London. Some months later, McCormack let him borrow his chauffeur and Rolls-Royce or Bentley, Sorrell can't recall which, to impress a first date, Sandra Finestone, whom he would marry. They had three sons, were married for thirty-five years, and divorced in 2005. (The divorce cost him an estimated £30 million and a four-story townhouse.)

He left IMG in the mid-1970s with the idea, he told the *Harvard Business Review*, "to try to start a company with my dad, who was my closest adviser and mentor at that time. We didn't find a business that made sense." So he joined James Gulliver Associates as a financial adviser. The firm had invested in an ad agency that Saatchi & Saatchi acquired, and when Saatchi was searching in 1976 for a chief financial officer, Sorrell was recruited. For the next nine years he worked for Maurice and Charles Saatchi, often terrifying those sitting across from him as he crunched numbers in his head, stared down opponents, and orchestrated a spree of mergers that would transform Saatchi into a powerful holding company.

The pioneer who launched the "holding company" era was Marion Harper, Jr., president of McCann-Erickson, who acquired a number of agencies and by 1960 had placed them all under a new umbrella, the Interpublic Group. Advertising agencies began to go public, and attracted famed investor Warren Buffett, who in the 1960s took sizable positions in McCann-Erickson and Ogilvy & Mather. "You know the best business to be in?" Kenneth Roman, former chairman of Ogilvy said, recounting Buffett's words. "It's one where you're shaving in the morning and can look in the mirror and say, 'Today, I'm going to raise prices.' And you can do it."* As was true in most giant industries, the belief that size conferred advantages was rampant. Size conferred more leverage to raise prices and lower costs, provided a bigger global footprint to pitch clients anywhere, enabled synergies that offered efficiencies, and boosted profits by applying cost-cutting pressure on newly acquired assets to improve the parent company's margins.

The Saatchis realized that the industry was evolving into two tiers, a handful of giants versus Saatchi and everyone else in the middle, where they were prey. Harper understood this. Andrew Cracknell credits—perhaps condemns is a more appropriate word—Harper's push for a giant holding company because it subjected advertising to "the equivalent of its own industrial revolution." In the future, he wrote, agencies would be measured by "the bottom line," not the creative "quality of their work." And by coining the phrase "marketing communications" to describe his agency, and bringing under his IPG umbrella marketing functions and charging clients for their distinct services, Harper had more of an impact than the great Bill Bernbach, in Cracknell's view.[†]

Saatchi's first major acquisition came in 1975, when they partnered with the London office of Garland-Communications, whose clients included Procter & Gamble and who owned a piece of Compton Communications, which was much larger than Saatchi. The maneuver, which was a reverse takeover, would over the next decade help propel Saatchi to eclipse IPG as the world's largest ad agency. Sorrell was the financial engineer. "That was the cornerstone deal," Sorrell says. "The brilliant deal we did"—he invokes the word *brilliant* three times in a single sentence to describe the deal—"was when we squeezed

---

* Kenneth Roman, op-ed, *The Wall Street Journal*, March 28, 2017.
† Andrew Cracknell, *The Real Mad Men: The Renegades of Madison Avenue and the Golden Age of Advertising* (Philadelphia: Running Press, 2011).

Compton advertising," becoming the controlling owner. Under the terms of the deal, Compton would own 20 percent of Saatchi.

However, instead of paying Compton, Sorrell persuaded them to convert their one-fifth ownership into shares in a new subsidiary company Saatchi formed. Compton was a public company, and its market valuation generated a pool of capital for Saatchi to tap to make more acquisitions, including Compton's U.S. business in 1982.

In the nine years he worked there, Sorrell was often referred to as "the third brother," an identity he rejects because he says the brothers were shrewd strategists unto themselves and he was very clearly their employee. As the person who negotiated Saatchi's deals, Sorrell could be intimidating. Jerry Della Femina, the creative force behind the agency Della Femina, Travisano & Partners, was eager to expand in the 1970s. "I had a reputation as a wild man," he says. "I realized I would not get good packaged goods accounts, which is where the big dollars were. I decided in the seventies I had to buy an agency in the UK." He checked out London agencies and was told Saatchi might sell. "I visited the Saatchi brothers and Sorrell. They lacquered me with praise. I was their hero. They talked about how I could buy them. I said to myself, 'They are smart guys.' After a while I realized, 'They are smarter than I am. They would eat me for lunch!'" A few years later an *Advertising Age* reporter phoned Della Femina and asked for his reaction to news that Garland-Compton had acquired Saatchi. "'No,' I said. 'Saatchi will own them.' They did."

"The great thing about the Saatchis is they let you do what you wanted to do," Sorrell says, before adding, "as long as you got no public credit for it."

"I don't remember him being very happy," Simon Schama recalls. Sorrell cited three reasons he was unhappy: he thought the Saatchis were brilliant strategists and ad men, but too "showy," too unfocused on managing a now sprawling business, and "he didn't have enough power." Plus, he adds, "I left them because I wanted to do something on my own. I was forty years old and had male menopause." And he aimed not to suffer the fate of his father. "Some things I found difficult to accept. My dad had always said to me, 'Build a reputation in an industry you enjoy.' And building a reputation means that people respect what you did and as a result you get some leverage and clout." Until Jack Sorrell died in 1989, Martin spoke with his father daily.

With an eye on leaving, in 1985 Sorrell made a personal investment in a wire basket manufacturer, publicly listed as Wire and Plastic Products. When he left Saatchi the following year, he rechristened this shell company WPP and set up shop in a one-room London office he shared with an associate. His ownership stake in WPP amounted to 16 percent. Over the next eighteen months, WPP purchased eighteen companies. "We went from a market cap of 1 million pounds to 150 million pounds," Sorrell says. Up until this time, ad agencies were gentlemanly, refusing to launch hostile takeovers. Martin Sorrell disdained these polite unwritten rules. By 1987, the shark was ready to swallow a whale: he made a hostile bid to take over the venerable but troubled J. Walter Thompson, whose revenues were thirteen times greater than WPP's. Sorrell loaded up with debt and benefited from a Japanese real estate investment that was part of the acquisition and that helped him make the $566 million purchase, which included the world's largest public relations firm, Hill & Knowlton.

Jeremy Bullmore, who was the chairman of J. Walter Thompson in London at the time, and would become a close adviser to Sorrell, says he wasn't upset by the takeover. "I thought the company had become soft."

Sorrell would build his empire, as Jack Welch would build General Electric in that period, by purchasing companies, not starting them. Unlike Marion Harper, who was terminated for financial profligacy, Martin Sorrell erected the first financially successful advertising holding company. Within two years, he doubled Thompson's profits. By 1989, he engineered a hostile takeover of Ogilvy & Mather for $864 million, prompting David Ogilvy to publicly brand him "an odious little shit." (Martin is five feet six inches tall and likes to say, "Same height as Napoleon." Press accounts of Ogilvy's attack changed "shit" to "jerk.") Soon he would swallow two other huge agencies, Young & Rubicam and Grey. WPP would become the world's largest advertising and marketing company, with 205,000 employees in 3,000 offices in 112 countries. By 2015, WPP enjoyed profit margins of 16.9 percent, the industry's highest. He kept those margins high by aggressively diversifying WPP from a company reliant on North America and Great Britain to a company that produced up to 45 percent of its revenues "from the faster-growing markets of Asia Pacific, Latin America, Africa & Middle East and Central and Eastern Europe." China is today WPP's third biggest revenue producer, with 15,000 employees, and WPP has a 45 percent market share in India. Sorrell was knighted Sir Martin by the Queen in 2000, and chose for the motto on his shield, "Persistence and Speed."

Sir Martin's ambitions brought WPP perilously close to bankruptcy in 1991. A combination of taking on too much debt coupled with a worldwide recession slashed WPP's stock price and revenues and menaced his dream. Banks were pressing him for payments. Schama recalls a lunch with him at the Connaught when Sorrell shared that WPP was "in real deep trouble and close to going under." To extricate WPP, Sorrell humbly accepted a deal that reduced the company's debt by granting WPP equity to the banks.

By 1992, WPP regained its stride. If Michael Kassan earned the title of "the connector," Martin Sorrell earned his as "the consolidator." WPP aggressively buys majority or minority stakes in marketing companies all over the world. According to WPP's website, it owned all or part of 412 companies. Enter the bright yellow door to its two-story London townhouse, walk past a fake cactus plant, and settle on a short faux leather visitors' couch, and you find yourself staring up at a massive mounted orange drum. On it in small black letters are the names of WPP companies. A sleek office building on a nearby street houses many of these companies. Its public relations holdings include Hill & Knowlton, Burson-Marsteller, and Finsbury; its data, technology, and polling companies include—in addition to GroupM—Xaxis, Kantar, the Benenson Strategy Group, and Penn Schoen Berland; its public affairs and lobbying roster includes the Dewey Square Group, Glover Park Group, and Wexler & Walker Public Policy Associates; its various companies are major players in health-care communications, design, and direct mail. It owns sizable pieces of digital content companies like Vice Media, Refinery29, and Fullscreen. It owns a piece of the movie and TV production enterprise the Weinstein Company. It owns one fifth of a digital measurement company that competes with Nielsen, the combined Rentrak and comScore. Back when she was recruited by Sorrell to become CEO of Ogilvy & Mather and became a trusted colleague, Charlotte Beers says, "I disagreed with him buying all these below-the-line companies. I was wrong. It's why my WPP stock is so strong today."

Today, three quarters of WPP's $20 billion in revenues spring from what Sorrell describes as "stuff that has nothing to do with Don Draper advertising" and everything to do with "communication services." WPP, like the other ad and marketing giants, set out to acquire not just advertising but marketing agencies. Today, outside the United States, most marketing dollars are spent in England, France, Germany, Japan, and China. But late in the last century, one did not need a crystal ball to see that China and India would each house more than one billion people. The two countries now rank number one and number two in Internet users. "In Don Draper's day," says Sorrell, who has devoutly watched every episode of *Mad Men*, "he was wrestling with working with the New York office or the Chicago office or the Detroit office and would be very focused on the United States. The U.S. was the biggest market. It still is. But when I started thirty years ago, up to three quarters of worldwide advertising was controlled from the East Coast of the U.S. That's no longer the story."

* * *

Even Sorrell's critics acknowledge he is a nearly peerless long-term strategic thinker. It is customary for him—in his annual reports, in meetings with analysts, in press interviews—to lambast corporations for their preoccupation with the short term. "It's the demand for quarterly performance" issued by CEOs who only average six or seven years in office, he grouses. In an article he wrote for *The Economist* in early 2017, Sorrell assailed American corporations for share buybacks and dividends that in the year up to June 2016 exceeded their retained earnings. He claimed that corporations were choosing to reduce their investment dollars even though they sat on more than $7 trillion in worldwide cash. "One survey," he wrote, "revealed that nearly 80% of executives admit they would 'take actions to improve quarterly earnings at the expense of long-term value creation.' In this environment, procurement and finance departments (rather than growth-drivers such as marketing and R&D) have the whip hand."

Sorrell was early to see that data and technology and the ability to target individuals, as opposed to demographic or income groups, would one day transform marketing, so he invested heavily in data and tech companies. A turning point, says David Moore, was in 2007, when Google acquired DoubleClick, the automated digital ad-serving platform that buys and sells ads. Moore was a founder of 24/7 Media, a similar but smaller automated ad-serving platform. The DoubleClick purchase aroused Sorrell's suspicions that Google intended to shove into the advertising business. "I wrote to Martin suggesting to him that we do a deal. He agreed," Moore says. "He said he wanted to acquire us, not partner with us." In 2011, Sorrell merged Moore's 24/7 with Xaxis, a collector of data and an early programmatic advertising adopter. They were placed under the umbrella of WPP's GroupM, and openly competed with DoubleClick and Facebook's Atlas (which has since been abandoned by Facebook).

Those who work for Martin Sorrell, like those who worked for the younger Rupert Murdoch, always feel he is watching. Sorrell answers e-mails almost instantly on his BlackBerry, even when attending tennis matches at Wimbledon. Miles Young, before he voluntarily stepped down as CEO of Ogilvy, said, "I probably get three to four e-mails a day from him. I'm a great fan of his. He has an ability to be broad and strategic when needed, but at the same time he has the ability to be very detail oriented." Sorrell is constantly in motion, jetting on commercial airlines to attend most ad conferences, be they in Los Angeles or Barcelona, to visit WPP offices in India or Brazil, to sit in on board meetings in Beijing or New York, to chair WPP's four times yearly Stream conferences in Greece, Cannes, and elsewhere, to attend Google confabs in Sicily and Burning Man in Nevada.

The incessant e-mails help forge his reputation as a micromanager, as does his fecund memory for promised but unmet executive goals. More than a few WPP executives, not wanting to be quoted, complain that Sorrell nearly suffocates them with his over-their-shoulder attention to detail. Sorrell describes the claim that he is a micromanager as "a compliment," explaining that the CEO of a company whose size is equal to "a ministate" must delve into details. Keith Reinhard, who orchestrated the ad agency mergers that became Omnicom, observes, "Omnicom is considered a holding company and WPP is a parent company." Others disagree. David Sable, then in his sixth year as the CEO of Young & Rubicam, said, "Martin is an overrated meddler.

Most people think he gets down in the weeds. I don't think that's true. Martin has rarely told me what to do."

To understand Sorrell as a manager one has to begin with his self-identity as a founder, not a manager. He flicks aside the shareholder critics, not to mention former London mayor Boris Johnson, who railed against his steep pay—£43 million in 2014 and £70.4 million in 2015, making him the highest compensated executive in England. In an op-ed page piece he wrote for the *Financial Times* in June 2012, Sorrell declared, "I have been behaving as an owner, rather than as a 'highly paid manager.' If that is so, mea culpa. I thought that was the object of the exercise, to behave like an owner and entrepreneur and not a bureaucrat." Today he owns 2 percent of WPP and chooses not to diversify his investments but to tie his wealth to how his company performs. "My dad said, 'Invest with companies you know best,'" he says. Despite his rich pay, Sorrell rarely chooses to fly privately, insisting that it would cheat shareholders. He feels liberated to opine on most any subject, from Brexit to Donald Trump's immigration policies (he was opposed to both), not to mention the unabashed joy he takes in belittling Maurice Levy, his Publicis rival.

Members of his WPP team bristle when he publicly disparages "the snooty" attitude of creatives, who play a diminished role in the advertising business. Interviewed by Michael Kassan before an Advertising Week audience in September 2015, he proclaimed, "Seventy-five percent of our revenues comes from things—$15 billion of nearly $20 billion—Don Draper wouldn't recognize." Often, he will declare that the folks who massage data, or buy ad time, or the financial types who shape an acquisition, or the engineers who devise ways to spread messages on social networks, are as creative as a copywriter. Miles Young doesn't disagree that many marketing professions can be creative, as can a plumber. "But there's a type of creativity concerned with ideas, and that's what Martin probably doesn't appreciate because he's never worked inside an advertising agency." It is not unusual to hear sneers that Sorrell is merely *a suit*, an accountant, as Bob Greenberg has described him. Jeremy Bullmore, who serves as an intellectual brain trust for Sorrell, would challenge that characterization. But he does disagree with Sorrell for bashing creative agencies: "That's the wrong signal to send, and I don't think it's accurate." He does not dispute Sorrell's assertion that various parts of an agency can be creative. But his problem with the signal Sorrell is sending is that "it gets interpreted that we're not in the advertising business anymore. That's not a sensible thing to say because he is in the advertising business. The WPP group is an advertising group. He often has this irritating habit of saying things that on one level are obviously true, but their interpretation is not only wrong but dangerously wrong."

Like any battle-scarred veteran, Sorrell has amassed detractors. In London, he is called "six twenty-one" behind his back, because June 21 is the year's shortest day. Michael Kassan believes the bad blood between Sorrell and Maurice Levy stems from when Levy and Sorrell were in a bidding war to buy the Cordiant Communications Group. "I was in the middle of it. That's why Martin and I didn't talk for three years," Kassan says. He had not yet started MediaLink and was representing Cerberus Capital, the private equity firm whose specialty is making investments in distressed companies. Cerberus owned $79 million of Cordiant's debt. But Cordiant had become overextended and slipped into default. Cerberus was unfamiliar with advertising agencies "and they brought me in." Kassan spent three months in London, going back and forth between Sorrell and Levy. "Cerberus wanted to maximize its investment. Maurice and Martin were bidding against each other and Martin won. But it cost him more than he wanted it to cost him, and he blamed me. He made it personal. It wasn't personal."

Months after the deal closed, Kassan remembers walking into

London's Connaught Hotel with a client who spotted Sorrell and went over to say hello. Kassan followed and offered his hand. "He wouldn't shake my hand." Kassan says they only began to speak again some years later when he was hosting a dinner at Nobu for his client, AT&T, also a WPP client, and Kassan told his friend Irwin Gotlieb that Sorrell was not welcome—unless he apologized. He says Sorrell apologized. Told of Kassan's account, Sorrell says he doesn't recall the hotel incident or the AT&T incident. What he does recall is this: "Michael was not involved in the Cordiant negotiations. He was paid a fee by Cerberus for advice."

Sorrell is famous for his intensity, which is almost exclusively devoted to WPP. His second wife, Cristiana Falcone, says he has few close friends, and even his oldest friend, Simon Schama, says they see each other maybe once a year. Longtime client Jack Haber of Colgate says of Sorrell, "I enjoy his company. He's very funny. . . . I respect him." But "I never for a minute don't remember that Martin is my buddy because I'm an important client to him. It's a billion dollars of business." He remembers attending a cocktail party at the Consumer Electronics Show and he and three WPP executives agreed to go off to dinner. "I said, 'Let's ask Martin.' They said, 'Nope.' He wasn't going to be fun at dinner. I don't mean any disrespect, but he's a very tough, demanding boss."

Cristiana Falcone likens her husband to the obsessive Dustin Hoffman character in *Rain Man*. Seeking to add variety to his life, she booked a vacation to Uruguay for ten days. He quickly developed a routine. "We must go to lunch at one P.M. He would have a tantrum if we didn't sit at the same table." He would ask the waiter what the dessert choices were, but he always ordered the same dessert. His BlackBerry and iPhone and iPad accompany him everywhere. "This guy lives and breathes for WPP. He's persistent. It's what makes him successful." Yet she takes care to introduce the testimony of three sons from his first marriage: "His sons say they had a great father."

To understand Sorrell's persistence, consider how he pursued Falcone. She was born in Rome in February 1973, the daughter of an airline pilot and senior Alitalia executive. After receiving an MA from the Fletcher School of Law and Diplomacy at Tufts University, she worked for Shell and for the UN's International Labor Organization. She eventually joined the World Economic Forum as a senior manager (and later, director) of the media and entertainment industries group, which coordinated with executives from these sectors who attended the World Economic Forum in Davos and elsewhere. When Sorrell laid eyes on the tall, slim, vivacious blonde with an Italian accent and a feisty I-don't-bow-to-anyone personality, he was smitten. "For four years," she says, "he invited me to join him for a drink in Davos and I did not go. He tried to convince me he was the right partner for me." She had a Swiss boyfriend, and she declined. When she attended the Cannes Film Festival, she left a general message on her office phone that she was in Cannes. He showed up there. He pursued her by appearing at Forum meetings in South Africa, India, and Japan. Knowing that the Italian name her parents gave her was "Savage," he says, "I named my dog [an Irish setter] after her." He wore her down. She worried about the three-decade age gap, but was taken by his ardor, and his charm. She says, "He listens very well. He takes it in. He's very inclusive." He treated her like an equal. They married in 2008.

Charlotte Beers, who once reported to Sorrell and remains a trusted associate, vividly recalls his bitter divorce in 2003 and how unhappy he seemed. She went off to work in George W. Bush's State Department and fell out of touch with Sorrell. When they reconnected after his marriage to Cristiana, she was struck by the change. "When I came upon him he looked ten years younger. He had a different energy. He had a delight in life. I think it's from having a very happy union. He's amused by it. He has a wonderful capacity for play. You'd never believe that because of how hard he works. But Cristiana is a player. She likes to dance. She likes to go to unusual things." She lured him to attend Burning Man in the Nevada desert. She gave birth to their baby daughter in the fall of 2016.

One can fill notebooks with the criticism heaped upon Sorrell. But these don't paint a complete picture. If we just froze the picture when David Ogilvy called him "an odious little shit" we would miss what happened next. After they met for the first time, Ogilvy wrote Sorrell: "To my surprise, I liked you. . . . I was flattered when you quoted my books, and even more so when you invited me to become chairman of your company, which goes by the name WPP. I accepted your invitation. . . . It remains for me to tell you that I am sorry I was so offensive to you—*before we met*." When Ogilvy was dying of cancer, Sorrell visited him and promised to look after his wife. He did, and according to Miles Young, "it was Martin who paid for Ogilvy's nurses. His image is as Genghis Khan of the ad world. But he's really very caring." When David Moore's wife was diagnosed with brain cancer in 2007 and was being rushed by ambulance to a New York hospital, Moore was in London. He told Sorrell he had to rush back to the States to be with his wife. "When I landed I had three voice messages on my mobile phone from doctors Martin had called. They called me to offer their services."

Sorrell's vivid personality can overshadow his professional accomplishments. "He's gone to places no one has gone," Shelly Lazarus, who was CEO and is today chairman emeritus of Ogilvy, says. "He's explored the future. He's taken chances. He thinks long term. Everyone thought he was crazy when he invested in his first research company. He was right. He diversified WPP. He invested in programmatic buying when no one was sure what it was or where it was going. He is constantly traveling, soaking up information, figuring out the next thing."

The *Harvard Business Review* ranked him as the fifth best CEO in the world in 2015. The only other marketing holding company executive to make the list of 100 of the best-performing CEOs was Maurice Levy. Sorrell had to be pleased that Levy only ranked thirty-ninth. In 2016, Sorrell was placed in the top three. All three were lauded for their courage in implementing long-term strategies.

Whatever their differences, there are many shared views in the agency world. They commonly believe advertising and marketing should be viewed as an investment in growth, not just a cost. They share a frustration that too many clients, led by procurement and chief financial officers, focus on the short term. By wrenching costs out of marketing budgets, they complain that clients are crippling agencies and failing to invest in their brands.

As Sorrell looks down the road, the two grave nemeses he sees to WPP's business are the digital giants, like Google and Facebook, and the consulting and software companies. This is particularly awkward since the holding companies place billions of dollars worth of ads with Google and Facebook, and often employ the services of consulting and software companies. This is why Martin Sorrell popularized the phrase "frenemy" to describe companies that both cooperate and compete. On this point, at least, there is no disagreement between Sorrell and Maurice Levy, who says they are now going "directly to clients." Uneasy lies the head that wears a crown, especially in an age of turmoil and revolution.

7.

FRENEMIES

"We are not trying to disrupt agencies. . . . I know people don't believe that."

—Carolyn Everson

arolyn Everson doesn't look like an existential threat or a frenemy, certainly not to Michael Kassan. Facebook's personable vice president of global marketing solutions evades the Facebook engineer clichés: no growling for her, no T-shirts and unwashed hair, no looking down at her shoes when she speaks. Her straw-blond hair is perfectly coiffed and curved into a helmet above her shoulders, her neck and hands are friendly to jewelry, her fashionable dresses might be featured in *Vogue*. Michael Kassan met Everson when she was COO and executive vice president of U.S. Ad Sales for Viacom's MTV Networks, and has served as a mentor for nearly two decades. They met when he was moderating a panel at CES and a debate between Everson and Publicis executive Pam Zucker ensued about how best to massage and employ data. To add a touch of levity, Kassan borrowed what he thought was a familiar joke from *Saturday Night Live*: "Pam, what you're really saying is, 'Carolyn, you ignorant slut! You don't know what you're talking about.'" The audience laughed. Everson did not.

The next morning, a Friday, a friend phoned Kassan and said, "You have a real problem with Viacom. You called Carolyn Everson a slut!" The CEO of MTV lodged a formal complaint with CES. Chastened, Kassan phoned Everson and tried explaining that he had borrowed a line from one of the all-time most popular skits on *Saturday Night Live*. "You actually think I would call you a slut onstage?"

Monday morning when Everson arrived at work she was greeted by a dozen roses and a signed note from Kassan: "Here's hoping I get a second chance at a first impression." He did, and says, "We became best friends."

Carolyn and her older brother, Bill, grew up in the middle-class community of Stony Brook, Long Island, where their mother taught elementary school and their dad was a midlevel executive at Grumman. From a young age she displayed the outgoing personality of a salesperson—taking part in ballet performances, public speaking, competitive sports, always eager to raise her hand in class, and "always in the good graces of her teachers," her brother says. She received a full academic scholarship to Villanova. She didn't have a career plan, but she located one of many future mentors, sociology professor Bernard Gallagher, who was impressed by the three papers she wrote that were published in academic journals. He fervently recommended her when Arthur Andersen visited campus to interview seniors. After graduating summa cum laude in 1993, she was hired as an Andersen consultant. Her first task was to help Merck & Co. and Astra smooth any kinks in a joint venture and to research strategic alliances. Demonstrating her knack for being adopted by mentors, she read a book by Robert Porter Lynch on strategic alliances, cold-called him in Rhode Island, and recruited him to advise the two companies. He would serve as another mentor. Carolyn also became friends with a divorced Merck executive, Douglas Everson, a friendship that would blossom one day into romance.

She left Anderson in 1995 to join Disney. By now she was dating Doug, and they married in 1997. Knowing that her career path was business, her brother urged her to go to business school. Aware of her large ambitions, her Disney boss, Charles Adams, stepped in as a mentor. "If you want to be a CEO or a general manager, the Harvard Business School is where you want to go." As an alumnus, he put in a good word for her.

After graduating with honors, she held a number of executive jobs over the next several years, including the ill-fated Pets.com, followed by two years at Zagat and three years at PriMedia, Inc., before joining Viacom. Then, in 2010, with a nudge from Kassan, one of his consulting clients, Microsoft, offered Everson a position as vice president of global advertising sales and trade marketing teams in Seattle. After Everson received the offer, she turned to Kassan for advice. "Michael told me not to move to Seattle," she says. He advised her to take the job, but persuaded her that the ad community she needed to work with was located in New York. Microsoft relented.

Only four months later a headhunter called and asked if she would meet with Sheryl Sandberg, the COO of Facebook. At first she said no. "Carolyn was really torn," Kassan recalls. "She's a very ethical and loyal person. But this was an opportunity of a lifetime." Eventually she weakened, and on the way to Australia for Microsoft she stopped in the Valley on a Sunday to meet with Sandberg and Mark Zuckerberg. She spent a full day at Facebook. "I knew in my heart that's where I wanted to be," she says. "It was so much more entrepreneurial. Advertising was the entire business of Facebook, whereas at Microsoft it was a tiny piece."

Everson was the same age as Sheryl Sandberg, forty, and like her was a former Baker Scholar at the Harvard Business School and extremely well connected. She consulted what she refers to as "my board of directors" for advice. They include Kassan and Wenda Millard, Irwin Gotlieb of GroupM, Bill Koenigsberg of Horizon Media, Andrew Robertson of BBDO, Nick Brien, now the CEO of Dentsu Aegus in the U.S., Jack Myers, chairman of MyersBizNet and a prominent marketing consultant, and Terry Kawaja, CEO of Luma Partners, an investment banker. She also phoned Martin Sorrell for advice. These are hardly people hostile to the interests of the advertising establishment. Nine months after joining Microsoft, she departed for Facebook.

No one played a larger role in her coming and going than the unofficial chairman of her board of directors, Michael Kassan. He provided one-stop service, for "behind the scenes" she says he helped persuade his client, Microsoft, to let her go, and promoted her talents to another client, Facebook. "She absolutely worships Michael," says her husband, Douglas Everson, who would take early retirement at sixty, after three decades as an executive at Merck, to care for their twin daughters when Carolyn's job at Microsoft and then Facebook required extensive travel. He says of Kassan, "He has been an amazing resource for Carolyn. Michael is like family to us." As they are to Kassan, who "treats me like his niece," says Carolyn. When one of Doug's two older sons from his first marriage had a child, they brought Kassan to the boy's bris. When the UJA-Federation of New York Marketing Communications Division honored Everson and Rob Norman, GroupM's global chief digital officer, in May 2016 and raised nearly a million dollars, the dinner chair for the past seven years and the person who selects the honorees was Michael Kassan, who also serves as the UJA's national cochair of its Entertainment, Media, and Communications Division. The Pierre ballroom was packed with advertising notables, for as Wendy Clark of DDB says, "Michael has convening power." And when Everson rose to accept her honor, after thanking her family she turned to offer a bow to Kassan: "Michael, you took me under your wing."

As Facebook's point of contact with agencies and advertisers, Everson receives high marks. "Her enthusiasm and relentless optimism stand out. She's very collaborative. The collaboration she's driven at Facebook has set the tenor for others. She's a connector," Wendy Clark says. "We are not trying to disrupt agencies. We are trying to help improve sales," Everson says. "We are getting a seat at their table, helping them think through real business problems, and the faster we help them move to become more nimble and understand how mobile is impacting marketing, we will benefit in the end because they will invest more with us because we happen to have the dominant mobile platform. I don't go to meetings and ask for money. I don't think I've done that in five years. I know people don't believe that." By "people" she means Martin Sorrell, who she believes—wrongly—stands alone in his wariness. "We are not a frenemy," she says. "Do you hear that coming out of John Wren?" At least not publicly.

※ ※ ※

Martin Sorrell was becoming alarmed about Facebook in the winter of 2016. When told what Facebook said about "not trying to disrupt agencies," he disputed the claim: "They are not agnostic. They are selling Facebook inventory." He knows Facebook benefits from the growing mistrust advertising clients harbor toward their agencies. And he believes they are selling under false pretenses, because "they are not a technology company. They are a platform, a media company. You wouldn't give your media plan to Rupert Murdoch, or Les Moonves, or Bob Iger. So why would you give it to Mark and Sheryl? That's a fact. There's a subsidiary point: If that is Facebook's case, then give us your data—which they don't." He went on to say that he agrees with Facebook that what is crucial to know is "the outcome" of an advertising campaign. "But the only way you can prove the outcome is through the data."

Michael Kassan agrees that Sorrell is not alone among agency people who complain that Facebook is a frenemy. Increasingly, he says, clients feel more independent and consult with digital companies like Facebook, with potentially ominous consequences for agencies: "If you and I find out we speak the same language, why do I need a translator?" Facebook is clearly competing for advertising dollars. Sometimes Facebook complements television, Everson says, because with TV viewing down among millennials, Facebook "is great at finding that audience." But, she concedes, "At the end of the day, we all compete for ad dollars." Where Sorrell is wrong, Kassan says, is when he objects to Facebook meeting independently with its advertisers by, in effect, exclaiming, "'You can't go to my clients!' Last time I checked, the Thirteenth Amendment outlawed slavery in this country."

Paranoia about Facebook's advertising intentions are ignited by several factors: by its size, by the walled garden it maintains when refusing to share much of its data, by the immense volume of data it gathers, and by fear that it aims to displace agencies. By 2015, Facebook's size as translated by its market cap or worth was equal to General Electric's; by 2016, its market cap zoomed past the world's fourth most-valued corporation, ExxonMobil. By the end of 2016, Facebook collected $27 billion from ads, and basked in profits of $10 billion. Facebook and Google's size advantage was revealed in the first quarter of 2016 when Mary Meeker of Kleiner Perkins Caufield Byers reported that of every new digital ad dollar, eighty-five cents went to Facebook and Google. Their digital dominance increasingly mattered because digital advertising by 2017 was expected to surpass the $70 billion spent on the number one U.S. ad platform, television.

Monopoly fears magnified: "Facebook and Google are a digital duopoly," Terry Kawaja says. "They have two thirds of mobile ad revenue, and it's growing. They have first-party data on people, which in a mobile world is the only way to identify people. . . . They are sucking up all the oxygen." Shane Smith, cofounder, CEO, and driving force behind Vice Media, speaks in sentences followed by exclamation points and shouts "FUCK" a lot. Facebook's power was a favorite exclamation, and after he boasted before an audience of Hearst executives in May 2016 that Vice was "going to become the fourth-largest or fifth-largest, or maybe the third-largest" media company in the world, he took aim at Facebook. "This is the biggest problem of the world: Facebook has bought two thirds of the new media companies out there without spending a dime because they own a majority of their mobile" and thus control access to media's content. Offering what he describes as "a reality check," Randall Rothenberg, president and CEO of the Interactive Advertising Bureau, the trade association that represents digital companies like Facebook, says, "How different is it from when most advertising dollars were going to just three television networks?"

Those who compete with Facebook believe it *is* different, and feel especially vulnerable. Longtime digital executive Patrick Keane, former president of Sharethrough.com, where he sold the native ads of publishers to digital companies and worked with brand advertisers to link up with these digital publishers, does not hide his competitive fear of Facebook. "It's a Facebook world we all live in," he says, noting that Facebook and Google leave advertising pennies for other digital platforms. "Facebook has this incredible, almost instantaneous, ability to be successful in anything. They turned their biggest liability—they were late to focus on mobile—into an asset almost overnight." Now they are trying to better compete with YouTube in video. And "they've become a publishing platform with Instant Articles." This program, launched in 2016, allows publishers to display entire articles within the Facebook app in much the same form as in their "home" environment. Harry Kargman, founder and CEO of Kargo, a MediaLink client whose business mission is to create a mobile advertising platform to spread ad dollars to media company clients, is worried. He says, "The question is, What's Facebook's mission? Their mission is to get people to spend one hundred percent of their time on Facebook. Their mission is to become the Internet."

If Facebook were to become the Internet, the site people never leave, where they share pictures, IM, get their news, shop, search, watch television and, one day, movies, it would create a nearly impregnable walled garden. And in the meantime, the complaint from both agencies and brands, which grew louder in 2016, was that Facebook, like Google, takes ad dollars but shields much of its data from advertisers, disabling them from targeting consumers on other platforms or in their future ad campaigns. "The less data we get from them, the harder it is for us to decide where to allocate our own dollars," says Rob Norman. The more information agencies can extract from Facebook about what else their users like and do, the more precise their ad targeting.

Norman is clear about what agencies, and clients, want from digital companies that know much more about their users than do nondigital platforms like television, radio, or print. Comparing three digital giants—Facebook, Google, and Amazon—he says, "You could argue that Facebook has the best data on users based on their social interactions. You could argue that Google has the best because a search signals a person's intent. If you're thinking of purchasing intent, Amazon has the deep spear, which is actual purchasing data." Agencies and advertisers would like the data from all three. Facebook, Google, and Amazon have a financial incentive to safeguard this data. Their public defense is that they are protecting the privacy of their users and their pledge not to share names or personal information.

The assertion that Facebook and Google compete with agencies gathered force in 2016. Agencies were agitated that neither Facebook nor Google shared data with measurement umpires like comScore or Nielsen, which would have enabled an independent assessment of an ad's effectiveness. Martin Sorrell regularly accused Facebook and Google of seeking "to grade their own homework." This fed into suspicions that their real aim was to displace agencies.

Facebook and Google are also seen as poaching talent from agencies. Facebook hired a creative director from Saatchi & Saatchi to work for its own chief creative officer, Mark D'Arcy, who had spent two decades as a copywriter and as a chief creative officer for agencies and media companies. D'Arcy later hired Andrew Keller, former Crispin Porter + Bogusky CEO, as global creative director of what it calls its Creative Shop. Everson demurs, saying, "We have zero interest in creating competition with agencies." Facebook employs a staff of 220 under D'Arcy and Keller, and their mission, Everson says, "is to inspire the creative agencies," not compete with them. Few would see the line between inspiration and competition as being as clear and bright as Everson does. Certainly, Facebook's chief creative officer does not. D'Arcy concedes that his team does at times compete with agencies. He says Facebook "partners with ad agencies sixty percent of the time," which of course means they don't forty percent of the time. "We have absolutely no interest in serving as an ad agency," he insists. But he adds, "Nor do we think any business has a monopoly on creativity."

Facebook's business is reliant on selling ad space, so of course Facebook pitches advertisers. Smaller advertisers routinely reach out to Facebook directly, as do many larger advertisers. *Advertising Age* reported that half of the top fifty global advertisers assign teams of their people to embed with Facebook and Google teams to figure out how to better reach their consumers. "Facebook is not saying to us, 'Why do you work with agencies?'" says Anne Finucane of Bank of America. "They are saying to agencies and to us, 'Don't put up a brick wall between the client and us.' We agree. But the agencies don't want this.

The agencies make no less money. But they want control." For a company like Facebook that helps advertisers shape creative approaches to its users and seeks to better understand client needs, it is probably inevitable that they will usurp some agency functions, including that of go-to adviser.

* * *

Each quarter Facebook rents a large space in Manhattan and invites client and agency representatives for a full-day briefing on how mobile, and particularly mobile video, is the new frontier of advertising, the new television. The audience of three hundred to four hundred is dominated by people under thirty-five. To emphasize the reach of mobile video, a Facebook executive told them: 100 million hours of video was watched daily on Facebook, more time than viewers spent before their TV sets. They screened an old Bulova watch black-and-white TV ad as a warning that the ad formats and length, and how mobile ads were presented, had to be very different. They offered the testimony of Facebook advertisers who extolled the success of their Facebook ads. They invited to the stage Zach King, a young video star with thirteen million Facebook followers who described how he became what is known as an "influencer," casually selling products by integrating them into stories he told. They emphasized that video ads would fail if they didn't capture the attention of viewers quickly, certainly within the first three seconds because "you don't have the luxury of time on mobile." They spoke of Facebook's Dynamic Ads, which rely on algorithms to "hypertarget" ads to people whose Facebook data predicts whether they might be receptive.

Everson closed out the day at 5:30 P.M. by telling her audience that a mobile phone "is the most personal device people ever had. No other medium in marketing has ever been this personal." We carry it with us always, unlike a TV set. We store our personal information and pictures and preferred apps on it. We don't loan the phone to others. And because a mobile phone is so personal, to be effective, ads can't feel like an interruption and have to be more personal. "So my biggest point," Everson concluded, "is that you have an opportunity to communicate to consumers in new ways that will evoke emotion and will drive business results." The entire day was an advertisement for why clients and agencies should divert ad dollars to Facebook.

However impressed the audience was—and to a reporter individuals affirmed that they were—there are a couple of barriers Facebook won't easily scale. Unlike agencies, Anne Finucane says, "They are not neutral. That is the core of what bothers clients. Objectivity is enormously important to us. Facebook is selling its own product, so how can they be objective? The same for Google." There are those in the ad business who foresee Facebook or Google trying to compete with Irwin Gotlieb's GroupM as a buyer of media. But would a media plan drawn up by Facebook include a substantial buy for competitors like Google or Snapchat? The other barrier impeding direct Facebook competion, Andrew Robertson cautions: "Why would they trade their forty percent profit margins for ours?"

At their peril, agencies forget that Silicon Valley companies like Facebook take pride in being disrupters, in reducing costs and better serving customers by offering less "friction" and shoving aside what they see as superfluous middlemen. Mark Zuckerberg's famous corporate mantra at Facebook used to be "Move fast and break things." (In 2014, Facebook changed it to "Move fast with stable infra," which doesn't have quite the same edge to it, no doubt deliberately.) Unlike most agencies, Elliot Schrage, Facebook's vice president of global communications, marketing, and public policy says, Facebook takes "the Wayne Gretzky approach to business. Most businesses go where the puck is—where the business is today. Facebook is building a business for where the puck will be." Facebook, he says, does not aim to unseat agencies. However, "certainly companies like ours will offer more and more tools."

A glance at Facebook's history confirms that this is the opportunistic pattern the company has followed. Like Google and many Internet enterprises, Facebook began with an aversion to advertising. From its launch in 2004, Mark Zuckerberg had what David Kirkpatrick, whose book *The Facebook Effect* offered the first definitive account of the company, described as "ambivalence toward advertising." He accepted ads on Facebook "only so he could pay the bills." Zuckerberg's priorities—user growth and a better customer experience—"were more important than monetizing." It wasn't until he recruited Sheryl Sandberg away from Google to serve as his number two in 2008 that Facebook woke up. At Google, Sandberg oversaw its primary revenue source, online advertising sales. With Zuckerberg off on a monthlong round-the-world trip, deliberately allowing Sandberg to establish her authority, she organized daylong executive meetings to figure out how to monetize Facebook's proliferating user base. With 250 million Facebook users at the time, the choice was clear. They emerged from these sessions and Sandberg told Kirkpatrick, "The revenue model is advertising."

Like Mark Zuckerberg, Google cofounders Larry Page and Sergey Brin also formed their company with a belief that advertising was corrupting and would ill serve users. In a paper they presented at an Australian Web conference in 1998 that was unearthed by Tim Wu, they wrote that "advertising-funded search engines will be inherently biased towards the advertisers and away from the needs of the consumers."* Today, like Facebook, Google competes for ad dollars and

---

* Tim Wu, *The Attention Merchants: The Epic Scramble to Get Inside Our Heads* (New York: Alfred A. Knopf, 2016).

the attention of clients. It performs services for advertisers—from targeting their dollars using its DoubleClick automated buying, to designing search ads, to pitching that its YouTube is a more effective medium than standard television, to not charging advertisers unless an ad is clicked on, to offering data that highlights the user's intent—what they want—when they do a search. By the end of 2015, Google far eclipsed Facebook in the global ad dollars it amassed—$74.5 billion to Facebook's $26.9 billion—but Facebook ad revenues were growing faster.

■ ■ ■

When Carolyn Everson joined Facebook in 2011, the company had about half a million advertisers. By March 2016, Sheryl Sandberg told an Advertising Week audience, three million advertisers flocked to Facebook, a number that six months later zoomed to four million and soon, five million. Part of this extraordinary growth is a reflection of the expansion of the Facebook platform—the average Facebook user clicked on the site 150 times a day. And part is attributable to the company's ceaseless efforts to develop new tools for advertisers to target clients, resources unavailable to an advertiser who spent $5 million in 2016 for a thirty-second Super Bowl ad and had to guess who watched it.

Advertising is easy for Facebook's five million advertisers. Any company wanting to market a product can circumvent an agency and choose from multiple Facebook Lead Ads. Just click on the marketing message they wish to send, specify the amount they wish to spend, share their contact information for online customers, and specify the type of people they wish to reach. If they're unsure which marketing message might work best, the Facebook AI can test how well the message works. The Facebook software can also help choose the best targets. Companies can monitor the results hourly if they wish. And

Facebook analyzes and shares the results of what marketing messages work, and which don't. While Facebook shields some valuable data from advertisers, on its Web site it tells potential advertisers they can target audiences based on a variety of characteristics. In addition to age, gender, education, and job titles, their data offers personal interests like hobbies or preferred entertainment, past purchase behavior, location, so an advertiser can choose where "you want to do business," and they can even identify "look-alike audiences" with characteristics similar to those of the advertiser's customers. With that much data on its users, Facebook can target hundreds of thousands and even millions of users—"at Facebook we call it personal marketing at scale," Everson says. "The definition of creative advertising has changed. It's not just Don Draper creating ads." Targeting and the technology that allows it becomes part of the creative recipe.

By way of illustration, she recounted how Lexus launched a new Lexus NX model, a crossover SUV, in a thirty-second ad for the 2015 Super Bowl, and also made this part of a larger campaign by creating unique video ads targeted to individual Facebook users. Instead of a single TV or print ad, working with Facebook Lexus produced a thousand different online advertisements. If you were a male living in Silicon Valley, or a female surfboarder living in Los Angeles, or a golfer, or you were a past Lexus owner, or planned to buy a car in the next three months, Facebook merged its anonymous user data with Lexus's, along with so-called third party data they purchased. The result was tailored Lexus stories aimed at the interest of individual consumers.

Everson reports to David Fischer, vice president of business and marketing partnerships, who has worked alongside Sandberg as her deputy at the Treasury Department in the Clinton administration, at Google, and now at Facebook. To facilitate better communication, Everson initiated a Client Council in 2011 composed mostly of major brand CMOs like P&G and Unilever, along with some top agency executives, and a Creative Council in 2012 composed of creative agency executives. Each meets quarterly, and sometimes, as in Cannes in June 2016, they meet jointly.

※ ※ ※

At the Cannes quarterly in 2016, Everson stood at the front of a large Majestic Hotel conference room wearing a white dress with large blue pearls circling her neck. In a strong voice that did not need a microphone, she welcomed the forty or so client and agency representatives whose chairs were arranged in a large rectangular pattern with only carpet between them. She began with a status report, first mentioning a plan for a September session to which she was planning to invite several upstart companies that aim to disrupt various industries, her hope being that those in attendance might better understand how disrupters think and this might spark ideas about how to face future threats. She thanked the assembled for the fact that both quarterly councils offered early warnings that they were missing mobile, spurring Facebook to move aggressively into mobile. With alacrity, Facebook shifted from a desktop to a mobile company, and today mobile provides over 80 percent of its ad revenue.

She offered an update on some of the councils' other past suggestions: "You told us to get serious about emerging markets. Since then we've opened sixty offices around the world." They warned that video worked great on mobile devices with 4G, but what if users were on Facebook with a 2G mobile device or even a feature phone? So Facebook created a slide-show format that glided effortlessly across the screen. They complained that "Facebook felt like a walled garden, so we started giving you more data."

She updated them on some Facebook numbers: Its Instagram photo-sharing site has reached 588 million users, having doubled in the past two years, and 68 percent of its users visited on a daily basis;

the total time spent watching Instagram videos has grown 150 percent in six months; its Messenger IM was now used by 900 million people, up from 150 million in two years; Facebook had 158 million users in India, and it would not be long before India passed the United States' 203 million; Brazil was not far behind with 110 million users.

She invited Graham Mudd, director of monetization product marketing, to discuss what Facebook was doing to improve how it measured the effectiveness of client marketing efforts. A key thing to measure, he said, is whether the message is "engaging" to the potential consumer, not just whether it gets a click. To decipher that, Facebook was trying to gauge "the emotional connection" to the marketing message and "the attention" it gets by measuring the time spent with the message and contrasting this with the average time each individual usually spends with other ads or content. They measure whether the person presses the Like button or shares the message with friends. They have made good progress on measuring "attention," the easier of the two. They learned, for example, that millennials and teenagers "consume content two and a half times faster than older people." And the larger the screen the more time they spend with videos, meaning that to accurately measure attention they needed to know the device the person was using. In general, if the message kept the person's attention for at least two seconds, that was probably a good sign, though just two seconds probably skews the audience as younger. If the person spent three or more seconds, 85 percent were likely to stay for a thirty-second message. They had the data to compare whether the time spent with an ad was longer than the time the user spent with other ads. What they are also able to do "is target what type of people actually pay attention to that type of ad." Thus: "You can stipulate to us that you want to reach ten million people and we can target the right ten million people."

A CMO asked if the varied tools Facebook was creating could be shared and integrated so clients could use the data on other digital platforms. A Facebook executive admitted, "for us this is a hard one." Performance data could be shared, he said. But since there was no "universal platform" on which all data could travel because companies employed their own formats, shared data was illusory. What the Facebook executive did not say was that since they don't like to share some data, and since they were so dominant, Facebook had no interest in a universal platform.

The tension over data sharing between Facebook and agencies and advertisers did not disrupt this meeting, though it might have. As noted earlier, a reason clients and their agencies grouse about Facebook's walled garden is because they want information about consumers that Facebook is unwilling to share, including targeting data they could utilize for non-Facebook ad campaigns. Facebook refuses to allow its users to be targeted on non-Facebook platforms, for that would weaken Facebook's leverage. Facebook says its bigger concern is that agencies and their clients are asking them to share personally identifiable information about Facebook users, the names and e-mails and phone numbers that would allow advertisers to track them and serve them marketing messages. Facebook says that would violate their privacy pledge to users. Advertisers deny they would ever ask for personally identifiable information. They each exaggerate their virtue.

Council members are generally appreciative of these gatherings. "The Facebook Council—I was there from the beginning. This is the most clever idea," Keith Weed of Unilever says. "This is Carolyn Everson's baby. You get all the leading clients and agencies in a room and they're very open about what they're trying to do, and Facebook gets feedback. It's free consulting with all the people who really matter." But one is never far away from the frenemy issue. One agency attendee, who did not wish to be named, said afterwards, "This is the greatest grin fuck. To grin fuck is to keep smiling when you're fucking us." He believes Facebook is conditioning clients to believe Facebook has all the answers, which one day might lead clients to abandon their agencies.

※ ※ ※

There are many complaints about Facebook ads. In late 2015, James Murdoch, the CEO of 21st Century Fox, questioned the value of Facebook's video advertising formats, insisting that when Fox sold a product placement to Pepsi for $20 million and integrated its soft drink into the plot of its hit series *Empire*, it was a lot more effective than "a two-second viewable in the corner of a screen as you scroll through your Facebook feed. I feel like those sorts of impressions are not really earning anybody's attention." (Maybe not their attention but certainly Facebook's, because these ads provide lucrative ad dollars.) In early 2016, Patrick Keane, a Facebook competitor, extended Murdoch's argument: "A huge percentage of Facebook's revenue is sort of the underbelly of the Internet. Just direct response, shitty stuff. Punch the monkey stuff. Silly ads. They're just trying to get users to download and engage. And they're able to do it because it's quantifiable. If it's on the screen for a second, it counts. There's no outside referee that certifies that it worked." Keane's argument dovetailed with a view repeatedly expressed by Martin Sorrell. It troubled him that clients were paying for ads that often were not viewed by human beings but rather by bots, or automated software. "There's no way a three-second view on Facebook, and fifty percent of the time the sound is turned off, can be equated to a thirty- or sixty-second TV commercial," Sorrell complained publicly.

Unverified ads are a burgeoning challenge for Facebook and Google.

So too are efforts by agencies and clients to boost strong digital competitors to the two giants. Their private agenda was not unlike that of nineteenth-century Austrian chancellor Metternich, who maintained the balance of power by building up other nation-states to help resist Russia's expansion. Some of the other dominant digital companies are not legitimate rival advertising platforms. Apple relies not on advertising but on the sale of its hardware and software and on an iTunes subscription model for music and the sale of apps. At the moment, Amazon's and Microsoft's business models rely little on selling ads. Twitter is ad reliant, but Twitter has never earned a profit.

By late 2015, many agencies and clients hoped two digital competitors might bust out: AOL, which was armed with new financial resources when Verizon decided it was too risky to be a dumb pipe and acquired AOL in May 2015, or Snapchat, an emerging social network Facebook competitor. With AOL and the *Huffington Post* providing content and Verizon providing the pipe and data on its 135 million telephone customers, AOL CEO Tim Armstrong boldly proclaimed to an Advertising Week audience in September 2015 that the new entity "has dreams of being the largest mobile media company in the world." The competitive target, he said, was Google and Facebook.

The cofounder and CEO of Snapchat, Evan Spiegel, openly aspires to disrupt Facebook, which he mocked as passé. "If you look at the next generation of social media, it's really pinned on this concept of instant expression," Spiegel said over a breakfast at Manhattan's Four Seasons Hotel in October 2015. "And it was only technically possible with the advent of the smartphone, because you have a camera connected to it. People underestimate this transformation. So you can express yourself in real time, in the moment. So you no longer have this weird phenomena, which is really what Facebook is built on, which is that you collect all these experiences and you upload them later. So on Instagram you see these photos three days later. On Snapchat, you see Snaps the moment they are created."

Martin Sorrell decided in 2016 to ride the Snapchat horse as a rival worth betting on. He decided to sweeten the ad dollars WPP earmarked for Snapchat. "It does become a threatening alternative to Facebook," he told CNBC, "and I think that's the big opportunity for them. . . . I think Facebook is concerned about the potential opposition."

Not that concerned. Sorrell's threat was pure bluster. Although WPP would over time double the ad dollars it steered to Snapchat, from $90 million in 2016 to $200 million in 2017, it was akin to throwing pebbles in the ocean: WPP's ad spending on Google rose five times as fast in 2016, totaling $5 billion; WPP purchased $1.7 billion of ads on Facebook in 2016. While Snapchat's revenues jumped seven times faster in 2016, they only reached $404.5 million. By contrast, Facebook's ad revenues totaled $27 billion that year. The looming threat to Facebook and Google, which would prompt Sorrell and the agencies and their clients—as well as Facebook and Google—to quake, would not come from Snapchat. It would come from Amazon.

8.

THE RISE OF MEDIA AGENCIES

"We always had the view that the less a media owner knows about what our objectives are and what our needs are, the more leverage we have in a negotiation. If he knows what I need, why would he discount it?"

—Irwin Gotlieb

n Hollywood, if you utter only certain first names—*Warren* or *Barbra* or *Jeffrey*—the film community knows you mean Warren Beatty, Barbra Streisand, or Jeffrey Katzenberg. In the advertising community, if you say *Irwin*, people know you mean Irwin Gotlieb, the global chairman and architect of GroupM, the powerful media agency. Michael Kassan refers to Irwin as "my closest friend," usually speaks to him at least once a day, and says of him, "In our industry, Irwin Gotlieb is Yoda."

Comparing media agencies to creative agencies, Gotlieb's boss, Martin Sorrell says, "Media agencies are better compensated than creative agencies. The engine room of WPP is the media agency's billings." Of the many companies that fly the WPP flag, GroupM is the largest single profit contributor. And media agencies were the target of

Jon Mandel's attack on the holding companies. Traditionally, a media agency supervises marketing campaigns: planning strategy, targeting where ads will appear, negotiating ad rates, and buying ads or promotional messages on media platforms. By the end of 2015, the foremost competitors to GroupM were the media agencies of Publicis, Omnicom, Dentsu, IPG, and Horizon. GroupM has ten companies under its wing, including Mindshare, the biggest of its four media planning and buying entities, and Xaxis, the world's largest programmatic buying arm. Together, GroupM's companies lavished on various platforms a total of about $75 billion advertising dollars, which in 2015 represented almost one fifth of all global ad dollars. GroupM is paid primarily on what is known as Scope of Work, or SOW, which means the agency submits how it will staff the account and the client approves a preagreed profit margin, one that goes up or down based on the success (the key performance indicator, or KPI) of the campaign. Generally, GroupM's profit margins are a couple of percentage points higher than WPP's 17.4 percent.

In appearance, Irwin Gotlieb looks as if he just slid out of a barber's chair. Not a silver or black hair is out of place; he keeps it swept back at the sides and combed flat atop his head, like the deck of an aircraft carrier; he wears tailored suits, and if not adorned with an expensive tie, the top two buttons on his starched shirt are open just so. He speaks slowly, as if inspecting each word. This very careful man has traveled a long, circuitous path from his birth in Dalian, China, formerly Port Arthur. His parents, Genya and Jacob, were refugees from Belarus who after World War I separately traveled by train across Siberia to China, because Japan allowed Jews to relocate to Japanese-occupied China and each had relatives who had immigrated there. His mother's family fled to Harbin seeking business opportunity; Jacob followed a more circuitous route. His parents died when he was young, and as a child he joined the youth organization of Ze'ev

Jabotinsky, the commander of Betar, a radical Zionist organization that was at war with the British who occupied Palestine. By eighteen, Jacob Gotlieb was a fervent Zionist serving in the Polish army and, according to his son, was deemed "a troublemaker as a Zionist and had to get out of the country." Desperate, Jacob tried to flee from Poland to Palestine, but was blocked. He came to Harbin seeking safety.

Jacob and Genya met and married in China. Irwin was born in June 1949, and in 1950 Irwin and an older sister and their parents boarded a coal tanker that was retrofitted to sardine 1600 refugees. The journey took six months to reach Israel, where his father's brother owned movie theaters and meatpacking plants. Irwin says his father came to Israel carrying precious stones, and had managed to bring on the boat thirteen crates containing crystal and silverware and even a refrigerator, half of which he traded to Chinese officials in order to escape China. "He kept the good stuff," Irwin says. To this day, it's a mystery how his father collected this haul. "This is hearsay, I never got it from him because there were things the man would not talk about." He's uncertain how his father, though thirty-seven at the time, not only wasn't in the Israeli military reserves but had been excused from service. "From what I was told he made a deal to serve in the foreign ministry for a year without pay in return for a deferment of his reserve duty." He knows this wasn't the total truth. Nor does he know why his father flew alone to Tokyo in 1952 and three months later summoned his family to join him at their new home in Kobe, Japan, where he had started a thriving pearl and diamond business. Jacob Gotlieb, his son says, "did other things that were strange." He maintained an apartment in Tel Aviv, and would regularly fly there and visit his good friend, Menachem Begin, who had been the commander of Irgun, the clandestine underground militant organization that grew out of Jabotinsky's Betar.

His dad was stubborn and difficult, and Irwin was closer to his mother. "My mom was the brilliant one," Irwin says. "She was an incredible mathematician and pianist. She pushed me on both." She made him practice piano three hours a day, and by the time he was thirteen "I was concert level." The day after his Bar Mitzvah he stopped playing. (He resumed in 2014.) A precocious student who skipped grades, Irwin learned to speak nine languages, and by age fifteen his parents decided to send him to college in the United States.

He came to New York and enrolled at New York University. But he never attended, and never told his parents. Like his father, he lived a double life; for the next several years, "they thought I was in school." What did he do? "I partied a lot." He got a job in the media department of Norman, Craig & Kummel. He met Elizabeth Billick at Fridays, a popular singles bar on East Sixty-first Street and First Avenue. Much like he would later do in shrewdly negotiating advertising deals, he asked for her phone number but waited three weeks to call. Why? "I didn't want to show my cards!" They've been married forty-eight years and have a daughter and two grandchildren in California.

Irwin worked for a variety of agencies—his second ad job was at SSC&B, followed by associate director of broadcast programming at Benton & Bowles in 1977. He grew deeply frustrated by the parochialism of America and the advertising industry. "In the seventies I was a closet sushi eater," he says. He'd sit at the bar of a sushi restaurant on West Forty-eighth Street and be the only non-Asian in the restaurant. "The United States has historically been a very parochial country," Gotlieb says. "We're an island. We're separated from the rest of the world and there was this attitude at Benton and Bowles in the mideighties that London was a branch office. The difference in my DNA was that I always knew there was a very large world out there." In 1989, Benton & Bowles changed his title to global head of broadcasting. He left in 1993 to found and serve as CEO of MediaVest Worldwide, the first time a U.S. media department was spun out as a stand-alone company.

Martin Sorrell recruited him in 1999 to serve as chairman and CEO of Mindshare Worldwide, which he forged into a global power-house by bringing into its fold the media agencies of Ogilvy and J. Walter Thompson. In 2003, WPP consolidated all agencies under his watch into GroupM, anointing him global CEO. A passionate technologist, Gotlieb was early to spot the growing strategic impor-tance of data in marketing campaigns. By 2015, he had hired a total of 2,500 engineers and analytics specialists.

Gotlieb's ascent reflected a trend in the advertising business. With their deep pockets, holding companies started acquiring media agen-cies. In the United States, one of the first acquisitions was IPG's pur-chase of Western International Media, the company Michael Kassan sold. This 1994 acquisition had been preceded in France, when the WCRS Group bought Carat in 1979 (later acquired by Dentsu), and in the UK in 1988, when Saatchi & Saatchi spun off Zenith into a separate agency (now owned by French giant Publicis).

Eventually each holding company would have its own media agency with a primary seat at the client table. Each agency had a large pool of ad dollars, which gave it more leverage to demand lower prices from the ad seller. With clients ever more reliant on the data and targeting and media-buying prowess of media agencies, their profit margins came to exceed those of the creative ad agencies.

"A big difference between today and the *Mad Men* era is that Bill Bernbach and David Ogilvy were media figures," says celebrated ad man Jeff Goodby, cofounder and cochair of Goodby, Silverstein & Partners. "Today, the business-side people tend to be the public fig-ures." Martin Sorrell, not David Droga or Bob Greenberg, is the adver-tising celebrity featured in ads for the *Wall Street Journal*. Observes another creative from *Mad Men* days, Jerry Della Femina: "My agency has my name, Della Femina, on it. There isn't any agency with a human name on it anymore. No Carl Ally. No Papert, Koenig, Lois. No Doyle Dane Bernbach. Agencies are named very much like rock groups— 72andSunny." Della Femina overstates, neglecting Droga and Goodby and several others. But his argument is more valid than not.

A second consequence of the ascendancy of the media agency was the further erosion of trust between client and agency. The media agency's hefty profits, coupled with assurances to clients that "we can buy you media at a lower price aroused the suspicions" of clients that "we are making millions," moans Publicis CEO Maurice Levy. There were reasons to believe agencies were extravagant. In *Mad Men* days, many agencies had private chefs; profligate liquid lunches and dinners were billed to clients; Interpublic CEO Marion Harper once commanded a fleet of five airplanes, including his private DC-7 with French Provincial furniture, a king-size bed, and a sunken bath. Harper flaunted his ostentation, once telling an interviewer, "We can't support people with little thoughts or little dreams."*

There are those, like former Ogilvy CEO Miles Young, who believe Gotlieb's famed negotiating skills can be traced to his upbringing in China: "He's very Mandarin. He's very opaque, but in a good way. He reads the market well. He's subtle." Gotlieb declines to attribute his approach to the lessons learned in China, though his self-description qualifies as an endorsement of Young's observation: "We always had the view that the less a media owner knows about what our objectives

---

* Recounted in Michael Farmer, *Madison Avenue Manslaughter: An Inside View of Fee-Cutting Clients, Profit-Hungry Owners and Declining Ad Agencies* (New York: LID Publishing Ltd., 2015).

are and what our needs are, the more leverage we have in a negotiation. If he knows what I need, why would he discount it?" Yet he ap-
preciates that when the negotiation ends, both sides need be able to
claim victory: "I tell this to my people all the time: negotiation isn't
about shouting louder, or hondling longer. It's not about wielding a
heavier sledgehammer. You have to have a strategy. And you have to
have some level of insight into what shaped the other party's position.
And then as gently as possible you back them into a corner and force
the outcome. And if you do it right, it doesn't get unpleasant, and
both sides feel pretty good about it as they walk away because it was
the right thing for both sides. And don't put anyone out of business,
because you're going to need them."

The Chinese-born Gotlieb and the British-born Sorrell shared a
conviction that to grow, WPP had to expand globally. By 2015, only
37 percent of WPP's revenues came from North America, with 30 percent generated in Asia, South America, Africa, and the Middle East. In
non-Western countries, Stephan Loerke, managing director of the
World Federation of Advertisers, says, "Understanding of the value of
advertising has increased appreciably in recent years." In many countries, Loerke says, governments push harder to support advertising.
"You go to China or Brazil and it's different. The first question they
ask is, 'How do we maximize the economic engine that advertising
represents?'" Not surprisingly, the Chinese government banned ad
blockers.

Unlike Facebook and Google, or media companies like Rupert
Murdoch's News Corp, that confronted a red stop sign in China, Gotlieb and WPP received a green light. GroupM has more freedom to
mine customer information since there are fewer privacy restrictions in
China. Why? "Because in China people know they're being watched,"
and because people are more willing to share their data, says Bessie

Lee, who until 2017 was WPP's CEO in China.* With China now its third largest market after the United States and the UK, WPP in November 2015 combined three thousand GroupM and other agency employees into a single Shanghai campus.

Keith Weed describes a week he spent in Shanghai, where three companies—Tencent, Alibaba, and Baidu—dominate nearly three quarters of all time spent on mobile, and where Tencent's thriving WeChat alone had 650 million customers. He experimented by touring the city with a local Unilever employee who carried no cash and only her mobile phone. They relied totally on the WeChat messaging app that afternoon. Using the app, they ordered a car. From the WeChat platform, "We booked ahead on Alipay and she paid for lunch on WeChat." They ordered merchandise from Alibaba and paid via mobile. They fetched movie tickets on WeChat. Six years ago, he says, China was "a pale copy of Silicon Valley. Now there's real innovation there. In messaging, they're ahead of us. They want messaging to be the portal to the Internet."

In India, where the population is projected to one day exceed China's, the government is more welcoming to capitalism. Visiting with Prime Minister Narendra Modi in October 2015, Sorrell told a local reporter that "India will be one of the great advertising and marketing places in the world." The advertising and marketing agencies his company owned or partnered with gave WPP a market share in the country of about 45 percent. Part of India's appeal, Rishad Tobaccowala says, is that half of all Indians are less than twenty-five years old. Facebook expected India to soon surpass the United States as its largest market. With a contract from the energy department in India, Edelman public relations opened a twenty-eight-person advertising department in Mumbai. India is an alluring marketing opportunity, albeit

---

* Bessie Lee at a September 21, 2016, *Financial Times* panel in New York.

with pitfalls. India's advertising expenditures are only 5 percent of those in the United States, Tobaccowala says, and that's because there are not enough consumers with disposable income for advertisers to reach, and because a creaky digital infrastructure impedes the Internet and mobile phones.

※ ※ ※

While Irwin Gotlieb worked hand in hand with Martin Sorrell to transform GroupM and WPP into a global enterprise, the future challenge that consumed much of Gotlieb's waking hours was how to master big data. Digital cookies yielded data that allow marketers to better target individuals rather than amorphous groups, but also to measure the effectiveness of a marketing campaign. Big data was the promise Carolyn Everson and Facebook employed to entice advertisers. And big data did one other significant thing: it granted more power to media agencies who used data to shape marketing campaigns. But this was so only if the media agency was big enough to hire the data engineers and convince clients it could unlock consumer secrets.

"The kinds of stuff that we are focusing on, the technology, the data, all of these things benefit from scale, which is a real amplifier of those capabilities," Gotlieb said one day from his Garment District office on Seventh Avenue and West Thirty-seventh Street. "The more touch points we have, the more volume we have. The more data we gather, the more we understand. Let me give you an example of something I could foresee: the GroupM shops are going to be the guys who do the major ideation. What I see us doing is that we are increasingly able to slice and dice audiences into microsegments, each of which will need customized communication. When you logged into a client's e-commerce site, we custom built an offer for you in real time. How did we do it? We know what you purchased in the past. We know what you own. And we know what the next thing you're likely to need is.

That's different from what I need. Each of us gets a highly customized offer." To customize, however, will mean that the media agency may encroach on some creative agency's function, as Gotlieb concedes: "We might be doing creative executions" to customize messages.

Customized messages beg another question: How to define creative marketing? CMOs like Keith Weed like to say that the Holy Grail separating effective from ineffective advertising is a "big idea" executed by "good creative." But when messages are customized to individuals and not aimed at a mass audience, does the individualized message shove aside some big creative idea? If it did, it would cement the rising power of media agencies like Gotlieb's GroupM. We saw this occur when one of GroupM's media-buying agencies, MediaCom, created the "Love Is On" campaign for Revlon, inducing women to carefully apply lipstick and fragrances to open up to love and romance. One could argue that this was a "big idea," but the idea was conceived not by a creative agency but by a media agency and it was targeted at individuals. We would see a manifestation of the rising power of media agencies in 2016, when Omnicom won a bid to create a single agency dominated by its Hearts & Science media agency to represent AT&T, the fourth largest advertiser in North America. These "Mediapalooza" accounts, as they've been called, start with data, for the data shapes the narrative. "This is not brain surgery. You don't need a big idea," Gotlieb says, choosing not to dwell on the classic big ideas crafted by those who'd qualify for an advertising Hall of Fame—Bill Bernbach, David Ogilvy, Mary Wells Lawrence, Lee Clow, Keith Reinhard, Bob Greenberg.

Big data is siphoned from three sources. Generally, first-party data is gathered by the companies that interact with customers directly and usually retain their credit cards; plus from department stores, credit card and car companies, Amazon, magazines and newspapers, and companies reliant on subscriptions. First-party data has the names of individuals, which the company can use and can share. Second-party data is anonymous but also contains a rich trove of individual information from various sources, including clients, data companies like Nielsen, comScore, and a WPP-owned agency, Kantar. Anonymous third-party data is purchased from catalogues and stores. GroupM assembles all this data and strives to match the products of its clients with targeted consumers.

More than a few obstacles impede the data collection efforts of media agencies. Companies like Facebook and Google, who bank some of the richest first-party data, resist sharing much of it. Eric R. Salama, CEO of Kantar in London, its thirty thousand employees rivaling Nielsen and making it the world's second largest research company, expresses a common frustration with Facebook and Google among agencies. "We really have to get into these walled gardens to really understand what people are doing and how they're behaving," he says. Mobile phones pose obstacles as well; marketing on mobile phones is complex. Salama cautions, "How do we test ads on mobile?" And if the mobile phone lacks a flash drive, they can't show the ad. Talent may be big data's most crucial impediment, Salama thinks. "Everyone wants to hire data scientists and engineers." The supply is limited, the competition intense.

■ ■ ■

In the data arms race, Irwin Gotlieb set out to build a state-of-the-art data weapon, known internally as the Secret Sauce project. Gotlieb was intent on building GroupM's own proprietary data system because, as he would publicly complain in 2015, Facebook and Google had their own ad tech vehicles to target ads and were, in effect, muscling agencies and clients by warning: "If you want to buy ads on our properties, you have to use our ad tech tools." He saw other holding companies making inexpensive deals to utilize Google's DoubleClick or Facebook's tech tools, and he thought they were crazy to become dependent on a frenemy. He liked Carolyn Everson, was proud to be listed on her long list of mentors, but was not seduced by her luminous smile. "They want to sell their impressions for the highest possible price," he says. "I want to buy them for the lowest possible price. In order for me to accomplish this objective, I have to keep them in the dark as much as possible."

With the support of Martin Sorrell, he says he spent a total of $2.5 billion to build GroupM's own tech stack, the unique operating system and supporting programming to run a complex application, in this case their secret sauce. One day in a GroupM conference room, Gotlieb and Harvey Goldhersz, CEO of GroupM Analytics, shared its ingredients. The initial ingredient came when WPP acquired digital marketing company 24/7 Media. Gotlieb says the two biggest attractions of 24/7 were its hard-to-recruit two hundred engineers, and WPP's desire to block competitors from acquiring the company. Earlier, WPP bought KBM, or KnowledgeBase Marketing, a company that had relationships with three thousand retailers and stored a cornucopia of what is known as personally identifiable information (PII), including the people's names and their behavioral traits. Now KBM gathered sales data from companies WPP either owned outright, like Kantar, or those in which it was a major shareholder, like Rentrak and comScore. In addition, KBM vacuumed additional data, providing GroupM with a range of about forty thousand personal "behavior attributes"—what people purchase, eat, read, watch, their interests and hobbies, along with their age, sex, and neighborhood. GroupM only has anonymized data, but it assigns each individual a digital identifier or persistent identifier. "We know you're number 001," Gotlieb says. In all, of America's 200 million adult population, Gotlieb says Group M has anonymized data on almost all of them, the exceptions usually being those who don't have a bank account or e-mail address.

What's key, Gotlieb says, is the anonymized PII. "We rely on persis-tent identifiers, not cookies," and convert them into cookies. He offers this example of how it would work: "Assume we have a client who wants to sell tomato paste." From available data on people who buy lots of tomato paste and tomato sauce, GroupM then matches these people with its database and comes up with a universe of regular tomato paste and sauce consumers. GroupM then aims a marketing campaign at them and can tell whether they saw the marketing messages. Then they go back to the sales data to learn whether the targeted consumers pur-chased more. "That's one measure of whether the marketing campaign worked," Gotlieb says. It also allows them to match this data with other data they've collected on the individual, Gotlieb continues. "This also allows an assessment of the same group's other attributes. Do they drive similar cars? Do they watch similar TV shows? Do they fit in the same income segments?" GroupM knows a tremendous amount. But, he insists, they don't know their actual identity. "We know the family. We know the income. We know the credit score. We just don't know the name and the address. KBM does. It's not the law in the U.S. that prevents us from knowing the names, it's WPP's internal policy."

"Think of it as a spreadsheet," Gotlieb continues, "with two hun-dred million rows and forty thousand behavioral characteristics." To illustrate the difference targeted marketing can make, he turns to the consumption of rice: "Seventy percent of the U.S. population has not bought rice in more than two years. It doesn't mean they don't eat rice." But the 30 percent who do buy it "tend to be ethnic—Asians and Hispanics—because rice is endemic to their cuisines. And they buy a lot," usually in bulk. "Only ten percent of the population buys convenience rice products, like Minute Rice and Uncle Ben's." These convenience rice products each only have a market share of 2 to 4 per-cent, and an American consumer typically buys only two boxes a year. If GroupM represented one of these 2 to 4 percent brands, what he would do is create a marketing campaign offering enticing rice recipes. "If I can move them from two boxes a year to three boxes a year, you've got a fifty percent increase in volume." An even bigger marketing opportunity for Minute Rice and Uncle Ben's is among those who buy rice in bulk. Since GoupM would be able to identify these consumers, for the 20 percent of them who might be potential customers, his marketing message would be, "'One day you will come home and not have time to cook your rice.' Maybe they will buy one box. If I can penetrate five percent of that twenty percent, my convenience rice has gone from two- to three-percent penetration."

Gotlieb believes they have reduced the guesswork. "Today we have evidence that this person saw two commercials and bought this product," he declares. With clients increasingly asking agencies to prove their return on investment by demonstrating that their marketing campaign was effective, and with clients willing to pay them a bonus for success, Irwin Gotlieb is convinced his secret sauce will enhance GroupM's bottom line.

But not just yet. "It is going to take another couple of years for this to be fully deployed," he says. "We haven't exposed it to all of our clients because we can't retrain our people quickly enough. We're changing out the engine while the plane is flying." There is also a security concern. Media agencies usually share clients with other creative agencies outside of WPP, meaning that Gotlieb works with an Omnicom or IPG creative team. How much of his secret sauce does he want to share with competitors? Like Facebook and Google, he has reasons to wall off his data.

He also knows that the era of shared campaigns may be shrinking. Media agencies like his are changing in profound ways. If his secret sauce works, more clients will push for the media agency to serve as the pilot of the marketing plane. The definition of "what is creative will keep changing," Gotlieb says, and "the creative function will bifurcate," with media agencies, as his friend Michael Kassan believes, planning and executing entire campaigns, perhaps even the creative.

A number of impediments may be thrown in the path of Irwin Gotlieb's future vision. He is aware that digital and consulting giants pose a competitive threat, but is he guilty of assuming that his holding company competitors are more inert than they are? Can he galvanize his own organization to discard the familiar legacy model they have relied on for decades and embrace a more scientific approach to targeting? Can media agencies retain the trust of their clients? But perhaps the primary impediment to Gotlieb's secret sauce centers on privacy.

What is the privacy line Gotlieb won't cross?

Although they could collect real names, he says, "We will not cross the line to know their name." Of course, since they know "a tremendous amount" about each individual and have assigned a personal identifier to each, their name is not crucial for marketing purposes.

Did he worry that GroupM's abundant data on individuals is too much information and might be abused?

"No," he instantly responded. "Could I get to a place where I have too much? It's possible, but unlikely. And to be blunt, we have nowhere near what Facebook, Google, Apple, and Amazon have."

Gotlieb's statement won't discomfort the digital giants, for he is acknowledging their data dominance. But it would discomfort consumer advocates. They are shocked that privacy limitations are set by companies like WPP, not the U.S. government, which doesn't impose the same strict privacy laws of other countries, particularly Western Europe's.

Perhaps because he lives in Western Europe, Eric Salama is acutely aware of the threat stricter privacy laws pose to his data company. "I think the privacy issue is going to become a bigger issue," concedes Salama. "In Germany, it's massive. In the United States, less so. I think it's going to be huge because I don't think most people have a clue how their data is being used. There is an implied contract where people are getting all this content for free. But someone has to pay for it. And the pay-for-it comes through advertising. But that's an implied contract, not an explicit contract. And people are being targeted on the basis of their behavior, and we need to be much more open with people that when they sign up for something, that they know what they are signing up for. If I go on my computer or my mobile, I'm quite happy that a cookie has been stored there. It means that I don't have to reload everything, and I'm getting stuff that is relevant to me."

What Salama does not say is that media agencies are wary of giving consumers the choice of opting in, meaning that instead of allowing consumers to follow labyrinthine instructions to opt out of sharing their cookies with companies, consumers would have to voluntarily opt in before their data could be shared. While consumers choosing to opt in would advance privacy protections, it would derail the targeting dreams of Irwin Gotlieb and media agencies.

9.

THE PRIVACY TIME BOMB

"The key thing we see in privacy is that companies have made a decision to privatize privacy."

— Christian Sandvig, associate professor of communication studies at the University of Michigan

D ata—big data—and its benefits are cheered by client and agency and platform alike. But when data is the subject, privacy inevitably becomes a part of the conversation too. So it was at an early April 2016 Monday staff meeting at Media-Link. Often at these weekly meetings MediaLink invites a client to bring them up to date on what they're doing. On this day, it was Foursquare's turn. The location-based mobile app was launched in 2009 to much fanfare, then lost altitude, and more recently had climbed to fifty million monthly users, $100 million in annual revenues, and attracted clients like Microsoft and Capital One. Wenda Millard turned over the floor to Michael Rosen, Foursquare's vice president of sales, who sketched how his company had changed. They still rely on the GPS in smartphones to follow and locate people and allow friends to share where they are at any moment. But they've abandoned awarding stickers and badges and encouraging users to be christened, say, mayor of a local Starbucks, which was cute but didn't generate much marketing dollars.

Rosen said Foursquare currently provides "data intelligence marketing that can help marketers" by gathering information from hundreds of apps like Snapchat and Twitter, allowing Foursquare to offer "foot traffic location data" at ninety-three million locations around the world. And they're not just reliant on the fifty million who have signed up to be part of the Foursquare community. Foursquare thinks of itself as a public utility. When people visit the app the very first time, they are asked: "Allow Foursquare to access your location even when you're not using the app? Foursquare needs your location to help you find nearby places you'll love." Even if you don't use the Foursquare app, if you tap "Allow," they follow you. As is true on all sites, consumers can opt out of being tracked, though this process is often cumbersome and confusing. Privacy advocates like former senator Al Franken (D-MN) champion what he calls antistalking legislation that would require location data apps to first offer consumers a choice to "opt in" before they can collect or share consumer data, a policy fiercely opposed by digital companies and marketers. Opt in is required in some Western European countries, as well as in Japan and South Korea.

Although Foursquare—like hundreds of other apps that use location data—doesn't know your name, they follow people, as Irwin Gotlieb does, by assigning them a digital personal identifier. They can tell Bed Bath & Beyond the "path to purchase" followed by their customers because they can tell what stores their customers first visited and what store they went to afterward if they exited without a purchase. By comparing prior and current foot traffic, Foursquare can predict when business is falling off or rising, and who the foremost competitors are.

They rely on three sources of data, he explained, including first-party data "on millions and millions of vendors," which is data from stores or credit card companies or vendors or brands that have a direct relationship with their customers. Like other companies, Foursquare fattens their consumer profiles by purchasing less direct second- and third-party data from a variety of sources, including government agencies like motor vehicles and the vast array of data traffickers—Palantir, Acxiom, Experian, IBM's Watson, Oracle's Datalogix, among others—who sell nonpersonalized data to marketers.

In addition, Foursquare has data on those who see an ad on television and then visit a store. They can tell whether you've visited Shake Shack or a bar once or twice that week, and can target you as a likely hamburger eater or beer drinker, which advertisers will pay for. They can compute the wait times at checkout counters, which stores seeking a competitive advantage will eagerly pay for. By wirelessly communicating with in-store Bluetooth radio transmitters known as beacons, stores can transmit a discount coupon to a mobile phone, directing the consumer to a bargain counter. Being able to predict foot traffic is an enticement for retail clients to flock to Foursquare, as Target, Home Depot, and Whole Foods have done.

When Michael Kassan is asked about privacy, he skates over the surface of the question, acknowledging that there is "a delicate balance. We all like to get Amazon recommendations for this book or that book. We like it because it makes our life more efficient. In part, we think it's great that people can predict where we want to go and lead us to places we're interested in. But the delicate balance is that you don't want it to be scary. . . . You start to get worried as an individual when *they* know too much, whoever *they* are." Like his brethren in the marketing business, however, Kassan doesn't see "a delicate balance" when it comes to requiring companies to have consumers opt in. "I don't think we've figured out a good way to have an opt in really work, because nobody reads the fine print. We still live in a world where as a lawyer I would say that if you shop for a hotel and you go online and it says, 'Agree,' have you ever read what you agree to? I don't think people read the language." Translation: Companies and advertisers would be denied valuable marketing data because confused consumers would not opt in. Kassan is a true-blue marketing man. His first instinct is to protect marketers.

※ ※ ※

Marketers are awash in data. Think of Irwin Gotlieb's secret sauce and many of the 40,000 personally identifiable attributes it plans to retain on 200 million adult Americans, each assigned a digital identifier. Of the 130 billion daily ad pages displayed on the Internet each day, a senior executive at WPP's Xaxis says they can follow about 40 percent of all online ads, allowing them to better understand what advertising results in sales. This is small potatoes, he suggests, noting that over time Carolyn Everson's Facebook sees trillions of online ads. But by tracking what users search and watch and do online, GroupM's Brian Lesser says, hopefully exaggerating, "We know what you want even before you know you want it."

Among its two billion worldwide users, Facebook assembles about a hundred personally identifiable attributes and purchases, including personal information from many of the five thousand data brokers around the globe who gather pharmacy records, store loyalty cards, voter registration, mortgages, pay stubs, and other data, according to author Sue Halpern, a scholar-in-residence at Middlebury College.* *ProPublica*, which has ferociously chewed on the privacy issue like a dog on a bone, wrote, "Facebook offers advertisers more than 1,300

---

* Sue Halpern, "They Have, Right Now, Another You," *The New York Review of Books*, December 22, 2016.

categories for ad targeting . . . Every time a Facebook member likes a post, tags a photo, updates their favorite movies in their profile, posts a comment about a politician," browses the Web, or taps WhatsApp and Instagram on a mobile phone, "Facebook logs it."[*]

Google has merged all the data it collects from its 3.5 billion daily searches and from YouTube and other services, and it introduced a Google About Me page, offering advertisers your date of birth, phone number, where you work, mailing address, education level, where you've traveled, your nickname, photo, and e-mail address.[†] Airbnb CMO Jonathan Mildenhall says of the many millions of people who rent homes, "We know everything about our hosts. Likewise with our guests," though it's a bit less specific for the latter. As for Amazon, since it is the world's largest store and knows what individuals have actually purchased, its data is unrivaled.

With Amazon's Alexa in the home, the company can gather more: Alexa is an agent that not only knows what you purchased but when you wake up, what you actually watch, read, listen to, ask for, and eat. In addition to posing a potential threat to privacy, Amazon poses a threat to Google. By 2017, roughly half of all product searches were being done on Amazon, not Google. And in challenging Amazon and Google's digital assistants, Apple tried to use the privacy issue against them, vowing not to sell your private information to advertisers. When 2017 ended, Apple announced that it would place its Siri digital assistant in a new HomePod that will be "less creepy" than Amazon or Google because it would deny advertisers the data they desire.

Many other companies are also awash in data. Bank of America has comprehensive information on its 50 million customers. This data-rich

---

[*] Julia Angwin, Terry Parris, Jr., and Surya Mattu, "What Facebook Knows About You," *ProPublica*, September 28, 2016.
[†] Sarah Perez, "Google's New 'About Me' Page Lets You Control What Personal Info Others Can See," TechCrunch.com, November 11, 2015.

customer base is replicated by every bank, Wall Street investment firm, and credit card company. Comcast, the nation's largest cable company with 22 million subscribers, has stored in its set-top boxes a wealth of personal information, from credit cards to most-watched programs, and can combine this with third-party data to compare ads viewed with purchases made. Comcast and other cable companies that span the United States collect actual viewing numbers on millions of citizens. Verizon and AT&T each had over 100 million wireless subscribers in 2016, with a mind-numbing array of personal information. Telephone and cable broadband providers retain data about what TV you watch, what banks you use, what Web sites and apps you visit, what newspapers and magazines you subscribe to, what you purchase online, what stores and restaurants you favor. Those who sweep up data can chart what drugs a consumer purchases, and "inferences about your health can be used," warns Joseph Turow, a professor of communications at the Annenberg School at the University of Pennsylvania.

Data can be weaponized by marketers to target messages and ultimately to create what's called addressable advertising. Prowling his London office in jeans and royal blue socks, Keith Weed of Unilever grows excited as he describes how mobile phones have elevated data as a marketing tool. "When I started in marketing we were using second-hand data which was three months old. Now with the good old mobile, I have individualized data on people. You don't need to know their names. . . . You know their telephone number. You know where they live because it's the same location as their PC [and the IP address this data yields]." They know what times of the day you usually browse, watch videos, do e-mail, travel to the office or dinner, and what routes you take. "From your mobile I know whether you stay in four-star or two-star hotels, whether you go to train stations or airports. I use these insights along with what you're browsing on your PC. I know whether you're interested in horses or holidays in the Caribbean." By using programmatic computers to buy ads targeting these individuals, he says, Unilever can "create a hundred thousand permutations of the same ad," as they recently did with a thirty-second TV ad for Axe toiletries aimed at young men in Brazil. If they knew the target was fond of cars, or sci-fi movies, a particular soccer team or type of music, each ad could be personally tailored.

Tapping new technologies that can compute the emotional reactions of consumers reduces the guessing done by marketers. In recent years a number of companies have emerged to create a database of thousands of different facial expressions, and software translates these into algorithms that describe their meaning. Using Webcams and security cameras, marketers monitor the facial expressions of consumers as they shop, decide to exit a store, watch ads, or video chat. Apple's iPhone X, introduced in late 2017, recognizes faces, not just the owner's: Obviously, the same technology can help detect whether a child is in pain after an operation or an alleged terrorist is lying.

If big data was one of the flavors of the year in late 2015 and into 2016, targeting and addressable messages was an accompanying flavor. It was a flavor sampled all over the world. In 2015 and early 2016, Tencent's Online Media Goup in China entered partnership agreements with WPP, Dentsu, and Omnicom to access Tencent's consumer database of about 800 million monthly users. Together, they set out to develop models to trace the online behavior of Tencent's consumers. Tencent was trading its valuable data for the marketing dollars of agency clients. A new slew of start-ups emerged, hoping to either partner with or nudge aside agencies to help brands identify targeted customers.

SocialCode is one of these start-ups. Its CEO is Laura O'Shaughnessy, and it is funded by her dad, former *Washington Post* owner Donald Graham. After graduating from business school and working in digital start-ups, O'Shaughnessy believes that a "complete transformation" is coming in the way "brands can connect to consumers. Back in the days when my grandmother ran the *Washington Post*, there were four or five channels to reach people in Washington, D.C. There were two newspapers and three television stations. Period." Today platforms have proliferated, as have the marketing messages hurled at consumers. "Marketing became offensive. I was seeing messages that were irrelevant to me, that I didn't care about. It was a waste of my time."

Like those at Foursquare, to her way of thinking SocialCode and its 230 employees, half of them engineers, were serving consumers, not just making money on clients such as Macy's and Budweiser. By targeting individuals on social media, by sometimes creating the ads, and then using programmatic buying to deliver individualized messages, they were offering ads "that are relevant to me, that are useful to me. And I can tell when I serve the ad whether that person made a purchase and checked it out in a retail store." The way it works, she explains, is they decide on a target group, say those who drink a particular beer brand. Their client, another beer brand, pays for ads that are created by her company or the ad agency. These ads are relevant, she thinks, because they are aimed at persuading a group of beer drinkers to switch. They serve up the ads, track whether the individuals saw the ads, and then, relying on store data assembled by Oracle's Datalogix from its many store clients, they track whether "user 123 who was served an ad" switched beer brands.

They are no longer doing what she thinks "advertising has been doing for a long time, which is guessing." She dubs this her "customer-centric model." They chart for clients: What messages worked? What doesn't work? Who comes to the store? Who doesn't come to the store? It becomes, she believes, "a game changer." Using this data, the brand can make changes to improve the customer experience and convenience, as Warby Parker has done for eyeglasses and Uber and Lyft have done for transit. Unless big agencies learn to shed old habits, to move faster, she believes they are in danger of plunging down the same rabbit hole as most newspapers.

* * *

Big data excites Laura O'Shaughnessy, as it does Irwin Gotlieb, Martin Sorrell, Carolyn Everson, Michael Kassan, and the entire marketing industry and its clients. It alarms Nate Cardozo, senior staff attorney and one of eighteen lawyers who work for the Electronic Frontier Foundation, a nonprofit based in San Francisco, whose mission is to repel privacy threats. "I want companies to be honest with what they're collecting and what they do with it, and right now that information is really difficult to figure out. The companies don't need to make that information public, and they do their best not to." Under the long, densely written contracts most consumers "sign" when joining an app or buying a product or service, the "terms of service" that we agree to empower a Tesla or Ford to track where we drive and stop, or allows DMVs, credit card companies, Facebook, or Google to sell data to secretive data-collecting companies like Palantir in Silicon Valley or Acxiom in Arkansas, who in turn can sell it to marketers. Google, Cardozo continues, "tracks every YouTube video you watch, every search term you enter, every result you click on. All of that data is tracked. And they're still using it. . . . We just don't know how they use it. They say they use it to improve products and services. What does that mean?" Even if marketers don't know your name, he says, as long as they have your IP address—the Internet Protocol number assigned to every computer—they can in most cases locate your building.

Cardozo says he has two nightmares. One is the danger "of identity theft on a massive scale. It's only a matter of time before there's a breach." (That nightmare occurred in 2017 when there was a massive theft of personal data from consumer credit reporting agency, Equifax.) Second, "If the data is there, advertisers, civil litigants, government agencies, you name it, are going to ask for it. What if you could subpoena someone's entire behavioral profile? What if you have a knee replacement that failed and you sue the manufacturer and the manufacturer goes to Acxiom and subpoenas your behavioral history to show you viewed ads about canoeing? Does that mean you went canoeing? It means you're interested in canoeing." Advertisers would be keen on having access to medical records so they could market pharmaceutical products.

The accumulation of data to predict future behavior has been labeled surveillance capitalism by Shoshana Zuboff, a professor of business administration at Harvard Business School. Its pioneers have been digital companies like Google and Facebook that derive their marketing power from shadowing citizens and using data to become fortune-tellers.

"The game," Zuboff wrote, "is no longer about sending you a mail-order catalogue or even about targeting online advertising. The game is selling access to the real-time flow of your daily life—your reality—in order to directly influence and modify your behavior for profit. This is the gateway to a new universe of monetization opportunities: Restaurants who want to be your destination. Service vendors who want to fix your brake pads. Shops who will lure you like the fabled Sirens." Success at this "game" flows to those with the "ability to predict the future—specifically the future of behavior."*

Success is more likely to come to marketers who harness this data to make it more personal, more useful to citizens annoyed by inter-

---

* Shoshana Zuboff, "The Secrets of Surveillance Capitalism," *Frankfurter Allgemeine*, March 5, 2016.

ruptive ad messages but who welcome messages about their hobbies, pets, or favorite vacation spots. Michael Hussey is the CEO of Stat-Social, a data company that has constructed consumer profiles of 600 million citizens from around the world based on their public activities on Twitter, Facebook, Instagram, YouTube, blogs, along with the e-mail addresses of 170 million citizens purchased from data companies he says he is not contractually free to identify. In a separate partnership with IBM's Watson, its artificial intelligence arm, Hussey says they have identified 50 million citizens and segmented each into "the fifty-two personality types" Watson tracks, such as adventurous, conservative, liberal, conscientious, or open to change. In work they do with Irwin Gotlieb's GroupM for Ford, they track consumers seeking to buy a new car. "The personality type that is 'conscientious,'" Hussey says, "should get a different message—maybe the eco-friendly car—than the 'adventurous' person. . . . Everything is about personalization, microtargeting your audience with different messages."

To an engineer, data is virtuous. It offers clues to the mysteries of human behavior, suggests efficiencies, offers answers that will better serve consumers. Data yields facts, advances engineers' quest to be more scientific. But as first Google, and then Facebook, discovered, that data made it possible to attract advertising dollars. "The more data it has on offer, the more value it creates for advertisers," Sandy Parakilas, who was Facebook's operations manager on the Platform Team from 2011 to 2012, wrote in a scathing November 2017 *New York Times* op-ed page commentary. "That means it has no incentive to police the collection or use of that data—except when negative press or regulators are involved."* The mix of genuine engineering

---

* Sandy Parakilas, "Facebook Won't Protect Your Privacy," *New York Times* op-ed page, November 20, 2017.

curiosity and business greed inevitably relegated privacy issues to the nose-bleed bleachers.

The privacy issue draws too little attention, says Christian Sandvig, associate professor of communication studies at the University of Michigan, because corporate America and the marketing universe have succeeded in submerging it. "The key thing we see in privacy is that companies have made a decision to privatize privacy." Companies insist that citizens make the choice whether something is private when they go to their settings or they click on opt in or opt out. He disagrees. "We've seen the privacy debate pushed into settings. The point of that feature is to inoculate the platform from criticism."

* * *

People don't march in one direction when it comes to privacy. Advertisers assert that targeted ads serve consumers information they desire, and this would be impossible without personalized data. The Interactive Advertising Bureau warns that strict privacy regulations will slow economic growth because they "threaten to hamper the data-driven growth of the Internet economy." Without ads, content companies would die. Since there is no single universally accepted definition of privacy, contentious debates will persist. In his attempt to wrestle this ambiguous term to the ground, the great Louis Brandeis defined privacy as the "right to be left alone." But where to draw the line? If I view advertising as intrusive yet it subsidizes my free television, is it really violating my privacy? If I physically bump into someone, I am certainly not leaving that person alone, but am I violating his or her privacy?

Some, like Ricky Van Veen, cofounder of CollegeHumor, the still popular user-generated Web site, who in late 2016 joined Facebook as its head of global creative strategy, thinks "privacy is overrated." In the early days of CollegeHumor, "college kids would send in photos of themselves with a beard at a party," and years later when they were looking for a job they'd write in to ask if CollegeHumor would please take it down. "Today, everyone has a photo of them with a beard at a party. It's the new normal. About forty percent of all Instagram photos are deleted within the first ten seconds." Why? Not because of privacy concerns but because "it won't get enough likes. People still care about how they're perceived, but the idea of privacy counts much less. Everybody is broadcasting themselves constantly!"

There is a body of evidence supporting the notion that privacy is losing popularity. In the studies he's overseen for Lippincott, chief content and strategy officer John Marshall believes the sharing economy advanced by social networks like Facebook and Snapchat has helped dramatically alter the attitudes of the young toward privacy. "As you start to connect seven billion people together much more seamlessly, you're moving toward a connected state being the natural state and the private state being the exception." He holds up China as an exemplar of future attitudes toward privacy, as if a dictatorship heralds how democracies will evolve. "When you talk to a sixteen-year-old in China about this issue and they're living on WeChat, what you learn is they think of privacy differently from you and me. They know there are things they want to hide, but the hiding is the exception rather than the sharing. Having the public state that it is sharable can be equated with them being a good person."

And the sixteen-year-old in the United States?

"Same thing."

What is similar among Generation Z and millennials, he believes, is the realization that data about them is abundant and "their data has value and they want to get something out of it." Traditionally, citizens willingly traded their attention and accepted advertising in exchange for free content. Today, he believes, a younger generation may be willing to trade their personal data, perhaps for discounts or partially subsidized content. Joseph Turow has coauthored a paper, "The Trade-off Fallacy," which agrees that many Americans of all ages "believe it is futile to manage what companies can learn about them." But their "survey results indicate that marketers are misrepresenting a large majority of Americans by claiming that Americans" are eager to make a trade. Although many are reluctantly resigned to the power of corporate data collectors, if a trade has to be made they want better terms.

Before tradeoffs can be made, a critical question intrudes: Who owns the data, the company or the citizen? And have citizens really ceded their ownership when they click "Accept" or "Agree"? "The entire economics of marketing depends on the answer to that question," Marshall says.

It depends on one other question as well: What does government say?

The U.S. government has at times stepped in to regulate advertising. Inspired in part by Upton Sinclair's *The Jungle*, Congress in 1906 passed the Pure Food and Drug Act, requiring what was advertised on food and drug labels to accurately disclose all ingredients. In the 1930s, a variety of New Deal legislation was adopted creating oversight of how certain products, including drugs and cosmetics that might pose health hazards, could be advertised. Defying enormous political pressure from tobacco companies and broadcasters who benefited from their ad dollars, Congress in 1971 agreed that cigarette smoking could be a health hazard and regulated cigarette advertising. To protect consumers, the Federal Trade Commission is empowered "to prohibit unfair or deceptive acts or practices," including false or deceptive advertising. And although privacy regulations are fragmented and not as strict in the United States as in Western European nations, the FTC has on occasion enforced privacy protections. Nor is it uncommon for the FTC to reach financial settlements with companies who are accused of false or nontransparent advertising.

By early 2016, pressures were rising on the government to become more assertive. Federal Communications Commission chairman Tom Wheeler proposed, and the commission later that year imposed, privacy regulations on cable and telephone broadband providers, preventing them from collecting user data and sharing it with advertisers without user consent. The rule paralleled the restrictions placed on telephone companies, which are prohibited from selling information describing which companies consumers contact and do business with on the telephone. The FCC declared, in Chairman Wheeler's words, that as with the telephone, "the information that goes over a network belongs to you as the consumer, not to the network hired to carry it." The new rule that applied to Internet service providers was vehemently opposed by the advertising industry, which has long argued that if they so desire consumers should be allowed to opt out. "There is no record of consumer harm to justify treating web viewing" as requiring "opt-in consent," declared a statement jointly issued by the ANA, the 4A's, the Interactive Advertising Bureau, the Direct Marketing Association, and the Network Advertising Initiative.

Less than seventy days after the new Trump administration took office, with attention riveted on Trump tweets and news of the possible Russian hacking aimed at sabotaging Hillary Clinton, the Republican-led Senate and House passed, and President Trump signed, legislation permitting cable and telephone Internet service providers to sell data about consumers' online activities to advertisers. The legislation also bans the FCC from ever establishing similar privacy protection restrictions. The government, in effect, declared privacy privatized.

10.

THE CONSUMER AS FRENEMY

"There really isn't any significant difference between the various brands of whiskey, or the various cigarettes, or the various brands of beer. They are all about the same. And so are the cake mixes and the detergents and the margarines and the automobiles. And, I might add, the different brands of salt."

—David Ogilvy

f Jon Mandel's March 2015 speech to the ANA sparked a client revolt that year, by 2016 signs were growing of a wider and more ominous revolt, a revolt by consumers against all advertising, as mobile technology brought ads more intimately and insistently into people's lives but at the same time gave them new tools to block them.

The marketing community gulped when Apple, which three decades before had famously aired a TV ad that declared a rebellion against the ruling IBM computer Goliath, now seemed to want to smash most advertising. Tim Cook, the CEO of Apple, stood on a San Francisco stage late that summer and announced that Apple would offer a new operating system for iPhones and iPads that would contain apps empowering users to block ads. Apple, which received less than one percent of its revenues from advertising, was helping consumers seal their devices from ads.

For consumers annoyed by intrusive pre-roll and banner ads, sluggish ad page load speeds, and uninvited marketing messages draining their batteries, or worried that their privacy was being invaded, this was a happy solution. The user experience must be paramount, Apple proclaimed. No, no, proclaimed Web sites, media companies, marketers, and ad-reliant companies like Facebook and Google: our ability to inform users and subsidize content is crippled by ad blockers. Those dependent on advertising accused Apple and ad blockers of murder. Apple and ad blocker advocates accused advertisers of committing suicide with mindless and intrusive ads. What neither Apple nor Google said publicly was that Apple's maneuver was part of a raging war between Apple and Google for smartphone supremacy. Apple made its money selling hardware and software; Google made its money selling ads. Apple was strategically offering consumers something Google couldn't.

In a June 2015 speech to the Electronic Privacy Information Center, Cook came down hard on how his neighbors in Silicon Valley "have built their businesses by lulling their customers into complacency about their personal information" and were monetizing it. "You might like these so-called free-services, but we don't think they're worth having your e-mail, your search history . . . sold off for god knows what advertising purpose." And consumers were getting Cook's message. As Tim Wu puts it in *The Attention Merchants*, Internet users have begun "to realize that when an online service is free, you're not the customer. You're the product."

Within weeks, Apple's ad blocking foray was duplicated by rival Samsung, which announced that it would include ad-blocking plug-ins to the operating system of its popular Android phones. For the communities dependent on the flow of advertising dollars, the speedy adoption of ad blockers conjured nightmare images of Napoleon's final battle at Waterloo. A study by PageFair and Adobe estimated that 200 million consumers worldwide and 40 million in the United States used ad blockers, a number that jumped 41 percent in 2015, wiping out an estimated $20 billion of ad sales. This number was expected to double in 2016.* It was akin, the study concluded, to the largest consumer boycott in history. In one sense, ad blockers are not novel. As we've seen, more than half of consumers who record programs on a DVR or the equivalent skip the ads. But at least they have to make the effort to do so.

AdBlock Plus, based in Cologne, Germany, is the world's largest purveyor of a free app users download to block ads. The app does not block all ads; AdBlock Plus offers a "whitelist" known as the Acceptable Ads Initiative, usually meaning ads they consider noninterruptive. However, for sites that wish to be whitelisted, AdBlock Plus taxes larger sites 30 percent of their ad revenue to allow the ad to appear; they say they don't charge smaller publishers, but will also block their ads if they are intrusive. Not surprisingly, members of the advertising community described the company's business plan, as the Interactive Advertising Bureau's CEO Randall Rothenberg did in a public speech, as "an old-fashioned extortion racket, gussied up in the flowery but false language of contemporary consumerism."

When Till Faida, a founder and the CEO of AdBlock Plus, and Rothenberg were to appear back-to-back at a TechCrunch confab in early 2016 on the Brooklyn waterfront, the 2,500 attendees expected sparks to fly. The topic: "The End of the Ad Era." Before the audience,

---

* As we see, data on the size of the ad-blocking community vary wildly.

Faida repeated his mantra several times: AdBlock Plus was "user friendly" and was installed because "you can't have a business that relies on pissing off your users." Instead of "personal rants," he said Rothenberg and his organization should have "set ad standards years ago." When he finished, Anthony Ha, the moderator, thanked him. As Faida, a large, burly man, exited the stage and the slight Rothenberg silently walked past, the moderator invited Rothenberg to pause and shake Faida's hand. Rothenberg kept walking. His aim was to state the opposition case, and he did. He assailed ad blockers for robbing publishers, particularly small publishers. Some Web sites, he claimed, were losing 40 percent of their revenues. If ad blockers were really "in the public service business" as they profess, he asked, "Why not do it for free?"

Faida sat alone backstage watching Rothenberg on a TV monitor. "He's making a point of not engaging in a dialogue with us," Faida said when Rothenberg finished. "By sticking his head in the sand he's pretending this will go away." Rothenberg later confirmed he had no interest in a dialogue with people he considers thieves.

Ad blockers were a clear and present danger, and marketers and publishers struggled to devise a counterattack. Worried clients turned to Michael Kassan and MediaLink for advice and reassurance, as they did after Jon Mandel's ANA speech. "It shook everybody," Wenda Millard says. "No one could predict what would happen." She and Kassan agreed that ad blocking was a menace, and a form of theft. But they also advised clients to create different kinds of ads, and to take more responsibility for lousy ads. "We said, 'Stop making Web sites that look like Tokyo at night,'" Millard said. "Improve the ads, make the ads beautiful."

The marketing community threw a number of countermeasures against the wall, hoping to see what would stick. German publisher Axel Springer filed a lawsuit asking that ad blockers be declared illegal.

Twelve hundred American newspapers joined in a cease-and-desist letter to ad blockers, charging that they were "blatantly illegal." Jerry Wind, from the Wharton School, decried this approach as dumb. "Blocking the ad blockers as some people in the industry want to do is the dumbest thing you can do," he said. "The consumer is sending you a message: 'I hate your advertising.'" Instead of saying, 'OK, let's change what we're doing, those idiots are trying to block the ad blockers. It's almost as dumb as what the record companies tried to do when Napster came out"—suing their customers. Thus far the courts do not seem to be an effective venue in which to defeat ad blockers; by the fall of 2017, both the lower and appeals courts in Germany upheld the right of consumers to block ads.

One-party states like China simply decree that ad blockers are illegal. Publications like the *Washington Post* and *Forbes* banned users from accessing their sites unless they turned off their ad blockers. The *Guardian* tried a different tack, using pop-ups to tell users that their ad blockers erased monies that subsidized good journalism and offered alternate ways for them to aid journalism. Instead of joining lawsuits, the World Federation of Advertisers agreed: "The Internet advertising experience is not satisfactory for consumers." They called for less alienating ads. Since Facebook is an app and ad blockers live on browsers, not mobile apps, Facebook was not as threatened as Google and others. But since it is an ad-dependent business, it took measures to try to prevent ad blockers from appearing on desktop computers using Facebook.

▨ ▨ ▨

The industry's preferred antidote to combat ad blockers was native advertising, which was unlikely to be blocked because its camouflage fooled the ad censors. Wherever one went in 2015 and early 2016— visiting a publication, a client, an agency—native advertising or branded content was invoked as a great hope. Michael Kassan was a believer. He saw ad blockers as an opportunity, not just a disrupter. Native advertising was the remedy he promoted to publishing clients like Condé Nast, Hearst, the *New York Times,* the *Wall Street Journal,* the *Washington Post,* Time, Inc., and Vox, and to brand clients like AT&T and Disney, among many others. Native ads would be much more effective storytellers than their beta version, advertorials. Sounding evangelical, he envisioned a world where consumers wouldn't be able to tell the difference between news and advertising. The creators of those ads would often be the publishers or the brands, not the ad agencies. "Hearst and Condé Nast are now content companies, meaning ad agencies," he said. "If every brand today wants to create content, as opposed to interrupting you with a commercial, then what the hell do I need a commercial for? I want to reach a point where premium content is like pornography. And Nirvana is when you can't tell the difference between the content and the advertising. You're actually in good shape because the consumer is going to get your message through branded content, or whatever you want to call it." Some would call it deceptive advertising.

Native does not offer salvation. Native ads in 2015 generated a total of only $7.5 billion ad dollars in the United States. A Facebook study projected that by 2020 worldwide native advertising would reach $53.4 billion. The *Atlantic Monthly* reported that three quarters of its online ad revenue in 2015 came from native advertising; *Slate* attributed half its ad revenues to native. (This sounds better than it is, for the same digital ad usually generates about 10 to 20 cents compared to $1 for the same print ad.) Unlike TV or print ads that are repeatedly shown, native ads do not readily lend themselves to repetition.

Native can take many forms. To market its *Narcos* miniseries, Netflix paid the freight for the *Wall Street Journal's* in-depth native ad report on the Medellín drug cartel, including motion graphics, video clips from the miniseries, and a Spanish language option. Separate from the *Journal*'s native promotion of *Narcos*, the newspaper reported a lengthy story on the Medellín drug cartel on which the series is based. When asked directly if Netflix helped sustain the cost of this reporting, its chief communications officer, Jonathan Friedland, a former *Journal* reporter, e-mailed: "It works like this: We go to news organization X and say hey, we would like you to come up with some ideas to enhance interest in show Y. They come back with themes and constituent elements in support of those and we decide which ones we like. . . . At Netflix at least, I have insisted when the marketing folks embark on this type of thing, they give the news organization complete freedom." This is but one example of how the traditional wall between the business and the news side was lowered.

Another prominent native campaign occurred in November 2015 when the *New York Times* teamed up with Google and General Electric and paid for one million Google Cardboard virtual reality plastic lenses to view a GE video produced in-house by the *Times*, "How Nature Is Inspiring Our Industrial Future." The viewer is drawn into an animated world where animals and butterflies alchemize into GE wind turbines and a city. This campaign, like many native ad campaigns, bypassed the agency middleman. "A lot of clients are frustrated," vice chair Beth Comstock says of GE and others. "We want more media properties to come to us like the *New York Times* did."

Inevitably, native ads create a tension between the interests of journalism and the interests of the advertiser. As the *Washington Post*'s Margaret Sullivan, onetime public editor of the *Times* put it: "If native ads look too much like journalism, they damage credibility; if they look nothing like journalism, they lose their appeal to advertisers. A fine line, indeed." A vocal minority of those in the advertising industry assail native ads for crossing a line because they undermine trust. "Native advertising is not new," the chairman emeritus of DDB Worldwide, Keith Reinhard, says. "We used to call it advertorials.

And it will not be around because it compromises both the media and the brand."

Trying to draw a line, the Federal Trade Commission in November 2015 did issue guidelines for native advertising. The FTC's aim was to prohibit native ads that "mask the signals consumers customarily have relied upon to recognize an advertising or promotional message." Although the FTC acknowledged that deception was not always clear cut, they insisted there was a line. Yet many publishers reacted as if the guidelines were invisible. MediaRadar, a cloud-based ad sales platform utilized by 1600 publishers, issued a study in 2016 revealing that nearly 40 percent of publishers did not comply with FTC guidelines. Surveys revealed that native ads tricked consumers because they did not notice the difference between a news story and a native ad; a nonprofit organization, the Online Trust Alliance, reported in 2016 that 71 percent of consumers were successfully tricked.

The introduction of ad blockers and native ads is a symptom of two much larger disruptive forces. First, of course, the surge of the mobile phone platform. Second, in addition to the advent of the mobile phone, we have two generations of computer-literate citizens who have grown up with access to ad-free options like Netflix, HBO, and to DVRs that enable ad skipping.

The year 2015 seemed to be the year mobile phones captured the full attention of the marketing industry. Speaking before the Mobile World Congress in Barcelona in early 2016, Martin Sorrell castigated big agencies and big advertisers for being late to comprehend the mobile upheaval. Mobile is not just "an extension of digital, just a way to reach consumers," he said. It is perhaps the most important channel to consumers "that has been developed, and it changes the way you live your life, by virtue of the fact that it is always on, it's 24/7, and we've never had this." In her much-anticipated annual presentation on "The State of the Web," Mary Meeker of Kleiner Perkins Caufield Byers reported that mobile phone users had rocketed from 80 million worldwide in 1995 to 5.2 billion in 2014, or three quarters of the earth's population. "We have never in history adopted a technology faster," Carolyn Everson told a CES audience in January 2016, noting that it took radio thirty-eight years to reach 50 million people and television only thirteen years. Mobile phones reached 7.2 billion people in just thirty years.*

Perhaps the most significant reaction to the mobile revolution came from Facebook. When Facebook went public in May 2012, its IPO filing said it did not "generate any meaningful revenue" from mobile. Yet founder Mark Zuckerberg knew his users were switching from desktop to mobile, and Facebook's mobile product, Carolyn Everson says, "was not good." Zuckerberg had to turn his ocean liner as sharply as a speedboat. Twice annually he holds an all-hands meeting with the staff, and he abruptly ended a 2011 meeting when members of a product team came in with a product markup for a desktop computer. He insisted that he wanted mobile mockups. "If you come in and try to show me a desktop product, I'm going to kick you out," he said. Over the next two weeks, Everson says, everyone canceled their product meetings with Zuckerberg, frantically seeking to devise a mobile strategy. Over the next eight weeks, all Facebook engineers were retrained. By the end of 2012, one quarter of Facebook's revenues came from mobile; by the following year, it was half. By 2016, 80 percent of Facebook's revenues came from mobile phone marketing. By 2019, the research firm eMarketer projected, ad spending on mobile would reach $65.4 billion and dominate 70 percent of all digital

---

* The disparity between Mary Meeker's figure of 5.2 billion mobile phones and Carolyn Everson's figure of 7.2 billion is a reminder that gathering global data involves some guesswork.

ad spending. Mark Zuckerberg knew Facebook was doomed if it could not reach its young audience on mobile.

The two younger generations were such a disruptive force because they are a prime audience targeted by advertisers since they are thought to shape future buying habits. They consist of millennials, those age twenty-one to thirty-four,* and of Generation Z, those twenty-one and younger, with teenagers being the heart of this generation. Of the two, we know less about Generation Z.

One Monday afternoon in early 2016, MediaLink invited to its conference room a client, AwesomenessTV, to share what they know of Generation Z. AwesomenessTV is a Santa Monica digital TV production company with its own YouTube channel that is wildly popular with this generation. To better understand Generation Z, they formed a youth marketing firm, Wildness. The chief strategy officer of Wildness, Margaret Czeisler, a former vice president at the digital ad agency Razorfish, was introduced by Wenda Millard.

Czeisler discussed what she said was the largest study of Generation Z ever conducted, a survey of 3,000 members of this generation, as well as in-depth interviews. She described Generation Z this way: It represents 34 percent of the world's population, and they see themselves as "culture creators," not passive receivers of information. Every 60 seconds they upload 500,000 hours of video to YouTube and 528,000 photos to Snapchat. They prize "authenticity" above all. "Ninety-four percent," the vast majority, "told us their highest social value is to be true to themselves." While surveys reveal that becoming wealthy is the second most-valued goal of millennials, she said, "It's not even in the top twenty of this generation. The opportunity for brands is to get real and to be consistent." By way of illustration, she reported that

---

* Again, not an exact science; Nielsen defines millennials as age eighteen to thirty-four.

70 percent prefer video streamed over the Internet to TV or cable. Why? "They don't want to be interrupted. They hate ads." They like YouTube because "people are real and authentic." They would prefer to subscribe to ad-free services, assuming they could afford to. "They also have the shortest attention span of any generation," she warned.

Although there are real differences between millennials and Generation Z, for marketers the similarities are meaningful, she said. Both share an aversion to being interrupted by ad messages. Both spend less time in front of television sets, get more news from Facebook than newspapers, multitask on multiple devices, tend to have attenuated attention spans, and are devoted to their smartphones. If a marketer wishes to capture the attention of both with a mobile ad, it has to be done in a second or two.

Whatever the obstacles, Czeisler said marketers can reach younger consumers. Their pitches have to be shorter, maybe using pictures and emojis and messages like six-second Vine videos rather than words. "The real challenge for brands is to create experiences" that are powerful and to understand their quest for "authenticity." Czeisler did not have to tell them that this is a reason brand advertisers increasingly emphasize in their marketing messages the services they perform, the social good they do, the "brand values" they share, as if makers of sugary drinks and fatty hamburgers are public servants. This generation, she said, is willing to hear from brands, and 91 percent said they would be willing to share their views with brands. "They like branded content because it is much more real," which is the same reason they like YouTube videos—they are "not overly polished."

The MediaLink staff perked up at the news that Generation Z was reachable, but in nontraditional ways. Just to be sure, Wenda Millard asked, "They really don't like ads?"

"Eighty-four percent told us they don't like advertising," Czeisler responded.

"That could be a problem!" Millard cracked.

"They like branded," Czeisler said. "They don't like to be interrupted."

The takeaway, Millard concluded: "They don't like advertising as we know it." The consumer was a frenemy.

※ ※ ※

Not liking advertising has a long history, certainly in America. Both in the Progressive era when the muckrakers exposed false marketing claims, and again during the Depression, when corporations and advertisers were in bad odor, federal agencies were forged to police false advertising.

Perhaps the most renowned critique of advertising and its manipulative powers was a book written by Vance Packard, previously an author of such fluff magazine pieces as "How I Lost 15 Pounds in One Month." Moved by a genuine sense of outrage, Packard published *The Hidden Persuaders* in 1957, and it quickly shot up to number one on best-seller lists. He lambasted advertisers for treating consumers as gullible children. The heart of Packard's thesis was this:

> This book is an attempt to explore a strange and rather exotic new area of American life. It is about the large-scale efforts being made, often with impressive success, to channel our unthinking habits, our purchasing decisions, and our thought processes by the use of insights gleaned from psychiatry and the social sciences. Typically these efforts take place beneath our level of awareness; so that the appeals which move us are often, in a sense, "hidden." The result is that many of us are being influenced and manipulated, far more than we realize, in the patterns of our everyday lives.

David Ogilvy granted ammunition to critics of advertising when in a 1955 speech to the American Association of Advertising Agencies he admitted, "There really isn't any significant difference between the various brands of whiskey, or the various cigarettes, or the various brands of beer. They are all about the same. And so are the cake mixes and the detergents and the margarines and the automobiles. And, I might add, the different brands of salt." The difference, he said, is found in the advertising and the emotion it creates. Or as MediaLink's Wenda Millard says, "At its heart, advertising is about creating desire."

Creating desire is what alarms James Steyer, founder and CEO of Common Sense Media, a children's advocacy organization focused on the harm media can afflict on children. He worries about advertising that promotes unhealthy sugary drinks or fast food, but he said his fear could be defined more broadly: "The ubiquity of advertising can turn little children into overly commercial human beings. They think of being defined by material things. Little kids don't know the difference between ads and programming. My twelve-year-old son constantly wants new sneakers."

Wanton consumerism has forever been blamed on advertising. Michael Schudson, who taught a course at the University of Chicago called Mass Media and Society, says he would freely assert in class that advertising was usually ineffective. He was inspired to study the impact of advertising because "I did not have an adequate response" to students who asked why companies would spend so much on ads if they got little return. In the book he would write about the industry, *Advertising, The Uneasy Persuasion,** Schudson explored advertising's sins. He compared advertising to the art of socialist realism because

---

* Michael Schudson, *Advertising, The Uneasy Persuasion: Its Dubious Impact on American Society* (New York: Basic Books, 1984).

"it does not claim to picture reality as it is but reality as it should be." He labeled it "capitalist realism" and said ads are designed, whether successful or not, to "subordinate" messy reality in order to spike sales of a product.

Among the hidden efforts of advertisers, critics most often latch on to how marketing manipulates our emotions. Industry leaders don't deny this, they extol it. Jack Haber, who retired as CMO of Colgate in 2017, says, "I'm a believer that consumers make decisions emotionally." As proof he cites Daniel Kahneman's esteemed best-selling book, *Thinking, Fast and Slow*, to demonstrate that most human decisions pivot on emotion. "If you look at how people make decisions to buy things, people make decisions emotionally. That's why we try to build an emotional connection to a brand." Colgate spent $5 million for a thirty-second spot in the 2016 Super Bowl that didn't mention toothpaste but instead urged viewers to save water by not leaving the water running. "Colgate is the most trusted brand in the world," he says, and he believes this Super Bowl ad reinforced the emotional connection people have with Colgate. One of the most celebrated ads ever was the Coca-Cola commercial that was the final scene of *Mad Men*. It featured children of all colors from around the world giving viewers goose bumps as they harmonized on a hilltop:

> I'd like to teach the world to sing
> In perfect harmony
> I'd like to buy the world a Coke
> And keep it company
> *That's the real thing*

The ad tells nothing of the product, or its ingredients, or why it's "the real thing." Keith Reinhard defends the ad and the emotions it evoked because "the ad is part of the brand experience," whatever that means. "We have always known, intuitively," he explains, "that people make their brand decisions—by the way, the same way they make their political decisions—emotionally, with that lizard part of the brain, the reptilian part." Marc Pritchard, chief brand officer of Procter & Gamble, tersely explained to an Advertising Week audience why his product, Old Spice, had rebounded: The advertising for "Old Spice is about ridiculous masculinity. And it works!"

It certainly worked for CBS, owner of broadcast rights for the February 2016 Super Bowl. The annual event offers the biggest audience of the year to advertisers, which is why CBS was able to charge up to $5 million for each spot. It was not exactly edifying fare. Bud Light had comedians Amy Schumer and Seth Rogen paired up to disagree whether the nation was divided this presidential year and to agree to canvas America to promote the "Bud Light Party." Audi was praised for its storytelling in their ad, "Commander," in which an elderly, utterly depressed former astronaut will not eat or talk and just stares ahead. His son enters the room, takes his hand, they walk outside, and in the driveway is an Audi R8 sports car that can reach 205 miles per hour. The father takes the keys, to the sound of David Bowie's "Starman," and he magically smiles. "There is no way for an Alzheimer's family to watch this without gasping" in shock, wrote *MediaPost* columnist Bob Garfield.

One explanation for advertising's constant stretch to transfix audiences is that advertising is really a form of show business. Randall Rothenberg, CEO of the Interactive Advertising Bureau and a longtime student of advertising, suggests as much: "Contemporary advertising is based on the deliberate, playful, wink-wink of P. T. Barnum. It's based on the idea that if you shout loud enough, tell clever enough stories, you can get people to do anything." No question, many marketing pitches are brilliant, and more than a few advance a social good, as P&G's Ariel detergent ads did in India, Unilever's Vaseline did for

Syrian refugees, Nike's "If You Let Me Play" ads did in promoting Title IX and girls participating in team sports, and as R/GA's inspiring antibias public service ad, "Love Has No Labels," did. But if one acknowledges that many marketing pitches are hyperbolic, then one holds hands with "truthful hyperbole," the phrase Donald Trump described in his book *The Art of the Deal* as "an innocent form of exaggeration—and a very effective form of promotion." From here, the distance to "alternative facts" is a mere step or two.

So as is often the case, two opposing things are true at once: the social mobile data revolution has made consumers more skeptical of advertising, even as ever more immersive and intimate technologies have given advertising more and better purchase over our emotions. And we've barely glimpsed the impact of virtual reality on the world of marketing. As Daniel J. Boorstin famously wrote in his 1961 book *The Image: A Guide to Pseudo-Events in America*, "We risk being the first people in history to have been able to make their illusions so vivid, so persuasive, so 'realistic' that they can live in them." More than fifty years later, this is still not a comforting thought.

11.

CAN OLD MEDIA BE NEW?

Lucrative new revenue streams explain why network television, unlike financially ailing traditional media like newspapers, magazines, and radio, is not on life support. . . . By 2016, Les Moonves's CBS was making more money than when he joined CBS twenty years before.

L es Moonves, the sixty-seven-year-old CEO and chairman of CBS, measured the success of the 2016 Super Bowl by the quantity, not quality, of the ads. It was the third most-watched Super Bowl in history, and CBS was charging $5 million per ad. "The ad sales went through the roof," says Moonves, arms folded across a blue pin-striped suit as he relaxed in the ornate, spacious thirty-fifth-floor Black Rock office that was once founder William Paley's. "It was the second highest day in ad revenues in the history of any media. The only time it was beat was by ourselves with the Mayweather versus Pacquiao fight," the so-called fight of the century. "We did four hundred million dollars for the day on the Super Bowl."

The ebullient Moonves had more than a Super Bowl to celebrate in February 2016. Under his leadership, by the end of the 2014–15 season

CBS had gone from last in the early 1990s to first in the prime-time ratings race for twelve of the last thirteen years, and 2015–16 would make it thirteen out of fourteen. He was handsomely compensated for his labors, receiving a pay package in 2015 of $56.8 million. He could also celebrate that CBS was no longer 100 percent reliant on advertising. The federal government in the early '90s initiated two measures with profound financial implications for the networks. The first came when Congress passed the Cable Act, requiring cable companies to compensate broadcasters for offering CBS and other programs on cable systems. The second was when the FCC rescinded the Financial Interest and Syndication Rules (Fin-Syn), allowing networks to own and sell their programs. In addition, unlike two decades ago, the networks no longer compensated their affiliated stations to carry their programs, and new digital platforms now paid the networks to show their programs.

By 2015, new revenue spigots enabled CBS to derive half its revenue from nonadvertising sources, including: the nearly $1 billion CBS got from retransmission consent fees paid by the cable companies and reverse compensation paid by local stations to carry network programs; the $1.5 billion CBS received from being able to syndicate and sell its programs internationally; the approximately $1 billion CBS received in 2015 from the sale of its archived programs to digital platforms like Netflix, Amazon, and Apple. Lucrative new revenue streams explain why network television, unlike financially ailing traditional media like newspapers, magazines, and radio, is not on life support. By contrast, the newspaper industry lost more than half its jobs between January 2001 and September 2016.

Les Moonves has been hailed as the Steve Jobs of television. "For me, Les Moonves represents the North Star," Michael Kassan says, calling him "a brilliant operator. You can never lose sight of the fact that he began his career as an actor. He's a showman."

Josephine and Herman Moonves raised three children in the

middle-class neighborhood of Valley Stream, just over the Queens border. She was a nurse, and her husband ran the three gas stations he inherited from his father. "I got my competitiveness from my father and my sense of art from my mother," Moonves says. He was a good student and skilled at both tennis and baseball in high school and at Bucknell University, where he also performed in school plays. "I was a very competitive athlete and competitive in virtually everything I did," he says. "I like winning."

After graduating from college in 1971, he moved to New York City with hopes of becoming an actor. After attending acting school and performing as a tough guy in TV series like *The Six Million Dollar Man* and *Cannon*, it dawned on him that acting was a dead end for him. "I knew I was a mediocre actor," he says. He segued to producing plays before joining the development office of Columbia Pictures to nurture and select TV sitcoms. After two years, he moved over to 20th Century Fox to develop movies of the week and miniseries. Recruited by Lorimar Television in 1985 to supervise its movies and miniseries, he would rise to be head of creative affairs and then president. When Lorimar merged with Warner Bros., he was elevated to CEO of their combined television operations. Warner Bros. Television thrived; one year he successfully sold twenty-three shows to various networks, including *Friends* and *ER*. Even as a mediocre actor, he believes his experience before the camera made him a better program executive. "I knew what to look for in a script and in talent."

With CBS lagging in last place among the four networks in prime time, the network recruited Moonves to become president of its Entertainment division in 1995. Ratings rose, as did he, first to CEO of CBS Television and then in 2003 to CEO of all of CBS. The corporate parent of CBS was by now Viacom, and its chairman, Sumner Redstone, divided the company into Viacom, with its cable and Paramount Pictures, and CBS. Although Moonves's range of responsibilities is wide—in addition to the network he oversaw its TV stations, its TV studios and distribution arm, its HBO pay-TV competitor Showtime, its CW network, CBS Radio, CBS Interactive, outdoor advertising, and Simon & Schuster, among other divisions—he still micromanages the Entertainment division. He says he reads twenty scripts each week and "no pilot gets green-lit without my approval. And none of the four or five lead actors on a show gets hired without my approval." He has programmed some series worthy of the "Tiffany Network" tag that originally attached to CBS, like *The Good Wife*. But he does not pretend to be a highbrow. This is reflected not just in the many formulaic programs that helped propel CBS to ratings glory, like *NCIS*, *The Amazing Race*, and *Hawaii Five-O*, but also what he describes as the "delicious candy" of series he wishes he owned, like the ten episodes of *The People v. O.J. Simpson* on the FX network.

Moonves attributes part of his success to a core team of executives who have been at his side for a minimum of a dozen years. His favorite movie is *The Godfather*, and to members of his team he is seen as a benign version of Don Corleone. "He is one hundred percent accessible to me and my team," Jo Ann Ross, the lauded president of CBS Sales for more than two decades says, "I never want to disappoint him." His second wife, Julie Chen, once told the *Hollywood Reporter*, "If you cross him, he doesn't forget. You're dead to him."

He feared he was, figuratively, dead in late 2005 when Sumner Redstone announced that the parent company would be split into two separate entities, Viacom and CBS. Moonves was unhappy, believing he was stuck with slow-growing assets like radio, publishing, billboards, and even the CBS network, all of which Wall Street punished because they were pigeonholed as old media. He wanted some of Viacom's fast-growing cable assets and its movie-manufacturing arm, Paramount Pictures. However, within a few years Viacom's stock tumbled and CBS's soared. By February 2016, Viacom had a market value of $12.4 billion, half its former worth, while CBS was now worth nearly twice as much as Viacom. "He is the only guy since Bill Paley who is both a businessman and a showman," says George Schweitzer, president of CBS Marketing for two decades. "We've had businessmen and showmen. We've not had both."

※ ※ ※

The showman might have to be waterboarded to publicly admit the perils ahead for CBS. As newspapers are more reliant on Facebook to distribute its content, Moonves privately knows he is increasingly dependent for revenues on digital platforms that lustily compete for the attention of viewers. He says he is comfortable with this because "we are a content company." Now that CBS is allowed to own and produce programs, it is a television studio, not just a network platform for other studios. "Netflix is a friend. They pay us a lot of money," he says. "Netflix just paid us $5.5 million per episode for *Star Trek* outside of the U.S. All in, it's hundreds of millions of dollars."

Netflix is also a classic frenemy, for while CBS receives revenue from them it has built up a competitor. Irwin Gotlieb thinks Moonves and the other networks that sell programs to Netflix and Amazon and other streaming platforms are "potentially sowing the seeds of their own destruction by selling their content to Netflix and any other subscriber VOD [video on demand] system." Netflix is a colossus. Already, it estimates that its subscribers watch one billion hours per week, and by the end of 2017 it expected to have 116 million subscribers, nearly half of them in the United States. CBS and the other networks today have smaller programming budgets than Netflix or Amazon. And at the same time, Google and Facebook are siphoning more of CBS's ad dollars.

Moonves's optimism is predicated, in part, on his bet that cable system owners will continue to pump more dollars into paying retransmission fees to the networks to air their programs, a sum he believes will climb close to $2 billion by 2020. His bet relies on three assumptions. He assumes that growing consumer pressure to break up cable bundles will not weaken cable's ability to make those payments. He assumes that by selling network programs to cable competitors like Netflix he will not retard cable's willingness to make those payments. And he believes, as he says flatly, that cable "needs the networks."

Moonves the salesman does not wail publicly about the perils ahead for CBS. Michael Kassan will surely advise his clients to invest more ad dollars elsewhere, including digital platforms like Google and Facebook, which by 2017 were poised to receive more ad dollars than the traditional ad sales champ, television. Irwin Gotlieb may refuse to pay steeper prices for ads on CBS because its audience is not growing and the number of those who watch ads on CBS shrinks. A generation accustomed to not watching ads will drive brand clients away from expensive thirty- and sixty-second ads. Les Moonves is not deaf. He's heard marketers like Michael Kassan say quite publicly that at some point soon advertisers will insist on paying less and will shift dollars elsewhere. He has reason to fear how CBS will pay for expensive quality drama series that after several seasons of star salaries can cost up to $10 million per hour. And while CBS has nicely diversified its revenue streams, with only half its revenues now coming from ads, one out of every two dollars is still an irreplaceable revenue stream.

These perils became public in the summer of 2015 when Disney CEO Bob Iger acknowledged that ESPN was for the first time losing subscribers—3.2 million subscribers, Nielsen reported—and thus "there's an inevitability to ESPN peeling itself away from the traditional pay-TV bundle." Iger went on to say, "eventually" ESPN would be "sold directly to the consumers," streamed over the Internet just as Netflix is. This unsettled the easily rattled financial markets. Because ESPN had always been a financial juggernaut, Wall Street clamored to ask: If ESPN bypasses the cable middleman, with the most popular programming in the cable package removed, did this doom the cable bundle? Did it mean more viewers would rebel against the expensive cable bundle and cut the cord? With cable stressed, did this mean broadcasters would lose some of the retransmission fees cable pays? If ESPN's growth has stalled, did this mean popular sports programming has hit its ceiling? Didn't this demonstrate that broadcasters substantially overpaid for sports rights? And if Disney would pull ESPN from cable, did this mean that Internet TV, like Netflix, is destined to replace traditional television? Didn't it mean viewers are fleeing from familiar television channels?

As questions mounted, media stocks cratered, losing more than $100 billion of their value by the end of 2015. CBS's stock price fell by one third. "Wall Street went crazy," Moonves says. Wall Street was reacting, he told a reporter for *SportsBusinessDaily*, as "if the whole ecosystem is failing. And that is just not true." The financial community was straining for a new narrative, and he defined it thus: "'Digital is taking over the universe. The old guys are dead.'"

Moonves didn't believe that. CBS's profits belied it. But Michael Kassan among others believed the networks, like ESPN, were in a long-term downward spiral. "The last bastion is sports," Kassan says. "That's why the market crashed when Bob Iger made the comments about ESPN. Everyone said, 'Oh my God, we know this is happening on ABC. But ESPN?' That's like the joke about the guy who comes home and sees his wife in bed with his best friend and he looks and says to his friend, 'I have to. But you?'"

Broadcast viewing tumbled badly between the start of the new season in September 2015 and December. The ratings of only three returning programs improved, *Advertising Age* reported, while 42 fell by an average of 25 percent. Cable programs also nose-dived. As viewing choices multiply—the average TV home had 206 channel choices, according to Nielsen—so audiences bifurcate, leaving fewer viewers for each platform. And this does not include their Internet and app options. Advertising dollars drifted down as well. The Upfront sales marketplace, which usually begins in May and runs into summer, and where roughly three quarters of ad dollars for the 2015–16 season would be invested, sank by an estimated 10 percent for broadcasters and 5 percent for cable networks. About $2 billion shifted from traditional to digital media. It is now conventional wisdom that the young, impatient with constant advertising interruptions and spoiled by being able to watch what and when they want without commercial interruption, and to be able to binge on it, will continue to abandon traditional television.

David Poltrack, the venerated chief research officer for CBS who has worked at the network for nearly fifty years, rejects this notion. He believes those who shun advertising and television are a passing fancy. The young may be tuned out to advertising and television today, he says, but that has always been true, and as they age they will become more like their parents. Millennials between twenty-five and thirty-four watch 43 percent more TV than those eighteen to twenty-four, he says. Although one third of each broadcast hour is devoted to advertising interruptions, and slightly more on most cable channels, he merrily insists, "People do not object to advertising. They object to bad advertising and irrelevant advertising. People like advertising. Advertising informs people. Advertising entertains people." When you ask millennials whether they would pay even as little as a dollar not to have to watch ads, he says, 90 percent say they would prefer to watch ads.

In a modest-size office surrounded by piles of research reports, Poltrack made another counterintuitive argument: Since 80 percent of those between eighteen and thirty-four are simultaneously on the Internet with another device when they watch their TV screen, "that has resulted in the fact that they are more tolerant of advertising because they have something to do during the commercial breaks. They need those breaks to keep up the IM-ing with their friends and the tweeting."

What? But they are not watching the ads?

They are, he insists. "There is research that shows those active on their devices are more likely to recall the advertising than those who weren't."

Why?

Because without a device, "when you're sitting there and doing nothing you'll look for something to do," and you are more likely to leave the room. "But if you're still in front of the TV" and you're accustomed to multitasking and the only sound in the room is the TV, this "means their hearing is totally centered on the sound from their television set."

Poltrack made a more startling claim during the annual summer 2015 press tour in Los Angeles: when you count current CBS programs on cable, and those streamed over the Internet by CBS, and those that are recorded by DVRs or on video on demand from cable or satellite companies and watched over a full month, if measurement services could track all these programs and the multiple devices they are watched on, he claimed, "Our programs are being viewed by more people today than a decade ago." And millennials, he guessed, were not watching less TV. He suspected the devices they viewed them on were not measured by the ratings services. He did acknowledge that the American population had swelled by twenty-five million in the ten years he was counting, and this partly explains his thesis. Poltrack, like Moonves, chants this thesis like a mantra. In May 2017, CBS published a full-page ad in newspapers proclaiming that "more people watch CBS today than 16 years ago."

Does this claim have the virtue of being true? In 2016, Nielsen added a measurement tool that allows them to estimate the number of viewers up to thirty-five days after the program originally airs. They measure those who watch CBS prime-time shows live, and those who watch them later on their DVRs or on VOD from their cable or satellite company. Even though the number of viewers does not account for those who watch CBS programs streamed digitally on multiple devices, Nielsen still confirms that CBS's claim regarding its shows is accurate. The ratings for a hit show may be a third of what they were sixteen years ago, but the cumulative audience is slightly larger. But, and here's the rub: with ad skipping the advertiser reaches a smaller audience, even though the overall audience is slightly larger. Plus: advertisers don't pay for CBS shows that appear the next season on ad-free digital platforms like Netflix and Amazon.

■ ■ ■

Netflix, in the meantime, thrives. By 2016, Netflix had nearly as many subscribers as the entire U.S. cable industry. Television watching on all channels declined 3 percent in 2015, according to a study by Michael Nathanson, senior media analyst of MoffettNathanson, and Netflix viewing accounted for half the decline. One reason for that decline is ad fatigue. "We have overstuffed the bird," Kevin Reilly, president of cable networks TBS and TNT confessed to the Television Critics Association in early 2016. In a halfhearted attempt to reduce ad clutter, Reilly's networks and the Fox network announced that they would reduce their ad loads, however slightly. NBC's *Saturday Night Live* said it was paring its commercial breaks by one third. Others gingerly followed. Mindful that his cash register was filling nicely, Les Moonves declined to join. Asked if she worried about ad clutter, Jo Ann Ross says she doesn't. "Maybe down the road this model gets tweaked. But so far, people haven't come to us and said, 'I'm not buying you because you have too many commercials.'"

Moonves was aware of other competitive threats, including Google's YouTube and Facebook, each of which commonly—and incorrectly—boast that their audience exceeds that of network TV. In June 2014, RBC Capital Markets's respected television and video analyst, David Bank, released a study revealing that for advertisers the ratings value of watching YouTube for an entire week would only match the value of a single original episode of CBS's *The Big Bang Theory.** YouTube executives invented new ways to assert that their audience was bigger than it was. They proclaimed that their twenty-three videos from *Jimmy Kimmel Live!* averaged 9 million views, more than the average 2.2 million viewers of the ABC late night show in May 2015. Yet Steve Hasker, Nielsen's global president and COO, notes that TV viewing is measured by how many viewers watch in an average minute, while digital outlets like YouTube measure the gross number of times the video is viewed for either one minute or one second. Since Nielsen was only measuring the average audience in any given minute, the average hourly *Kimmel* show in May 2015 had 5.3 million views nightly and 43.1 million adults for the month.

Unlike television, which has Nielsen to grade it, Hasker pointed out that Google and Facebook did not allow "independent third-party measurement."

Another long-term problem awaited Moonves, one that paralyzed most newspapers and magazines when they were first confronted by the digital threat in the late 1990s. Broadcast television could offer advertisers vast audiences, but they could not offer targeted ads and could not tell advertisers who actually watched their ads and bought their products. Unlike most newspapers and magazines, broadcast television remains a robust mass medium. However, unlike Internet or digital video, it lacks the tools to target audiences, the addressable

---

* Bank joined CBS in 2016 as senior vice president of investor relations.

advertising that helps explain why digital advertising spending would catch up with the $70 billion ad dollars devoted to television.

Moonves and his network brethren also resist computerized programmatic advertising that automates the targeting of audiences. Brian Lesser, the North American CEO of GroupM, is not alone in predicting that "all media will be digital"—meaning the TV networks will be streamed over the Internet just as Netflix is—and "all TV will be bought and sold programmatically." Moonves resists, believing that if he turned over ad sales to machines it would take the skill and the timing of the salesman or saleswoman out of the equation, reducing CBS's leverage. "Programmatic buying is fraught with peril," he says. "Somebody is selling inventory cheaper than you're selling it for." Networks like the mystery that the only way you can reach, say, women eighteen to forty-nine is by watching *Scandal*.

* * *

Also assailing Moonves and the networks was a six- or seven-year-old digital advertising bazaar—the New Front—meant to vie with traditional television's Upfronts, the period in which the four major broadcast networks sell up to 80 percent of their $9 billion worth of ads for the year. For several weeks in May 2016, thirty-nine digital companies sponsored presentations at which they made their pitch to about ten thousand advertisers and agency representatives. The New Front is organized by Randall Rothenberg's Interactive Advertising Bureau, and MediaLink kicked off the New Front at a May 2 breakfast at the New York Times Center on West Forty-first Street, presided over by Michael Kassan. MediaLink served as host and sent the invites, though the breakfast was paid for by two MediaLink clients, Vox Media and Kargo, a mobile marketing firm. The large hall was crowded with agency representatives and with many of Kassan's digital clients. By his count, Kassan says he represents 80 percent of the digital companies seeking to sell ads at the New Front. Surveying the crowded room, Harry Kargman, the founder of Kargo, said he saw the breakfast as an opportunity. "MediaLink allowed Kargo to be in front of people we may not have had the ability to get in front of," he says. "We want CMOs to say, 'What are we doing with Kargo?'" That's what he hoped happened when he spoke at this breakfast. And after this breakfast, he said, "Michael can pick up the phone and say, 'You've got to know this guy Harry Kargman.'"

This schmoozefest was gently interrupted by two panel discussions, the first moderated by Kassan, at which Jim Bankoff, CEO of Vox, without ever mentioning CBS or the networks, sought to distinguish "premium" digital video ads, primarily native ads, offered on Vox from the "interruptive" ads on television. Bankoff defined a "premium" ad as having three qualities: It's "creative," it "loads quickly," and "it engages me rather than interrupts me."

Bankoff and Kargman nodded their agreement on the second panel when Kassan concluded by declaring an end to the networks' Upfront monopoly: "I am a strong believer in this becoming a Video Front. It's all one. And at the end of the day, we subscribe to all the platforms and love all of the children equally. . . . If you adopt that view, it's all the same. The siloes are broken down."

The New Front brought bombast as well as competition. At YouTube's well-attended New Front presentation at the Javits Center, CEO Susan Wojcicki declared erroneously that YouTube "reached" more 18- to 49-year-old mobile viewers "during prime time than the top ten shows combined." But as noted earlier, "reach" does not equal viewing. Nielsen reports that the average audience per minute on television accounts for 95 percent of video watching, with smartphone video accounting for only 1 percent (and PCs 4 percent). Dave Morgan, the CEO of Simulmedia, a marketing technology company that designs targeted TV ad campaigns, says TV's ability to attract eyeballs far exceeds that of Internet darlings like YouTube. "*Judge Judy* today in thirty minutes," he says, "will deliver more seconds of advertising consumed by more people than all of YouTube will in all of America all day. One show!" Actually, more than YouTube delivers in an entire month, an RBC Capital Markets 2014 analysis reported. With 260 episodes per year, each containing 8 minutes of advertising for *Judge Judy*'s 9 million daily viewers, an estimated 1.6 billion minutes of ads were offered viewers, or twice as many as the 830 million minutes of ads per month on YouTube.

Some disruptions occur more slowly. At least in the short run, even with traditional TV's vulnerabilities, CBS and the networks have strengths other legacy and digital media can only envy. Networks may one day lose some leverage if programmatic advertising becomes dominant, but in 2015 Martin Sorrell said WPP sold only about 3 percent of its ads programmatically. Networks like CBS still command the attention of a vast audience. Ten of the top-ten-rated shows on network TV in February 2016 were on CBS, the first time ever that a single network captured all ten. By 2016, CBS owned just over 80 percent of the programs it aired in prime time, allowing the network to sell those shows to TV outlets in the United States and abroad. And by 2016, Les Moonves's CBS was making more money than when he joined CBS twenty years before. "When I first came here," Moonves says, "the CBS television network was losing money." Other parts of CBS, like the local stations it owns, were making money. Today, the network is the primary profit engine, one of several reasons CBS outperformed all media stocks over the previous five years.

*　　　　*

Entering the 2016 Upfront marketplace, all the networks knew that the 2015 Upfront fell below expectations, with lower volume of sales and CPMs, or cost per thousand viewer. In the months leading up to the 2016 Upfront and the ensuing negotiations between buyers (the agencies) and sellers (the networks), Moonves says, "It's always a cat-and-mouse game. Someone always has the upper hand." Because a disappointing 2015 Upfront was followed by ad prices jumping 15 to 20 percent over the rest of the year in what's called the scatter market, and because he believed "the bright, shiny object," as he referred to digital video, had lost its luster, in late April he predicted that "this Upfront will be a little bit of a renaissance for networks." His head of sales, Jo Ann Ross, would set a higher CPM price.

Several days earlier, Irwin Gotlieb of GroupM, the largest buyer, relaxing in his office wearing an open-necked pink dress shirt and tailored jeans, sat on a low couch and likened the Upfront to a futures market. "There was a futures market for Bordeaux in 2000 and 2003. But there wasn't in 2001, 2002, or 2004. You know why that was? The better vintages had scarcity. Good wine and reduced supply equals a strong futures market. Television continues to be a limited supply market. It will be a little more limited this year because I think people are looking very seriously at reducing commercial loads." Thus he predicted, as did Moonves, a buoyant Upfront for the networks. Which led Gotlieb to conclude that the buyer who jumps in early and makes a large dollar commitment to a strong network like CBS is likely to get a price break. To illustrate, he had his assistant place 10 bottles of water on the coffee table. "Let's say the total supply is 10 bottles and the cost per bottle is $100." Thus the total market demand is $1,000. "If I buy eight bottles at a two percent advantage because I bought early," the cost is reduced to $784. Similarly, if he chooses to buy late for a weaker network, the bet he is making is that the faltering network will offer a steeper discount in order to finally sell its ad inventory. For the buyer the question is always: "How do we read the futures market?"

What the seller always tries to do is steer the buyer away from a pure economic analysis by stroking their emotions in an Upfront presentation with the kind of showmanship the New Front cannot match. CBS invited thousands of buyers and the press to Carnegie Hall on May 18, where they were welcomed from the stage by Jo Ann Ross, who came out in a floor-length white fur coat, white top hat, and bedazzled cane. A video greeting from *Hamilton* creator Lin-Manuel Miranda was followed by late-night comic host James Corden performing as Hamilton in an eighteenth-century costume, surrounded by an ensemble, and rapping, "We just want your Hamiltons!" Lisa de Moraes of the *Washington Post* tweeted, "Another Hamilton segment at an Upfront! This makes three, or is it four?" But when Corden finished she tweeted, "James Corden's Hamilton performance puts other networks' Upfront Hamilton references to shame, including ESPN's Hamilton, ABC's Hamilton, and, sorry, Jimmy Fallon's Hamilton."

Corden introduced Moonves, who took shots at various competitors before stepping aside to allow the introduction of CBS's fall prime-time schedule, including the twenty new shows, all of them wholly or partially owned by the network. With Jo Ann Ross as orchestra leader—or "Momma," as she joyishly called herself—an array of well-known actors, newscasters, and executives trotted onto the Carnegie Hall stage.

When Upfront sales ended later that summer, Moonves blared that 2016 was "the strongest Upfront we have seen in many years." He said CBS enjoyed "double-digit price increases." Irwin Gotlieb concurred: "CBS did extremely well. Jo Ann Ross is as good as there is in the business. She knows how to read the marketplace."

What didn't change is that since network TV was the only way to reach a mass audience, the networks continued to get higher prices for shrinking live audiences and thus less viewing of ads. How long will this CBS advantage last? Will the advantage erode as technology enables buyers to cobble together a digitally targeted mass audience? Those two questions will hover over Les Moonves's head in coming years.

Michael Kassan, among others, believes Les Moonves will not like the answers to those questions. True, Kassan reflected, 2016 was "one of the best Upfronts. There was a flocking back to television as a safe place." Why? Because buyers in 2015 decided to spend less on the Upfront, wagering that the scatter market would be less expensive—and they guessed wrong. This year, he believes buyers said, "I don't want to get burned again." Nevertheless, he echoed a view shared by Gotlieb: for Moonves and the networks, "it was a short-term win, I think."

12.

MORE FRENEMIES

"We recast our business as communications marketing. The reason we did that was we wanted access to the marketing budgets, and we wanted to signal: you don't have to go to an ad agency to get marketing results."

—Richard Edelman

The advertising business is being invaded from all directions. A plethora of Michael Kassan's media clients—the *New York Times*, the *Wall Street Journal*, NBC, Condé Nast, Hearst, Vox, Refinery29, among others—are stealthily building out their own in-house advertising agencies. In 2015, Kassan believed that the primary disruption threat to agencies was to the media agencies that massaged the data, devised strategies, and purchased advertising time. He shared the view that Google and Facebook would one day go directly to agency clients and say, "Why do you need an agency in the middle?" By early 2016, Kassan's view had shifted: "I think the most likely to be disrupted now are the traditional creative agencies, and I'll tell you why. Every publisher from Condé Naste to Hearst to NBC to Disney now has creative agency units being built inside. So

Condé Nast has 23 Stories. Hearst is making all these investments in digital content creation. NBC has a content studio. Their mission is to sit down with Procter & Gamble and say, 'We can bring you ideas. We actually know how to create it.' They're not saying this, but the implication is: 'Why do you need a traditional advertising agency?'"

Today up to three quarters of the up to $2 trillion or so that is spent worldwide on advertising and marketing is not funneled through the creative ad agencies featured in *Mad Men*. The rise of below-the-line marketing expenditures, including public relations, polling, design, branding, lobbying, and in-store sales promotions, was why Martin Sorrell and rival holding companies vied to stave off disruption by acquiring marketing firms. Platoons of disrupters keep coming over the ridge. Among them, none is more surprising than publishers posing as ad agencies.

This ambition was on display on a visit to the *New York Times* in January 2016. The *Times* employed an advertising sales team of 325 people, and if you spied them at their desks you saw that nearly half were coders and designers and copywriters creating ads for clients rather than just selling ad space. Under chief revenue officer Meredith Levien, they worked for the T Brand Studio, whose purpose she described this way: "We are now in the business of making advertising. Our ad sales person goes out with a content creator to meet clients." The ads they create are interchangeably described as native ads or branded content, and they involve crafting stories featuring a brand. These look little different from a news story in the digital edition, except they carry a modest-sized advertorial label at the top of the page: "Paid for and Posted by . . ." With mobile becoming the dominant digital platform, native ads were necessary, she says, because the small phone screen "left no adjacent space on the page" for ads. Thus new ad forms were needed.

The T Brand Studio "is separate from the newsroom," says *Times*

CEO Mark Thompson, insisting that the church/state barrier has not been breached. Much of the sales force is composed of former journalists, which he sees as a calling card. "Clients come to us wanting to work with people comfortable with the idiom of storytelling. They don't have that with the agencies. And the agencies are locked into formats. We have a group of people who are used to inventing new formats. We offer a more open-ended approach." The *Times* aspired to serve as a near full-service agency. They bought a digital company, HelloSociety, that offers audience analytics and strategic alliances with influencers from its arsenal of 1,500 social media stars. They train ex-journalists and hire videographers to craft native video ads for mobile phones. They sell consulting services. They recruit employees skilled in distributing content on social networks. They are, Thompson says, "helping clients figure out how to use social media platforms. We're beginning to offer a broader portfolio of useful marketing services."

The *Times* is not yet a meaningful disrupter; its T Brand Studio produced revenues of just $35 million in 2015. But this represented a jump of 150 percent over the prior year. The incursions add up when you throw in the native ad revenues in 2016 of almost $600 million for Vice, $250 million for BuzzFeed, and about $60 million for the *Wall Street Journal*. Vice Media went a step further and formed a global ad agency, Virtue Worldwide, helping clients like Lululemon, and Unilever brands like Dove's personal-care products and Breyers ice cream shape marketing and ad campaigns to reach younger consumers. Refinery29 provides about two thousand stories per month targeted mostly at women and aiming to "help people discover and refine their personal style." Philippe von Borries, a cofounder, says, "We think of ourselves as a creative tool set for brands," helping them reach the 140 million women who visited his site each month by the winter of 2016. Of his 350 employees, 110 of them were tasked with creating native ads. "Brands need us because we have an audience and we have data." He would not disclose his ad revenues, but said they rose 70 percent in 2015.

In England, David Pemsel, the former marketing director of the *Guardian* newspaper and now CEO of the umbrella Guardian Media Group, doesn't sound as if he embraces that newspaper's leftist attitude toward capitalism when he describes the teams of storytellers and graphic artists that he has forged into Guardian Labs, with a staff of two hundred working directly with brands. "Guardian Labs is evolving into how do we help brands sell their stories. That could be by creating films. It could be producing print products or blogs. There are a whole bunch of assets I think we can create on behalf of our clients that will not deceive our audience." In appearance, Pemsel could pass for a smooth ad executive, with his fashionable stubble, square red-framed glasses, and a black V-neck tossed over a white shirt. In reality, he makes clear that he is taking aim at Martin Sorrell and cumbersome agencies, who he believes will be threatened by "media owners like the Guardian and Vice beginning to create advertising on behalf of our clients to get to the audience." The Guardian and Vice and the *Times* are hardly alone in creating internal agencies. Most traditional media companies—from Condé Nast to Hearst to NBC to Time Inc.—have molded what they refer to as content studios to work directly with brands.

■ ■ ■

The more immediate disruption threat to agencies comes from many former clients like consulting companies that are also invading the advertising and marketing business. "Several years ago, we thought Google was going to eat our lunch," Sorrell says. "Lately, it's become more of a Facebook threat." But the bigger menace, he says, may come from companies who have relationships with corporate CEOs or who have special skills to go along with their deep pockets. "People always said McKinsey would move into the marketing space, which they are increasingly doing. And Bain and the Boston Consulting Group. And then you're getting accounting firms that split their auditing and consulting functions. Accenture was our auditors. IBM buys three advertising firms in one week. Then there are the software companies—Salesforce.com, Oracle. So you've got layers." One reason Sorrell's WPP formed the marketing consulting firm Vermeer in 2014, as Publicis in early 2015 acquired the much larger global consulting firm of Sapient, was to better compete with consultants who had the ear of C-suite executives and were aggressively offering marketing services. The competitive threat from consulting companies was given a boost by Jon Mandel's vilification of the holding companies.

Unlike in Silicon Valley, marketing disrupters don't hide in a garage nurturing a new idea with the zeal of a founder. The threat usually comes from established corporations with a pool of capital and eagerness to seize a fresh business opportunity. "The largest digital ad agency in the country today is IBM," Michael Kassan says. "Accenture now has a digital agency. Deloitte has a digital agency. Ernst and Young has a digital agency. Maurice Levy spent $3.7 billion to buy, essentially, a consulting firm"—Sapient. He believes Levy was correct to do so because he wanted to confront the danger from companies like IBM. Levy had reason to quake, for at the end of 2015 the three largest global digital agencies by revenue, according to *Advertising Age*, were companies new to the marketing business: IBM, Accenture, and Deloitte. And the market cap or stock value of IBM (about $165 billion) was double the combined value of the six largest advertising and marketing holding companies—WPP, Publicis, Omnicom, IPG, Havas, and Dentsu.

IBM is worth a detour, for it has entered the marketing business at warp speed. In May 2015, *Advertising Age* named IBM's Interactive

Experience (iX) division the largest global digital agency. Later in 2015, IBM ingested live streaming and marketing software companies. Over two weeks in February 2016, it purchased two digital advertising agencies in Germany and one in the United States, and announced that it planned to open design studios in Prague, Warsaw, and Dubai. Worldwide, IBM had marketing offices in thirty locations and a staff of more than ten thousand performing creative and marketing design work for companies. Paul Papas, the global leader of its Interactive Experience division, announced, "We're raising the bar for experience-led digital marketing and commerce." Coupled with its October 2015 acquisition of the online assets of the Weather Company, weather.com, IBM made it clear that it was in the data business.

Joanna Peña-Bickley works for Papas and is the global chief creative officer for IBM iX. Her career started at ABC News, which she left to invent a video player to deliver streaming news videos and to design company Web sites. After the dot.com crash, she spent the next decade working for advertising agencies owned by WPP and Omnicom. Thinking that agencies were too focused on mass—like TV and full-page newspaper ads—and not focused enough on "solving the business problems of companies," she started a marketing company that grew to 150 employees.

IBM iX acquired her company and together she said they set out "to rethink the agency world." The "hole in the market" they saw was that data was not being used to zero in on what individuals wanted or needed and to solve large corporate problems. "Agencies are in a race to the bottom. They are losing talent, and the reason is that they have commoditized their creativity." Their corporate bosses at the holding companies, she believes, dwell too much on finances, including selling more thirty- and sixty-second ads. "The people that will win the race in the end will be the people who can fundamentally refine and make new products out of data." This data, for instance, tells IBM that large numbers of millennials don't want to own cars, they want to share them. So in representing an auto company, IBM iX brings a team to the auto company "to tackle this big business problem," and employing the data its engineers, writers, and designers assemble, they craft individualized messages to reach these millennials.

Although her creative department hired 1500 designers and writers in 2015, and would hire another 1500 in 2016, she said IBM would not supplant creative ad agencies. "Your ad agencies will still absolutely play a role in the innovation that we create. There's really room at the table for everyone. Our focus isn't ever going to be in the ad creation or campaign creation. It will always focus on innovation." She is sugarcoating, because her use of data and strategizing might not leave much "room at the table" for Irwin Gotlieb's GroupM.

In the world of data gatherers, IBM sees weather as a beachhead. Weather reports trigger emotional and very human responses that yield important marketing clues. Weather offers IBM an opportunity to marry data and marketing. For example, people tend to get depressed when it rains, which boosts both soup sales and movie watching. High pollen counts cue Walgreens ads. Inclement weather might trigger a company to advertise its all-weather tires. Steamy weather invites Gatorade ads. "We process billions of data points a day about the weather," says Jay Henderson, director of IBM's Marketing Cloud. "The weather," IBM CEO Ginni Rometty declared in a keynote speech at the Consumer Electronics Show in January 2016, "is the most pervasive impact source of data there is. It is why IBM acquired weather.com."

Another reason IBM acquired weather.com and its digital agencies was to mate them with Watson, a supercomputer that uses artificial intelligence and software to answer verbal questions, as Apple's Siri, Amazon's Alexa, or Google's Home strives to. But Watson's ambition is to be much more than a personal digital assistant. Its goal is to be capable of cognitive reasoning, like a human. Unlike a human, it would be capable of processing enormous amounts of data to unearth a single correct answer or to search for patterns to predict behavior. Watson searched weather.com and instantly awarded an IBM client, the Campbell Soup Company, with locations to invest their marketing dollars. Watson sweeps the Internet for what millions of people write on social networks and blogs. Instead of using standard measurement tools—clicks, CPMs, demographics, geography—it identifies personality types and interests that advertisers can precisely target. Instantly, Watson can scoop up sports fans, personalizing marketing messages to individuals. IBM is betting that ads directed at individuals will result in highly relevant marketing that may please rather than annoy.

It worked for Unilever when it partnered with IBM's Weather Company and created a new platform, Watson Ads, allowing consumers to tap into their mobile phone or computer and ask for a mayonnaise recipe using favored personal ingredients. "The big thing more than anything else," Jeremy Steinberg, the Weather Company's global sales chief, announced, "is that Watson is going to help humanize the advertising experience. It allows consumers to have a one-on-one relationship with brands like never before."

Of course, some part of what Steinberg and IBM hypothesize is blue sky. Artificial intelligence has been a holy grail since the birth of computers, and more than a half century later we're not there yet. Progress may be slower than visionaries predict.

Racing alongside IBM are consulting company giants. What was once known as Arthur Andersen, primarily an accounting firm, is now Accenture, the world's largest consulting company, which offers marketing as a new service. With 358,000 employees in 120 countries in 2015, including 80,000 employees in India, and three quarters of the Fortune Global 500 companies as clients, Accenture is a behemoth. By 2015, digital marketing revenues totaled 41 percent of all marketing spending in the United States. According to an analysis of more than a thousand agencies by *Advertising Age*'s Datacenter, Accenture Interactive's revenues ranked number one in the United States and the world, followed by IBM. Accenture Interactive offers digital marketing, shapes creative messages, provides strategy, data, analytics, and mobile services to clients. They have recruited almost 40,000 design and creative professionals to work in marketing. Companies like Accenture have an advantage in recruiting talent. "The average employee at Accenture makes three times as much as the average person at WPP," observes Terry Kawaja, whose small investment banking firm, Luma Partners, focuses on the marketing and tech sector.

Deloitte, with 225,000 global employees, has also aggressively expanded its marketing footprint. John Dunham, a former management consultant who today runs a branding consultancy in San Francisco, rates Deloitte as an especially formidable threat to agencies. Like Accenture and IBM and other consulting firms, they "already have an edge because they have relationships with top management. They had already been vetted. So it was easy for them to move over into the marketing side." They understood who the customers were, understood the data. "All they were doing was adding new services. Deloitte not only bought media companies, they bought a top-notch creative shop in San Francisco named Heat. All of a sudden they had capabilities to go against full service agency offerings." Deloitte, IBM, and Accenture confront intense marketing competition from other giants, including McKinsey, Bain, the Boston Consulting Group, PricewaterhouseCoopers, and Infosys.

     ❧ ❧ ❧

Tech companies also jockey to compete. Adobe, Oracle, and Salesforce .com race to offer cloud services that gather data on customers, target potential consumers, reach them on various company platforms, and generate information about what works to reach consumers and what doesn't. A "galactic war" is being waged between digital and tech companies, says Dan Rosensweig, a former COO of Yahoo and now CEO of Chegg, an online textbook rental and tutoring company, who serves on the board of Adobe. They vie to "let you know not only what does the person do but how do we get the person to come to your site? Once they're on your site, did they buy? How many steps did they go through? How can you make your site more efficient? And then testing which words and prices worked better? That's the modern-day ad agency!"

Anne Lewnes, the CMO of Adobe, saw Adobe's cloud services providing valuable data on its six million $10-per-month individual subscribers who use its Photoshop to edit and share photos or host Web sites. Adobe charges steeper fees to corporate customers like WPP and Publicis, who covet their data and have signed on as Adobe partners. Since they generate data and seek to know more about individual consumers, and WPP's GroupM or Kantar does as well, aren't they bound to collide? "We're not selling data," Lewnes says. "We're leveraging data. It's a little different." Rosensweig is blunter: "At the moment it is not competition." But he concedes, "Ten years from now, it could be."

Oracle did directly compete with Sorrell and Irwin Gotlieb to acquire Datalogix, a firm that massages data and helps analyze purchasing patterns, linking them to online ad campaigns to gauge how well or poorly an advertising campaign performed. When the bidding competition for Datalogix climbed north of $1 billion, Sorrell and Gotlieb dropped out. Gotlieb conceded it was "a company we lusted after," but admitted that WPP has a competitive disadvantage against companies with deeper pockets.

The company they lusted after took time to attain altitude. Eric Roza, the CEO of Datalogix, started out by sweeping up sales data from catalogue companies. He says he assumed "that what people purchased in the past was an indicator of what they would purchase in the future." He next went to grocery chains and their discount loyalty programs, collecting their data on what groceries their customers purchased. His big breakthrough came when Facebook contracted with Datalogix to learn whether ads on Facebook drove in-store sales. He induced Facebook to share what they would not with agencies—the names and e-mail addresses and information about its users—so he could match these individuals with those in the Datalogix database. "We could then say, these ten million people saw this ad and spent x dollars before the ad campaign and y dollars after the campaign. For the first time, the media impact on sales in terms of millions of people was done." Facebook told advertisers they could prove what drove sales, and publicly praised Datalogix. The company, Roza says, demonstrated that what products people purchased before was a much more valuable predictor of future purchases than clicks, page views, time spent watching or reading an ad, or search data. And not only could Datalogix demonstrate whether an ad campaign worked, Roza says, it had the ability to create addressable ads by marshaling its data to aim ads at likely consumers.

Today Roza is the co-senior vice president of Datalogix and three other companies that have been grouped together in what is now called the Oracle Data Cloud. In 2016, its database contained 2 billion worldwide consumer profiles, including 110 million U.S. households. Were they a threat to agencies? No, Roza responded. "We're a technology company. We partner well with agencies. Unlike companies such as Deloitte, we don't sell services. We don't place ads or create them." On the other hand, Silicon Valley companies like Oracle are not renowned for staying in their lane.

Salesforce.com has clearly veered into the agency lane. Entering 2016, Salesforce.com had acquired four companies—ExactTarget, Buddy Media, Radian6, and Brighter Option—to erect a marketing cloud. They aimed to serve as "the brain" for clients, assembling customer data, devising content messages to reach consumers, making these messages addressable to targeted individuals, and linking consumers directly with brands. Surveying tech companies who have jumped into cloud marketing, an April 2016 report by Pivotal analyst Brian Wieser concluded, "Salesforce.com appears best positioned to compete as a brain for marketers . . . and it contributes to our expectation that Salesforce.com should be the fastest-growing company in our coverage over extended periods of time."

* * *

Public relations firms also strive to disrupt agencies. Interviewed in 2016 at the annual conference of the Public Relations and Communications Association, or PRCA, Europe's foremost PR and communications membership organization, Martin Sorrell extolled public relations as "a good business" that was getting better for two reasons. "The first is because data has become more and more important. The other is digital. Digital has made public relations much more important than it was because of 24/7 communications at all levels. You can gain or lose a reputation at a click." Executives increasingly rely on PR crisis managers to douse fires.

Few public relations firms have expanded their reach more than Edelman, a privately owned public relations company with six thousand employees in sixty-four countries and such blue-chip clients as Unilever, Johnson & Johnson, Starbucks, Adobe, Samsung, Mars, and Kellogg's. The firm is run by Richard Edelman, son of the company's late founder. From his airy, open office high above bustling Hudson Street, where new buildings sprout up all around him, he says, "I decided that the only way to succeed in a world where classic distribution mechanisms"—newspapers and local TV news and radio opportunities—"were not only shrinking but evaporating," and where social networks became the primary distributors of news, and where consumers were allergic to ads and relied on ad blockers to defend against them, was for his firm to change.

Twenty percent of Edelman's business is now digital, he says. He disagrees with Martin Sorrell that PR agencies can't supply creative content to clients. "I believe earned media—pitching and telling stories—is the new paid. It's going to be very hard to get stuff through the ad blockers."

One of their campaigns that did evade ad blockers was, as noted earlier, for Vaseline, a Unilever product. Unilever prides itself on being a socially conscious company, and in its marketing often sells not just its products but the company's social mission, which Unilever also knows is a way to navigate past the skepticism of millennials. In 2014 they asked the Edelman agency to develop a social mission for Vaseline that linked the product to healing dry skin. An Edelman team conducted research and learned that dry skin can lead to infections and serious health issues. They came across a *Washington Post* story of two dermatologists who visited Syrian refugee camps in Europe and the Middle East and discovered that 70 percent of the refugees fleeing Syria had cracked skin and blistered feet. Working with Unilever in 2015, they launched the Vaseline Healing Project, donating one million jars of Vaseline and recruiting dermatologists to heal skin. The Healing Project was featured in sponsored content orchestrated by Edelman online, but also broke out as a TV and newspaper story. Referring to the tens of million of dollars Jeb Bush spent on TV ads before he dropped out of the Republican presidential primary contest in the winter of 2016, Edelman said, "There's a reverse relationship between how much advertising you buy and how trusted you are. You're trusted if you're seen as spontaneous." Or authentic. Unilever passed that test, and as we would stunningly learn, so did the winner of the Republican nomination, Donald Trump.

When public relations legends like Edward Bernays toiled earlier in the last century, their prime mission was to establish the public image of clients. They usually came to the table after the advertising agency shaped the advertising campaign. Today, they often sit at the table from the start. Richard Edelman explains that "classic PR" growth has stalled, requiring agencies like his to "evolve our traditional PR business into a communications marketing agency." To advance this goal, Edelman hired "four hundred creatives and planners" to work with clients like Samsung, Unilever, and Heineken. Edelman has entered advertising's inner kingdom, the thirty-second television ad. Richard Edelman recalls that when his employees created a Kellogg's YouTube story for the Winter Olympics of a four-year-old girl who one day became an Olympian, Kellogg's CMO told him, "'We want that as an ad.'" Edelman's four hundred creatives and planners now devise the kind of ads that were once the exclusive province of ad agencies. "We recast our business as communications marketing," he says. "The reason we did that was we wanted access to the marketing budgets, and we wanted to signal: you don't have to go to an ad agency to get marketing results."

If Edelman and other PR agencies are nipping at the heels of ad agencies, Martin Sorrell and the other holding companies are not standing still. A reason giant holding companies like WPP diversified and now own some of the most prominent PR agencies—Burson-Marsteller, Hill & Knowlton, Finsbury, Cohn & Wolfe—was both a defensive and offensive gesture. WPP aims to offer a full range of services. Donald Baer, who oversees 2300 employees in 110 countries for Burson-Marsteller, serves such clients as Bank of America, Microsoft, Intel, and Ford. He envisions two categories of growth in public relations. One is strategic counseling, helping shape the message and reputation and projecting a positive corporate image, as well as providing crisis counseling to companies. The second is what he refers to as "integrated communications. That's the injection of the digital, social, mobile, and content creation revolution that is transforming this business, and is the work that advertising and marketing agencies do. That's where we have had to move. Most of our growth is in this second category." Today, he says 25 to 30 percent of his employees work in integrated communications. Tomorrow, 60 percent will. Inevitably, Baer knows he will at times be competing with his sister ad agencies at WPP.

*　*　*

Reflecting the up-in-the-air nature of the marketing world, increasingly agency clients turn not just to public relations firms or consultancies or tech firms, but hire fresh start-up agencies or turn inward. The Association of National Advertisers announced in February 2016 that brands were increasingly abandoning old-school agencies as out of touch. They were turning to start-ups, particularly to help them navigate social media and incorporate new technologies. As we've seen, many of the largest brands have snatched their media buying away from agencies and established in-house programmatic media buying.

Prominent brands like General Electric and PepsiCo envision a day when they will spend less on advertising and become content creators, marketing and interacting with their consumers online. "GE wants to be a publisher, a content creator," says Sam Olstein, who as their director of innovation supervises GE's Disruption Lab. GE will expand their filmmaking and sponsorship of content—either "Brought to you by GE," or featuring GE scientists or engaging characters and selling their content to platforms, or placing content on GE Web sites. Olstein says, "We hope we can build an ecosystem or platform on a par with other media platforms out there."

Pepsi set up a content center and recruited creative talent to produce content they can sell. A reason Pepsi made this move, Brad Jakeman, president of the Global Beverage Group, told an audience at the 2016 Cannes festival, is because agencies are too rooted in the past: "I've been asking the advertising industry for years to evolve their business and they haven't. We value our agencies. But we also need the ability to produce fast." Fast may not equal effective. Few brands have been as successful as Red Bull in creating their own media platform that creates events that are covered by news organizations. It is costly, which is one impediment. And it may be delusional. Rishad Tobaccowala of Publicis cautions, "Brands want to talk about their brands, which in most cases is boring as hell and does not make an ongoing content platform."

Disruption is driven by frustration with agencies and by new business opportunities innovative technologies offer. On a deeper level, disruption is driven by a new reality: citizens are increasingly hostile to interruptive ads, as we've seen repeatedly. So advertisers experiment—with native ads meant to seduce users with narratives or ads that don't seem like ads; with new mobile ad formats, including six-second videos (instead of thirty-second ads) created by upstart companies like Kargo; with discounts and buy buttons. A popular and socially useful app aimed at reducing drunk driving fatalities was introduced by the Mindshare agency on behalf of Campari America, which makes Skyy Vodka, Wild Turkey, and Campari. They created in-app messages, sent Friday evenings to sports bars, containing a five-dollar discount coupon with the ride-sharing Lyft. Campari enjoyed a huge jump in its brand awareness, and probably saved lives.

Among the more effective marketing ploys to reach younger consumers has been influencer marketing. Young influencers have their own channels or platforms on YouTube, Instagram, Facebook, Snapchat, as well as their own Web sites. The route Samantha Fishbein, Aleen Kuperman, and Jordana Abraham took was unusual. They are not glamorous, wear little makeup, pin their hair up quickly, and enjoy the easy rapport of three girls who grew up around the corner from each other in Roslyn, Long Island, attended the same public schools and the same college. As bored seniors at Cornell, they started blogging and tweeting anonymously as the Betches. "We made fun of the ridiculous culture around us, without being a hater," Samantha says. After graduating in 2011, and getting jobs and returning to their parents' nests, they decided to try and popularize the Betches. As the Betches, they anonymously published a paperback book in 2013, *Nice Is Just a Place in France: How to Win at Basically Everything*. It became a national best seller. Success invited attention, and they promoted themselves in a *New York Times* interview, followed by others. Their Web site made fun of the lifestyle they enjoyed, including incessant partying; they posted pictures on Instagram with captions like, "The Best Emoji for Flirting & to Get You Laid." Their upper-middle-class audience of eighteen- to thirty-year-old females "doesn't take themselves too seriously and likes to have a good time," Samantha says. "No one would go and protest for something they believed in. It's very much about yourself, the ME generation." Not feeling comfortable that they could perform as well in a video format like YouTube, their preferred platform was Instagram. Impressed with their young female audience, advertisers sold ads on their Betches platforms, providing funds for them to rent an office on East Twenty-eighth Street in Manhattan.

There was rarely an agency between the Betches and the advertiser when they were hired as influencers. By late 2015, they were doing twenty influencer ads per month for such clients as Smirnoff, the Bumble dating app, and Captain Morgan rum. They assembled fifteen contract writers and an overall staff of thirty-five. They asked clients to send them the message they wanted conveyed. "Usually, we put it in our own words," Samantha says. "We said that the least promotional way to sell is the best." She continued, "When we started we didn't want people to think we are bought by advertisers." They quickly got over their qualms. "You can't sell out anymore. Everyone is doing it."

The key, says Jordana, "is doing it in a way that seems organic and natural. They don't want to know you're paid. Even if they do know, they don't want it in their face."

Asked if he believed the survival of advertising agencies was threatened just as newspapers and magazines and music companies have been, David Pemsel, the CEO of the Guardian Media Group in London, said, "I do. These agency guys are smart. However, they probably are surprised by how quickly change comes and the agility" of the digital world. "With the pace of change, it puts all of us under threat all the time."

13.

MARKETING YAK-YAKS AND MOUNTING FEAR

"We're weeks away from Armageddon."

—Michael Kassan

At the start of each year the entire marketing community—buyers and sellers, agencies, clients, publishers and platforms, Hollywood studios, digital and software and hardware companies—flock to CES in Las Vegas. Once, attendees came to tour the electronic exhibits, hoping to catch a glimpse of the future, and to meet and greet. Michael Kassan would come to CES with his friend Irwin Gotlieb to walk the floors of the various hotels that house the exhibitions. Then CES expanded its reach, and Michael Kassan assumed an outsized role. In 2010, to broaden their support in the tech community, CES called on Kassan to help lure Steve Ballmer, then CEO of Microsoft, a MediaLink client, to attend MediaLink's cocktail party. Ballmer has become a regular at this event.

Kassan started stumping for more advertisers to attend CES. Gary Shapiro, the president and CEO of the Consumer Technology Association, which produces CES, liked the idea, and Kassan offered a deal Shapiro welcomed. He would lobby brand advertisers and agencies to attend, and in return CES would give MediaLink VIP status to create a reserved space in an established hotel where Kassan and brands and clients could conduct closed-door meetings, as well as a separate venue where MediaLink could host and invite speakers and moderate panels. CES would also cosponsor with MediaLink the opening night kickoff cocktail party and would encourage a MediaLink dinner that became a must-be-invited-to meal for 350. Little wonder that after Peter Kafka of the online publication *Recode* followed Kassan around at CES in 2014, he lightheartedly described him as "the Godfather."

Kassan became the schmoozer-in-chief. His visits to CES coincided with the upheaval in the entertainment and marketing world. Members of the film and television communities started coming to CES in the late 1990s and early in this century when new technologies like HDTV were seen as disrupters and a debate raged as to whether the living room would be controlled by the TV or by computers. Advertisers followed not just because Michael Kassan invited them, but because they had the same curiosity about the companies and technologies that could disrupt their business. "Michael has put himself in the center of what's taking place," says Karen Chupka, CES senior vice president for corporate business strategy. By working together as partners, she adds, "I never walk away feeling, 'Oh, I gave something to Michael.' I always feel like we got something better together."

January 2016 was CES's forty-ninth anniversary, and 176,000 attendees filled 150,000 Las Vegas hotel rooms and walked the length of 50 football fields worth of exhibits. Stepping out of any hotel, neon signs beckoned visitors to come see the past perform—Donnie and Marie, Olivia Newton John, Wayne Newton. Or one could visit the future at just about any nearby hotel to see the 20,000 products on exhibit. Keith Weed of Unilever, who Kassan says was the first client to ask him to arrange a tour of the exhibition floors, explains why he comes to CES annually: "If you're going to get to the future, first you better have an idea of the future. . . . If I can stay ahead, it gives me an advantage." Plus, he adds, "Everyone is here." Like other clients, Weed told MediaLink what he was most interested in doing at CES. This year he wanted a curated exhibition tour to explore three subjects: artificial intelligence, virtual reality, and the Internet of things.

In addition to Unilever, MediaLink had a total of 100 clients attending and would curate 582 floor tours and meetings with advertisers, agencies, and digital companies. A staff of forty was in attendance, each person responsible for accompanying a group of clients—JPMorgan Chase, GE, McDonald's, NBC, Hearst, Gawker, the *New York Times*—as well as organizing public session panels for agency clients like Digitas, Publicis's digital media agency. "We're like the official sherpas for our clients," Wenda Millard says. Sporting his Christmas tan from Turks and Caicos, Kassan, casually attired in grey khakis and a wheat-colored crewneck thrown over a white shirt, met Tuesday afternoon with the MediaLink team to discuss their agenda for the rest of the week. They reviewed last minute additions to the 4,000 people invited to a party that evening billed as a MediaLink event, even though the names in small print at the bottom of the prominent posters were those who paid for the party—GroupM, Havas, Omnicom, IPG, Digitas, *Variety*, among others. They reviewed the 350 invites to their more exclusive Wednesday Executive Dinner.

At this CES, unlike many industry confabs, Jon Mandel did not seem to excite a fever of discussion. In between hugs and high fives, Michael Kassan mostly spent the day gliding from MediaLink's CES space in the Aria hotel, where it hosted panels; its private Aria Sky Suites, where he met with clients and visitors; and at another hotel where he was to interview NBCUniversal CEO Steve Burke on a main stage, just as he interviewed Les Moonves the year before and Twitter CEO Dick Costolo the year before that. Kassan constantly peppered staffers with questions. When he learned that PepsiCo CEO Indra Nooyi would attend their dinner, he asked, "Is this a Pepsi or a Coke hotel?" The answer did not matter. He wanted Pepsi served. He fielded a flood of e-mail requests, including one from Martin Sorrell asking if he could bring two guests to Wednesday's dinner, and one from a CMO asking to meet tomorrow for what Kassan guessed was personal advice on seeking a new job. Anxious that his Executive Dinner be flawless, accompanied by his daughter, Brett Kassan Smith, who was coordinating it, they visited the Foxtail at the SLS hotel, a combination indoor and outdoor space that she said could accommodate no more than 350. Aware that he had said yes to Sorrell and others, she addressed her father by his first name and warned, "Michael, you have to understand, we can't squeeze more than 350 in here." People pushed too far outside would not be able to see Lady Gaga perform. And she knew rain was in the forecast, which would close off most of the outdoor space.

He bobbed and weaved, never once agreeing. With Universal Music donating Lady Gaga, and with Condé Nast sharing half the $400,000 evening's cost with MediaLink but not half the branding credit, and with sports celebrities like Alex Rodriquez attending, he was the host of the hottest event of CES. He knew—his daughter knew—his guest list had already climbed north of four hundred.

Kassan's nights were devoted to drop-bys at a blur of agency, advertiser, and media parties. After leaving the Omnicom, Havas, and then MediaVest parties Tuesday evening, he raced by foot to the XS Nightclub in the Encore hotel for MediaLink's cocktail party. Coming toward him was an elderly man and a younger blonde, holding hands and wearing matching black sneakers. It was Rupert Murdoch, who

Kassan says is his biggest client, and Jerry Hall, soon to be his wife. After a warm exchange of hellos, Kassan quickened his pace and soon was escorted past long lines into the XS Nightclub, for what was billed as the MediaLink party.

Like Kassan, Carolyn Everson of Facebook had a packed schedule at CES. While being ferried in a black SUV to one of her many appointments in Las Vegas, she said of CES, "People moan and groan that it's the first thing they have to do when they come back from holiday. We all do it. And yet every top marketer and agency and media and technology company is here." Her Facebook team scheduled 122 meetings this week, 30 of which she would attend. They reviewed with brands what they did together in 2015, and what the new challenges for 2016 were.

Her task, as she saw it, was to help galvanize the marketing world to address disruption. Her pitch in meetings here, she says, goes like this: "The real challenge in the industry today is that consumer behavior has shifted already. More time is spent on mobile apps than on television. However, mobile is still an afterthought for most marketing campaigns. Companies are struggling with how to rejigger their teams, their skills, their work flow, their board structure, so they can be more relevant to consumers in a mobile environment. The real question is: How fast can they do that? Companies that have been around for a hundred-plus years? Really hard to change behavior and culture. New companies? They go right to mobile. Do you think Uber is worried about anything other than the experience on the mobile device?"

By selling mobile, she knows she is selling Facebook. But here, as elsewhere, she is both a self-serving and a supportive missionary. She knows companies will not shift to mobile unless they first transform their culture. "How can we help them learn from what Facebook is doing to hire people that are focused on impact, that are willing to move quickly, that are willing to have failures?" To prod them: "I start off by showing the photo of Facebook's headquarters in Menlo Park, which has the big Like sign." Facebook's sprawling headquarters was once home to Sun Microsystems, a seemingly impregnable tech company that fizzled and was sold to Oracle in 2009. She tells them what they don't see on the face of the Like sign: "If you peek behind the sign you will see the old Sun Microsystems sign. They say, 'Why?' Because every time a Facebook employee leaves campus we want them to remember that at any moment you could become irrelevant. Sun was an amazing company, and now they're no longer here."

One of the oddities of CES is that most marketers don't actually visit the exhibits. "No one wants to go to the floor," Andrew Markowitz, GE's director of global digital strategy said during a MediaLink panel on brand reinvention. "They want to be here for face-to-face meetings. There's a ton of meetings going on." And when people visit the exhibits, strange things can happen. The six thousand journalists who attend CES are asked to share their e-mail addresses, prompting a deluge of invitations to visit some pretty flaky-sounding exhibits. Like the invite from PetChatz, which was described as "the first-ever technology that lets dogs and cats 'call' their owners for a video chat and treat," and lets owners "call their pets while away." The e-mail invite said PetChatz was located in CES Booth 82646, which was in Hall G of the Sands. But a trip to the floor found Booth 82646 empty.

One objective of CES is to manufacture buzz. In 2016, virtual reality was the much-hyped new new thing, which would be supplanted at CES 2017 by artificial intelligence, and AI-centric products like self-driving cars and Amazon's Alexa. In previous years, drones, Google Glass, and 4K TVs had their moment. Writing about CES 2016, Farhad Manjoo of the *New York Times* observed, "If news from CES feels especially desultory this year, it might not be the show that's at fault. Instead, blame the tech cycle. We're at a weird moment in the industry: The best new stuff is not all that cool, and the coolest stuff"—AI, virtual reality, the Internet of things, drones—"isn't quite ready."

* * *

If CES had been a warm bath of relationship building, the American Association of Advertising Agencies conference at the Loews Miami Beach Hotel two months later centered more on conflict. The much-anticipated ANA report on agency kickbacks sparked by Jon Mandel's speech a year earlier hovered over anxious agency executives. Michael Kassan spoke of the K2/Ebiquity investigation for the ANA and evoked a common fear: "We're weeks away from Armageddon." The information he had picked up was that the report would be damning, and though it would not cite agencies by name he guessed that clients would then launch more audits of their agencies and maybe even ask: "Do I really need an agency?" One source who was said to be familiar with the report's conclusions even went so far as to tell *Business Insider* that some agency executives might face "jail time." Irwin Gotlieb was alert to the report, but less alarmist. He said he had heard "various versions" of what the report would say and expected it would be harsh. "It's being driven by Ebiquity," he said. "They want more business. They have a great deal to gain by fomenting distrust between clients and agencies. They want to get clients to hire them to monitor agencies."

On the eve of the 4A's annual March conference, war had broken out between the organization representing agencies and the organization representing advertisers. The joint task force the two organizations established after Mandel's speech, with the aim of agreeing to "transparency" principles, had ended in bitterness and recrimination. ANA board member Jack Haber says, "The 4A's said, 'We're not going to cooperate with you unless you do it our way.'" He says the 4A's would agree to transparency principles for agencies, but not for the worldwide holding companies. "We said, 'No go.' Then they issued it themselves." Haber says he hoped both sides could "take it down from an emotional pitched battle," but for him and the ANA the core question was simple, "Are you my agent or not?" Nancy Hill, the president and CEO of the 4A's, saw it differently. After working together for nine months to draft transparency guidelines, she said the task force splintered just before Christmas because the ANA suddenly "wanted to make a rash of changes" to the document. They wanted to "dictate contract language to an entire industry," while the 4A's believed contracts should be negotiated between individual clients and agencies. By toughening the language in the draft, agency reps believed, ANA members were behaving like cowardly politicians afraid to look weak to their foremost constituency, their CEO and chief procurement officer. As a counter, the 4A's rushed to release its own "transparency" principles.

On the surface, the 4A's Miami conference seemed like business as usual. The agenda was billed as Transformation 2016. MediaLink co-hosted an opening night after-party at a nearby hotel. A familiar array of speakers—Maurice Levy, Martin Sorrell, Wendy Clark, Bill Koenigsberg, Jeff Goodby, Carolyn Everson, Rishad Tobaccowala, and Rob Norman—appeared. There would be panels on how to drive business results with engaging digital content, how agencies can attract top talent, the future of the industry, the future of news, and the state of programmatic advertising. And, of course, there would be awards. As at most industry conferences, Michael Kassan would be spotted one moment in a choice seat at the chairman's table in front of the stage checking e-mails, the next moment walking about exchanging hugs with old friends, or slipping outside the ballroom to speak on his mobile, or surrounded by people enjoying his jokes.

What wasn't typical was the tension. It wasn't just the pending ANA report. Many delegates arrived on edge because of an ugly and well-publicized sexual harassment lawsuit filed just days earlier by

J. Walter Thompson's communication chief, Erin Johnson, against her boss, global CEO Gustavo Martinez. Johnson's court papers claimed Martinez subjected her "and other employees to an unending stream of racist and sexist comments as well as unwanted touching and other unlawful conduct." Once, she said, he approached her desk and told her to follow him "so he could 'rape' [her] in the bathroom." Another time he allegedly interrupted a meeting with sixty employees, including females, to ask Johnson "which female staff member he could rape." She alleged that he described African Americans as "black monkeys and apes," and said he and his wife disliked living in Westchester County because he "hate[s] those fucking Jews." Johnson said she complained to various officials at J. Walter Thompson and parent company WPP, and they either excused his behavior, assured her they would talk to him and didn't, or cautioned: *Don't harm your career!*

Martinez issued a public statement flatly declaring, "There is absolutely no truth to these outlandish allegations, and I am confident that this will be proven in court." WPP initially issued a statement saying an internal investigation found no evidence that Johnson's claims were true. The company placed her on paid leave while Martinez continued as CEO. Days later, WPP announced it had hired a law firm to investigate. On the eve of the conference, Martinez withdrew from appearing on a 4A's panel and, "by mutual agreement," stepped down as CEO and was replaced by Tamara Ingram, a seasoned WPP executive. Over coming months, WPP was assailed by Johnson's lawyers for opposing the lawsuit and for implicitly defending Martinez. Asked whether WPP was complicit, Martin Sorrell said WPP had offered Johnson another job and continued to pay her. As for Martinez, he said, "You don't try people in the court of public opinion." (WPP attempted to have the lawsuit dismissed, and in December 2016 the court ruled against them; in December 2017, the case was still alive and, despite the sexual harassment claims, it was revealed that WPP placed Martinez in charge of its operations in his native country, Spain.)

Erin Johnson did not attend the conference, but her story certainly did. It brought back memories. In *Mad Men* days at J. Walter Thompson, bathroom signs bellowed GENTLEMEN. Women found their bathrooms behind unmarked doors. When Marion Harper, the CEO of IPG, in 1966 offered Mary Wells Lawrence a promotion and the salary and authority of the president of Jack Tinker & Partners, he said he couldn't offer her the title. "It is not my fault, Mary, the world is not ready for women presidents." She promptly quit.* More recently, the 3% Conference, which promotes female creative agency leadership, reported that although women comprise half of agency employees, only 11 percent of creative directors are female (and less than 1 percent of marketing executives were black women). Reflecting a common perception among women in advertising, one hears complaints about the social activities that male colleagues organize—golf outings, watching sporting events like football, steak dinners—that make them feel like outsiders. "I don't want to whine, 'Oh poor me!' That's wasted energy," Wendy Clark said before going to Miami, recalling that several years ago when she joined a new company (that she declined to name), "in my executive package I was referred to as an employee and my husband was 'a trailing spouse.' He has an MBA, and he looked at me and said, 'Really? I'm a trailing spouse?'" She laughs, knowing the employment forms were created by men who assumed that women trail men.

The frustration of female executives spilled out at the 4A's. In her welcoming remarks to open the conference, Nancy Hill, whose career was in advertising, immediately raised the case of Erin Johnson: "Unfortunately, the alleged behavior does happen. And it happens more

---

* Mary Wells Lawrence, *A Big Life (in advertising)* (New York: Alfred A. Knopf, 2002).

frequently than we think." She pleaded for "a very frank conversation" about sexual harassment in the industry. "Real change," she insisted, "has to start at the top." In an address minutes later, Wendy Clark kept the sexual harassment issue alive by declaring, "Fundamentally, we have to pull back the curtain on this discussion and as an industry use confabs like this to share our best thinking and best ideas." In a fireside chat on the second day, Carolyn Everson was asked how the industry was doing in regard to gender equality. "I don't think we're in a good place at all," she answered, citing as evidence: "There's not a single country in the world where more than 6 percent of their CEOs are women. The needle hasn't moved." Choking back tears on one panel and sparking a rousing ovation, Chloe Gotlieb, senior vice president and creative director at R/GA, chastised her industry: "Where are the people of color? We're a white industry!"

Also, a white male-dominated industry. *Business Insider* released a report on the sixteen highest-compensated (salary, stock options, and other incentives) advertising executives in 2015 and all sixteen were white males. Topping the list were three holding company CEOs: Martin Sorrell ($87,500,000), John Wren ($23,576,047), and Michael Roth ($14,458,102), with Maurice Levy ($2,900,000) falling closer to the bottom of the list.

When Maurice Levy was the keynote speaker the first morning, he and Martin Sorrell wound up trading insults. For those who have long followed their clashes, the feud between the diminutive British bulldog and the tall, elegant Frenchman with a full head of wavy grey hair brings to mind Donald Trump's tweets: neither Sorrell nor Levy can resist the pleasure of inflicting pain on a perceived enemy. Their clash at the 4A's concerned the allegations of sexual harassment at WPP.

The Gustavo Martinez incident and Erin Johnson's lawsuit arose when Maurice Levy spoke. He did not attack WPP. Rather, he told the audience he did not believe the alleged extreme behavior of Martinez was typical. "It's a one-time mistake, a huge fault. But it's not a fair representation of our industry." Levy was not challenging the claims made by many female speakers at this 4A's that the industry lacked diversity, that it was guilty of offering too few opportunities to women, and had succumbed to what Carolyn Everson of Facebook would later tell the audience was "unconscious bias." He was simply claiming that Martinez's alleged extreme behavior was not the norm.

The next day, Sorrell appeared via a video hookup for an interview and deftly changed the subject from the behavior of the J. Walter Thompson CEO to Levy's behavior. He "violently" disagreed with Levy, he said. "Maurice has a habit of ignoring the facts in getting to his opinions." This was among the milder things Sorrell has said about Levy.

When asked about Sorrell after the 4A's, at first Levy said he did not wish to offer a description, and added, incorrectly, that in the past when he has offered criticism of Sorrell it "was always in reaction, unfortunately."

What was the crux of the problem between them?

"You should ask Martin." He paused as if he would say no more, but he could not contain himself: "I think the problem he has, besides the fact that I am twice as tall as he is, I think there is a problem with competition. . . . There are two brands in the advertising industry, Sorrell and Levy." Besides, he added several sentences later, "He doesn't like the French. He considers that we are second-class citizens." Levy traces their bad blood back to their competition to buy Young & Rubicam in 1999, and then in 2003 the British agency, Cordiant.

※ ※ ※

A fair amount of rage and gloom was expressed throughout the conference. The chairman of the 4A's, Bill Koenigsberg, stunned conferees with his opening remarks when he said, "I'm pissed off." What angered him is something that has long infuriated agencies: clients induce agencies to make free spec pitches during agency reviews, which burden agencies with about $400 million in free employee hours. "Our product is being devalued. We have to stop the insanity of giving away our work for free." On a panel with Vice cofounder and CEO Shane Smith, *New York Times* CEO Mark Thompson borrowed from *Game of Thrones* and predicted that winter was coming for the advertising industry; Smith chimed in, "You're going to see a bloodbath" of consolidation in the industry. In a talk on "Making Advertising Matter Again," Jeff Goodby, cofounder and cochair of Goodby, Silverstein & Partners, talked about some of the ad campaigns he crafted, not including the one he would do pro bono against Donald Trump's candidacy for president. (The Trump ad featured video of proud moments in American history—landing a man on the moon, inventing rock 'n' roll and the Internet—and closed by saying that we didn't do all this "just to be laughed at by the entire world in November." The ad closed with a close-up of Trump's face and, in large text, the words "History is watching."*) Goodby appeared in a black jacket and black mock turtleneck, with a long, silver ponytail sliding down his back, and made a declaration creatives have made for decades: the only way "to save advertising" from low morale and from 70 percent of employees seeking new jobs was to reinject enthusiasm into the business by regaining a sense of creative "vandalism." He explained: "Like good advertising, good vandalism is funny, loud, and still there the next day."

In "The Truth About Talent" panel, a LinkedIn senior director, Jann Schwarz, who is their liaison to the giant holding companies, recounted the results of a joint study with the 4A's to explore the

---

* A large number of voters tired of watching these ads, and a consensus jelled after Trump won that the Clinton campaign spent too much time seeking to define Trump and too little time defining why she should be president.

reasons professionals fled agency jobs. The survey sample was large, consisting of 300,000 professionals worldwide and 10,000 professionals who had switched jobs. While the foremost reason cited for leaving agencies was "lack of opportunities" to advance and a desire for "more challenging work," the survey also noted that the average first-year agency salary "is $45,000 less than in the technology sector." The median salaries for copywriters ($51,030), account executives ($45,338), or art directors ($56,263) ranked near the bottom among industries; the average starting salary at ad agencies ($25,000) was almost three times below that of management consultants ($70,000). Of college grads, thirty-one-year-old Rob Fishman, the cofounder of Niche, which recruits influencers to promote brands on digital sites, would say before the conference, "I don't know a single person who wants to work in an ad agency. It's not like it was in Don Draper's day."

Indeed. A study under the direction of Scott Galloway, a marketing professor at New York University's Stern School of Business, reported that 2,227 of WPP's employees left to go to work for Google and Facebook and only 124 joined WPP from the tech giants. "The ad world today is increasingly run by the leftovers," Galloway writes in his 2017 book, *The Four: The Hidden DNA of Amazon, Apple, Facebook, and Google*. WPP disputed his facts, saying their data revealed that only 200 left for Google and Facebook in the past year and a half and about 70 joined WPP.

Another panel, "The Future of the Industry," Rishad Tobaccowala of Publicis, Rob Norman of GroupM, and Scott Hagedorn, then CEO of Annalect, tried to inject some optimism into the proceedings. "We have a front-row seat at the nexus of disruption," which creates opportunities, Norman said.

"The future is likely to be far brighter than the past," said Tobaccowala, emphasizing that with the advent of digital and a proliferation of competing platforms, marketing opportunities will rise as traditional advertising declines. "We have to stop being insecure."

"There's no better time to be in this business," said Norman, mentioning the knowledge their global businesses could glean from the rise of video versus television in China, the different marketing successes in India (like P&G's Ariel detergent campaign), the e-commerce lessons taught by Amazon (which boosted sales by offering free delivery and streaming TV and movies for an annual subscription to Amazon Prime).

When asked why advertising did not seem to work in the Republican primaries despite huge TV expenditures by candidates like Jeb Bush, Norman, as marketers are apt to do, turned that negative into a positive: "If you have any doubt about the power of branded content, think of *The Apprentice*!"

14.

THE CLIENT JURY REACHES ITS VERDICT

A K2 investigator said he thought the rebates could be classified as "civil or criminal fraud," because "publicly traded companies are required to disclose their finances, and they didn't."

I t was a few days before the long-awaited ANA report was to be released on June 7, 2016, and Michael Kassan remained convinced its conclusions would be devastating for the giant holding companies, who he thought were in denial as to the seriousness of the claims against them. He had made a bid to conduct the investigation, seemingly unmindful that he would be investigating many of his own clients. In hindsight, he realized he had been lucky to be passed over to conduct the ANA probe; had he been awarded the contract he would not have been able to accept the new clients clamoring for MediaLink to review their agency contracts. He was also aware that the sleuthing work would inevitably strain relations with his friends, especially with Irwin Gotlieb.

Kassan was right about the report's harsh conclusions. After conducting 143 interviews and inspecting e-mails and other documents over 8 months, the core conclusion of the 58-page K2 report was that there is "a fundamental disconnect in the advertising industry regarding the basic nature of the advertising-agency relationship." Advertisers believed "that their agencies were duty-bound to act in their best interest. They also believed that this obligation—essentially, in their view, a fiduciary duty—extends beyond the stated terms in their agency contracts." In this expansive view, the agency was an agent of the client. The narrower contractual view publicly proclaimed by Irwin Gotlieb, and shared by many agency executives, the report said, was "that their relationship to advertisers was solely defined by the contract between the two parties."

The report affirmed the broad charges lodged by Jon Mandel. Rebates were common in the United States, the report concluded. "K2 interviewed 41 sources who reported that media rebate deals occur in the U.S. market." Of the 41 sources, 34 said the rebate information and monies were not shared with advertisers. Media companies who sold the ads secretly kicked back to agencies between "1.67% to approximately 20% of aggregate media spending, depending on the deal." The rebates took different forms, from cash to free ad inventory to debt forgiveness to benefits like equity in the media company. The most common way the rebate system worked, said the report, is that the agency holding companies used their purchasing power to buy discounted advertising time, which they then resold at a higher rate to their individual agencies who buy this ad time for clients. The lower purchase price paid by the holding company was not disclosed to the client. The report also said that holding companies often directed that ad dollars be shoveled to media companies they partially owned. This served the interests of the holding company, but these ad platforms were often extraneous to the client.

This would not be the first time a holding company was called out for extracting rebates. In 2008, the Securities and Exchange Commission imposed a $12 million settlement on IPG for rebates its McCann-Erickson agency demanded in violation of its contracts with clients. Nor would it be the last. Two months after the ANA report, the *Guardian* in England disclosed that it pays rebates to agencies, including "free advertising space, cash payments, or both." And in September 2016, a scandal surfaced in Japan when an important client, Toyota, complained that Japanese advertising giant Dentsu falsely billed them for digital ads that did not appear. After an audit, an embarrassed Dentsu announced that it would repay 111 advertisers a total of 230 million yen (roughly $200 million).

The report acknowledged the fairness of complaints agencies often lodge against clients. In new business pitches by agencies, the report said, clients were too often preoccupied, not with marketing strategy or fresh creative ideas, but with the agencies' fees. The rise of procurement officers, the report conceded, meant constant cost pressures since marketing was usually viewed as a cost, not an investment. And with the end of the commission system, agencies sometimes struggled to make money. Clients were often guilty of not auditing their contracts to learn if agencies were in compliance. And ANA president Bob Liodice admitted that his client constituents were often asleep when it came to rigorous audits and contracts, conceding that "the behavior on the client side was a little more paralyzed than one would have liked."

But the thrust of the report was a clear condemnation of the agencies. They were found guilty of engaging in secret rebates, of acting in their interests, not the interests of their clients, and of a basic lack of transparency. (Of the six holding companies, the report said they interviewed executives at all six but that only IPG officially cooperated.) The ANA emphasized the trust issue. "Advertisers and their agencies are lacking 'full disclosure' as the cornerstone principle of their media management practices," Liodice said in a prepared statement. "Such disclosure is absolutely essential if they are to build trust as the foundation of their relationships with their long-term partners." The report, Liodice declared at a press briefing, "represents an opportunity to rebuild agency/client trust."

He promised that by July the second company involved in the investigation, Ebiquity, would release transparency principles for his seven hundred members. The ANA urged its membership to reexamine all its agency contracts.

Requesting anonymity, a K2 executive was harsh, saying he thought the rebates could be classified as "civil or criminal fraud. In addition, publicly traded companies are required to disclose their finances, and they didn't. There are a number of different angles a regulator or a prosecutor could use as a hook."

The report was vulnerable to criticism. Because no guilty agencies were identified by name, and because the charges were anonymous— "K2 found substantial evidence of non-transparent business practices in Agency Holding Companies, as well as in certain independent agencies"—all but the smallest agencies were tarred with this broad brush. The name-no-names approach was promulgated by the ANA, as the report says: "From the outset, the ANA made clear to K2 that the goal of the study was not to embarrass or accuse any individual or corporate entity of malfeasance." Instead of singling out this or that agency for malfeasance, the report leaves the impression that all, or at least most, agencies are miscreants. Since the report fails to name client victims, all clients are left to wonder whether they might be victims.

The agencies were livid. In a public statement, the 4A's denounced the report, saying it is "anonymous and one-sided and paints the entire industry with the same negative brush." They bridled that the

ANA was treating their agency partners as targets of an investigation, even though the introduction to the report repeatedly claimed this was a "study," not an investigation. Yet when asked whether his failure to name names slandered innocent agencies, former federal prosecutor and principal author of the report, Richard Plansky, described his work as an investigation: "I don't think that's a valid criticism. When you do an investigation and sources are 'at risk,' it is standard industry practice to grant them confidentiality."

Attorneys for WPP and Omnicom had their law firms dispatch letters to the ANA demanding proof that they extracted rebates. Each holding company denied they pocketed rebates in the United States. Martin Sorrell and Irwin Gotlieb publicly questioned the motives of K2 and Ebiquity, charging that both firms had an ax to grind because they were angling to become the go-to auditors for advertisers. Irwin Gotlieb went further, questioning the assumption animating the ANA report that agencies are agents for their clients. Gotlieb measures his words carefully and his answers to questions arrive as if in slow motion. In his office, he was asked, "Does GroupM receive rebates in North America?"

He waited seconds to answer before stating flatly, "Zero rebates in North America." There followed another long pause, before he continued: "We've been very clear. We are not an agency."

If they were not an agent of the client, he was asked, were they a partner?

"I wish we were a partner. Ad agencies when they were formed acted like the seller's agent, not the buyer's agent. Look at who paid the commission. It was the seller. Somehow it evolved into a relationship where there was an assumed fiduciary responsibility to the client. However, contractual terms that have come into common practice, particularly over the last dozen years or so, are the kinds of terms that can't be reconciled with an agent-type relationship. I will give you three examples: An agent can't be held to deliver specific costs per thousands. Clients often ask us to provide guarantees and to put our fees at risk. It's become common practice." Second: "Agents don't offer extended payment terms"—meaning they will not get paid for months—"which are now routinely demanded by clients. We're not a bank." Third: "Agents aren't asked to indemnify clients for IP violations on technology. We're not an insurance company." Feeling pressured by clients to reduce their fees, and pressured by their holding companies to produce profit margins approaching 20 percent, and increasingly vexed by insecure relationships with clients, agencies don't feel as if they have signed a marriage vow.

This is one big takeaway from the ANA report: agency and client often don't share a common definition of their role, and thus mistrust arises. When agencies aggressively seek new ways to generate income, like employing their own funds to gamble on buying ad time and later selling it at a higher rate, they think they are serving their fiduciary responsibility to shareholders; clients think of them as unfaithful. Clients say agencies are taking rebates that deprive them of money; holding companies say they are taking risks with their own money and being rewarded for it. The drive by holding companies to tap new revenue streams serves as evidence to clients that the agency has mistresses. When Dave Morgan of Simulmedia looks at how agencies, backed by the 4A's, insist that in the new world they must be allowed "to trade on their own behalf" and maintain "undisclosable deals with media suppliers," he concludes that this translates to rebates: "It's pretty clear that the parsing of language became a big issue in the allegations and denials of rebate activities in North America. Not unlike, 'I didn't inhale.'"

After reading the report, Rishad Tobaccowala of Publicis came away with two opposite conclusions. Agencies are at fault, he says: "There's a lot of truth in that report. We're trying to sell all the time.

We don't listen enough to our clients. We have to help our clients prosper. Yet the ANA report is the biggest mass suicide of CMOs. The ANA hired the hit man who in hitting the agencies also hit them by making them look like they did not understand the space or how to steward the money. The report helps give power to the CFOs and procurement officers, which spreads more distrust between client and agency."

By mid-2017, there was scant evidence that as a result of the report clients had reduced their ad spending with agencies, or whisked their business from the large holding companies to flee to smaller, independent agencies. Agency executives, in effect, boasted: *Look, there have been no indictments or charges filed against any of us.* However, what is clear is that the ANA report has had a poisonous impact on the trust client and agency require to partner. Clients are wary, often maintaining more of an arms-length relationship with their agencies. And many agency executives are dispirited. "We've been assaulted in the trade publications as crooks, with no letup," says a senior agency official who does not want to be named. "By the way, your family reads this stuff too."

There was one other clear outcome: Once again, the report meant more business for Michael Kassan and MediaLink.

15.

CANNES TAKES CENTER STAGE

"MediaLink is the embodiment of one zealous man's unwillingness to say no. Michael built a giant dating service between circles that don't know how to talk to one another. . . . He connected all these pieces. He has a rare ability to create a prom that everyone wants to be at."

—Digitas CEO Tony Weisman

As his car inched along in clotted Cannes traffic, Michael Kassan's four smartphones vibrated relentlessly, a flurry of calls and e-mails pleading for a few extra invites to his annual dinner at the world's foremost advertising conference, the Cannes Lions Festival. Already he had approved four hundred media and marketing executive invitations to the exclusive June 2016 event he and MediaLink host at the Hotel du Cap, and some five hundred more people were clamoring to squeeze in. He had carefully added attendees to the $400,000 dinner from the cream of his media and platform client list, including NBCUniversal, Microsoft, the *New York Times*, the Walt Disney Company, 21st Century Fox, Facebook, Google, Twitter, Condé Nast, Hearst, Dow Jones, the *New York Post*, the *Washington*

Post, Gannett, iHeartMedia, Viacom, Turner Broadcasting, Bloomberg, Flipboard, and Vox Media. He had included the holding company executives who often have a love/hate relationship with Kassan, wanting his favor yet fearing he might whisper to his brand clients they should move to a new agency. Brand clients like Unilever, AT&T, Verizon, L'Oréal, Bank of America, Colgate, and American Express were, of course, also invited.

No other gathering during June's weeklong festival—not those hosted by Facebook or Google with libations on the beach, or WPP's afternoon buffet and Stream conference on the adjacent island of Ile Saint-Honorat, or even a luncheon invite from Rupert Murdoch—is more coveted.

As usual, in Cannes MediaLink was performing a role that was a cross between curator and concierge. It dispatched a total of forty-five staffers to service ninety-one attending clients and participate in over seven hundred matchmaker meetings over the course of the week, not counting the onstage speeches and panels MediaLink arranged for clients. Each staffer organized about six meetings per client. Scott Goodman, the MediaLink vice president in charge of coordinating staff assignments, said most media clients first requested meetings with prospective advertisers, and then with agencies. "The event itself is the easy part," Goodman said. "Even if you're the best wedding planner, the wedding itself is easy." What's hard are the months of planning.

Michael Kassan's ready smile camouflaged the stress he felt in Cannes. "Just imagine," he said as the chauffeured car headed to a dinner, "for five days at the end of June in a four-block radius on the Côte d'Azur, 100 percent of my revenue is there. Virtually every client is represented there. Here's the *Wall Street Journal*. Am I going to turn down Dow Jones? I'm going to say, 'You can have four dinner invites. You can't have seven.'"

An e-mail beeps from Revlon owner Ron Perelman asking to bring all the guests on his yacht. No, Kassan dictates to his chief of stuff, Martin Rothman, seated in the front seat.

Beep: An e-mail from a CEO at one of the companies that reports to his friend Bob Pittman's iHeartMedia, the powerful radio station owner who provides the dinner's entertainment. Pittman induced Chris Martin of Coldplay to perform this year, as he induced Sting in 2015, Mariah Carey in 2014, and Elton John in 2013. The iHeart executive asks for an additional five dinner invites. Kassan has a sly solution: "This is like when my son got married to the daughter of our best friends and we were making the wedding list and someone was friends with both sides. I said, 'This is on your fucking list!' Am I going to be the guy who tells him no? I'm going to have Bob tell him no." His chief of stuff makes a note.

In Cannes, too, Kassan is a celebrity. He gets the choice Hollywood star–named suites—Sean Connery, Sophia Loren, Cary Grant (renamed the Liu Ye suite)—at the festival's ground zero, the Carlton Hotel. He knows the names and embraces most folks who say hello or seek a private word. He slips from one meeting or panel to another, rarely staying long but always able to boast that he was there. Maître d's bow as he calls out their first names, no doubt remembering the many times he has generously schmeared them. After hosting a cocktail party Tuesday night, Kassan turned to his chief of stuff and asked Martin Rothman to book a table at the Le Maschou restaurant. Athough a long line in front of the restaurant snaked a good distance down the cobblestone hill, Kassan was immediately escorted to Le Maschou's exclusive outpost directly across the narrow street, where his party of three dined alone in a space that could accommodate maybe ten.

Tony Weisman, then the CEO of Digitas, which retains MediaLink to arrange meetings, speeches, and panels at industry events like Cannes, marvels at a feat Kassan pulled off here. Viacom was a client, and its CEO, Philippe Dauman, was on the cusp of getting fired, his cable ratings plummeting, his pay climbing to $54 million in 2015 as his stock dropped like a rock. Dauman would host a dinner Thursday, and he tasked Kassan with producing an A-list of guests. "I would love to know what Philippe Dauman pays Michael to get the four holding company CEOs to attend his dinner," Weisman said. One lure to attend was the reality-TV equivalent of watching how Dauman handled his pending corporate death.

Weisman salutes Kassan and MediaLink: "They do not have a competitor. MediaLink is the embodiment of one zealous man's unwillingness to say no. Michael built a giant dating service between circles that don't know how to talk to one another." Brand clients like Unilever and AT&T, which in the past did not have to think about new ad tech or digital companies like Facebook, and publishers like Condé Nast or Hearst, which "didn't have to worry about knowing the brands" because the brands sought their platforms, were suddenly at sea. "He connected all these pieces. He has a rare ability to create a prom that everyone wants to be at."

■ ■ ■

The Lions festival was launched in Venice in 1954, alternating between several cities, including Cannes, before making Cannes its official home in 1984. Initially, it was naturally dominated by the creative agencies. Philip Thomas, who was the CEO of the Cannes Lions before being promoted to CEO of Ascential Events by its corporate parent in 2017, remembers that in 2003 Jim Stengel, then CMO of Procter & Gamble, was the first client to make a point of attending, and this represented "a big, big shift. That attracted more of the media agencies." Today, Thomas says, clients comprise one quarter of all attendees. Next came the digital companies, then the media and publishing platforms, and most recently, the consulting and software companies. A breakthrough in getting celebrities to attend and bulking the press contingent up to six hundred, he says, was the arrival in 2014 of Kim Kardashian. "The *Mail Online* were very, very clever. They took a yacht at our festival" and invited her. It was the same year that the festival invited her husband, Kanye West, to appear. The *Mail* "got blanket coverage," providing an incentive for celebrities to flock to the festival. Hoping for buzz, more companies hired yachts or gave opulent beach parties and invited celebrities.

Some old-timers, like Bob Greenberg of R/GA, are devoted to Cannes. R/GA brings thirty executives. "I go and I come back and I can see patterns," he says, whether it is glimpsing the disruptive power of WeChat in China or digesting the creative work of competitors. Not all of his creative colleagues are as enamored. Jeff Goodby, who was anointed president of the Festival in 2002 and head of the prestigious Titanium jury in 2006, is troubled by what he sees as a diminution of attention for creative advertising. "It's about making money. It changes everything," he says. It changes the festival, he has written, into "a plumbers' or industrial roofing convention, after which I go home and begin to explain to a friend that there is an amazing new fiberglass insulation technology."*

The Cannes festival is owned by Ascential Holdings, a company based in the UK that organizes festivals and exhibitions, and provides economic information and analysis for clients around the world. The Lions festival is a lucrative business. Each of the fifteen thousand delegates who attended paid as much as 3,750 euros (approximately $4,400)† for the full eight days with "line-skipping privileges," or a somewhat lesser amount for fewer days and perks, down to 895 euros "for students and professionals under thirty." Each agency from the 110 countries that attends and submits creative entries in one of the

---

* Jeff Goodby, op-ed, *The Wall Street Journal*, June 24, 2015.
† The value of the euro was about 10 percent more than the dollar.

twenty-four Lions awards categories pays an average of 500 euros for most entries, rising to 1,399 euros for the most prestigious prize, the Titanium Lions. In 2016, there were 43,101 submissions and 1,360 Lions awards presented. If only four awards were given in each of the twenty-four categories (Grand Prix, Gold, Silver, and Bronze), the total number of winners would only be ninety-six. Cannes inflated the number of winners by giving multiple prizes for each category.

A third Lions source of revenue comes from its four hundred event sponsors, who Thomas says, pay from $20,000 to $700,000. This includes the cost to Samsung of its virtual reality exhibit, and the total of $300,000 for MediaLink's sponsorship, and two large LED electronic screens on the lawn outside the Carlton Hotel, which clients like the *New York Times* and the *Washington Post* subsidize to carry their news flashes and promos. Other revenues sprout from its archive of speeches and talks and ad campaigns presented at the festival or at its three regional festivals. (For 18,000 euros, 20 employees in a company get digital access for one year to 270,000 ad campaigns and 450 hours of talks.) Yachts receive a parking spot in the harbor plus five festival passes for $22,715. In all, the 2016 festival hauled in $62.5 million for Ascential.

Attendance is pricey, and not just because a Black Angus chateaubriand in the Hôtel Martinez costs $161 and Delta raised its round-trip first-class nonstop New York to Nice flight from $5,332 to $12,069. In addition to the attendance fee, MediaLink pays for its forty-five staffers' airfare, hotels, and food, plus the Hotel du Cap dinner they host, plus the separate Kassan-hosted Boys Night Out sponsored and mostly paid for this year by Hulu, and the Millard-hosted Girls Night Out party cohosted by Facebook and iHeartMedia. The cost to holding companies like WPP and Publicis works out to about $20,000 per employee. WPP had a thousand employees attend in 2016.

The awards are especially prized. "Awards fulfill a function in our industry," Philip Thomas says. Since choosing winners is subjective, "the only way to prove you're creative is the external acknowledgment of an award." Bob Greenberg's loftlike R/GA offices at Tenth Avenue and West Thirty-third Street contains a shrine of six walls of trophies and plaques, including the thirty-three Lions R/GA won last year, when he was also awarded the coveted Lion of St. Mark lifetime achievement award. Greenberg extols the awards: "By winning awards you are proving to clients you are good. It's not that different from the movie business. The attraction for me of the rewards is to attract and retain talent."

Amir Kassaei, the chief creative officer at DDB Worldwide, disagrees. Although Kassaei says his agency had won more Grand Prix Lions at Cannes than any agency, nevertheless he wrote in a 2016 newsletter that winning awards took too much time and money and did not prove the effectiveness of the advertising. He pledged that DDB would vie for fewer awards. Why? "Because we believe that winning awards only means that you are good at winning awards. Because we care more about selling our clients than ourselves. Because we care more about emptying our clients' shelves than filling our own with trophies."* (Kassaie's words are not matched by his agency's boasts. If one clicks on the DDB Web site, it touts the hundreds of creative awards won, including almost a hundred Cannes Lions.)

Strolling along the Croisette across from the Carlton on the way to the Palais, which houses multiple theaters where awards are presented most nights and where a crowded program of daytime speeches and panels occur and ad campaigns are displayed, one passes what Jeff Goodby has described as a strip mall of vendors. The festival calls this part of the Croisette, which overlooks the beach, Cabana Town. Along the way one strolls past the buildings containing the IBM, Oracle, Adobe, Accenture, PricewaterhouseCoopers, McKinsey, and Deloitte

---

* Amir Kassaei, *Campaign US* newsletter, January 13, 2016.

cabanas, among others; on the sand below are the private beach spaces—Facebook Beach and Google Beach and YouTube Beach, each featuring exhibits and talks and free-flowing rosé.

Walking past these consulting and tech company cabanas in Cannes is a reminder, if any is needed, that space at the marketing table is getting crowded. These companies have gobbled up ad and marketing agencies. In the two years before Cannes, IBM absorbed thirty-one marketing companies; Accenture bought forty; and Deloitte twenty-six.* *Advertising Age* has reported that eight of the top ten ad agencies are not traditional ad agencies but consulting and tech companies.

▓ ▓ ▓

Looking back at Cannes is also a reminder of another marketing change. No, not Unilever's Keith Weed's chartreuse sports jacket, one of two gaudy green jackets he brings to Cannes every year. With the jackets and his thick head of blondish hair that flops over his forehead, he could pass for an aging British rocker. Weed's Wednesday keynote to an audience packed into the vast Grand Théâtre Lumière was billed as "The Future of Brands." He made the case that to successfully engage with consumers in the future brands must convey that they are "a purpose-driven business." Weed and an increasing number of brand managers believe this is what younger generations expect. The way to win their trust is to demonstrate a social purpose. He displayed a number of film clips and Unilever commercials warning of climate dangers like deforestation, spoke of how their Ben & Jerry's brand promoted gay marriage, and showed a clip from a film Unilever made for a conference of world leaders that ended with their CEO, Paul Polman, declaring, "Help us by adding your voice in the battle for climate change."

Weed has more power than most CMOs, for not only is Unilever

---

* These numbers are from an internal Publicis Groupe report.

the world's second largest advertiser, but his reach in the company extends from marketing to communications to the company's sustainability efforts. He cited a survey Unilever did of a thousand ads, half of which "portray women in a stereotypical way," and of how his Dove brand has long created campaigns to lift "girls' self-esteem." He announced "#unstereotype," a global effort its four hundred brands would undertake to erode female stereotypes. He concluded by asking, "Do people buy products because they are more socially and environmentally safe?" They did, he said, because "more progressive advertising" produces stronger consumer engagement. He cited a Unilever global survey comparing nonsocial ads in 2014 with social ads for the same brand in 2015. Products with social message ads grew 30 percent faster, he said. "I think you could argue in the last few years with all that's going on with technology, that consumers have been ahead of marketing. Now marketing must be ahead of consumers. We can build our brands in whole new ways. This is the future of the brand."

Close your eyes and listen to Keith Weed and you hear Al Gore with a British accent. "We sold our salami brand because it was a product that would never have a positive story," he said one day in his London office. He spoke of making "marketing noble again." When he assumed his current position and latched on to the sustainability issue, he said colleagues resisted, asking, "What does sustainability mean?" What it means, he said, is: "We need to produce as much food in the next forty years as we produced in the last eight thousand years to feed everyone. We can do it by managing waste. If we continue to live like Europeans, we will need to produce enough food for three planets—and five planets if we live like the U.S. By 2050, there will be as much plastic in the sea as fish." He is appalled that, globally, 2.5 billion people have no access to a toilet.

"This motivates me. I tell my marketers they are coming to work to do good." But don't be fooled: Keith Weed is a businessman, not a do-gooder. "We tell our marketers, 'We are going to teach the world to wash their hands better. And if we do that, we'll sell more soap.' If we get people to brush their teeth twice a day, it would have a major impact on cavities and their health. And it would sell more toothpaste and toothbrushes."

What Keith Weed is promoting is not new to marketing. In a week-long class he volunteers to teach at the festival for about thirty young marketers from around the world, Jim Stengel shared his Pampers story. The young marketers listened raptly as Stengel told of when he was assigned to become brand manager for Pampers diapers in Germany in the 1990s. His mission was to reform what was a dominant but money-losing brand. Pampers simply sold itself as a product that would keep babies dry. "We had no empathy. And we had no purpose." A winning strategy "was right in front of us: Parents are obsessed with their babies' healthy development. And they crave information about their stages. Is my baby keeping up? Are they growing? Are they developing mentally? Sociologically? Psychologically? Pampers were in every hospital but they had no purpose." He hired people passionate about babies. He made sure that in every marketing campaign Pampers became an advocate for parents. He partnered with UNICEF "to help babies with the greatest need, especially with tetanus, which could be prevented." Pampers expanded, he said, from a $2.5 billion to a $10.5 billion business, with 20 percent profit margins. And soon Stengel was elevated to CMO of P&G.

※ ※ ※

When Cannes ended, there was no shortage of complaints. To some, Cannes reeks of Fort Lauderdale during college spring break, with late-night, loud crowds swilling drinks on the beach and spilling onto hotel and restaurant sidewalks. "I think Cannes is a fucking joke," one senior media agency executive who attends regularly said. "I don't know why it exists, other than to indulge a group of creatives who treat it like a frat party." It bothers this executive to see "people out cold on the beach from the night before." Irwin Gotlieb is upset that the Lions is a for-profit organization, unlike the Oscars, the Tonys, or the Emmys. "It may be a useful networking opportunity; after all, everyone attends. But I am deeply troubled . . ." He believes the almost nightly award ceremonies, the steep cost of applying for an award, and the large number granted cheapens the awards. "As an industry we deserve better."

Martin Sorrell complained that Cannes has "become a tech fair. It's a bit like a Bar Mitzvah party. Who can throw the biggest party!" Sorrell's foremost complaint is simply the cost. "It is too expensive." He said he was reviewing whether to attend again. Sorrell said this in the fall of 2016, prompting Michael Kassan to observe: "Martin is negotiating with them from a distance. He can't live without Cannes. The clients are all there, and they're not going to stop coming because he stops coming." It is fairly typical of Sorrell to place a public marker down as a negotiating ploy. After the 2009 Cannes festival, Sorrell publicly groused that to enter the awards was too costly, yet he returned each year. And when he hired new worldwide creative director, John O'Keefe, in 2009, Sorrell told him he was tired of coming in second to Omnicom or Publicis in the awards competition.

There is another takeaway from Cannes. Marketing may have great impact, but few of its denizens are celebrities. There are no paparazzi chasing them across the Croisette. Those who come to Cannes don't just come for the awards and the relationships. They also come out of insecurity. To be seen. To build relationships. To seek new business. To stroke clients. To size up frenemies. To escape and party and bask in the security that comes from the company of other members of what they fear is a dwindling tribe. As influencers often replace celebrities in selling their products, they know their business is losing glamour.

They know relationships don't matter as much as they once did. They are uncertain whether "the big creative idea"—the artist—matters more than the scientist and their targeting data. A Lions trophy offers a craved testimonial. So does a helping hand from Michael Kassan.

But the Cannes festival has many more champions than carpers. Keith Weed is a believer. "What I value is creativity, and anything that puts that front and center is fine by me. And that's why Cannes matters. Creativity is increasingly important to break through the clutter in a fragmenting media world. In addition, it's a highly efficient way to get the industry together." The founder and CEO of Flipboard, Scott McCue, said he was "thrilled" with the public platform and meetings with advertisers and agencies MediaLink arranged for him in Cannes. Michael Kassan was also pleased. At a MediaLink Monday staff meeting meant to look back at Cannes 2016, he said the meetings, speeches, and panels they arranged for clients, the dinners, the well-attended hospitality suite at the Carlton that welcomes visitors at cocktail hour, the MediaLink LED screens flashing client messages to most everyone walking to the Palais, left him to enthusiastically conclude that MediaLink's sway was undeniable: "For some reason, we crossed the river this year."

What Kassan did not share with his staff or clients was that such successes made MediaLink an attractive acquisition target. After a late Sunday dinner he hosted at Le Bacon restaurant in Cap d'Antibes for a couple of dozen guests, including magician David Copperfield and investment banker Aryeh Bourkoff of LionTree, he slipped off to secretly huddle with Bourkoff. After leaving JPMorgan Chase in 2012, Bourkoff founded a boutique investment bank that by 2015 ranked among the top 20 merger and acquisition deal makers in the United States. His foremost client was Liberty Media's John Malone, and recently he had orchestrated Charter Communication's acquisition of Time Warner Cable and Verizon's purchase of AOL. After years of nervously looking in his rearview mirror, of anxiety that his past brush with the law would publicly humiliate him and stain MediaLink, Michael Kassan was ready to expand internationally. In doing his due diligence, Bourkoff had come up with a menu of companies that might want to acquire MediaLink. They included agency holding companies, especially Kassan's friend Maurice Levy's Publicis, plus the consulting companies rushing to enter marketing, businesses like Ascential, plus hedge funds.

For a buyer, one condition of any sale was that Kassan would remain at the helm of MediaLink, which was also his wish. But three questions haunted their deliberations. Was MediaLink a company that could thrive when the sixty-five-year-old Michael Kassan retired? When the potential parent company kicked MediaLink's tires, would they think it was a real business or just the concoction of a charming connector? And would a bidder be scared away when their due diligence uncovered Michael Kassan's past skirmish with the law?

16.

MAD MEN TO MATH MEN

"The business of trying to measure everything in precise terms is one of the problems with advertising today. This leads to a worship of research. We're all concerned about the facts we get and not about how provocative we can make those facts to the consumer."

—Bill Bernbach, 1964*

Michael Kassan has a short, simple handle for how advertising and marketing has evolved over the years. "It used to be Mad Men. Then it became Media Men. Now it's Math Men," he says. "There's a mash-up that has occurred. The Mad Men, which was the creative agency, and the Media Men, which was the media agency, and the Math Men, which is the data and technology person, is now one person. And that's what clients want."

The industry has come to rely on the tools of Math Men—machines,

---

* Bill Bernbach, quoted in Andrew Cracknell, *The Real Mad Men: The Renegades of Madison Avenue and the Golden Age of Advertising* (Philadelphia: Running Press, 2011).

algorithms, puréed data, artificial intelligence—and on the skills of engineers. Among the many speakers and presentations at the Tech-Crunch confab in Brooklyn in May 2016, few were greeted with the same wide-eyed enthusiasm as Dag Kittlaus, who founded Siri in 2007, sold it to Apple in 2010, and left to cofound and serve as CEO of Viv, a next generation AI personal assistant. Standing before an audience of more than a thousand, he said Viv's AI software builds itself rather than just relying on data, and he said Viv was scheduled to be available commercially in 2017. He demonstrated a series of complex tasks he said the voice-activated personal assistant would answer in ten milliseconds.

He asked Viv: "Will it be warmer than seventy degrees at the Golden Gate Bridge the day after tomorrow?" The affirmative answer came back instantly.

"Send Adam twenty dollars for drinks last night." Done.

"Send my mom some flowers for her birthday."

"What kind?" the digital assistant asked.

"Tulips."

When Martin Sorrell repeatedly warned in early 2017 that Amazon was "the elephant in the room," the foremost threat to the advertising and marketing industry, he voiced this fear partly because he worried about its digital assistant, Alexa, and the data Amazon amassed. He worried it could make WPP an extraneous middleman. Why should a client consult with WPP when Amazon has evidence about what marketing messages generate sales? And by late 2017 it seemed clear that ever-secretive Amazon planned to capitalize on its rich data and ubiquity to begin selling ads to help subsidize the expensive television programs and movies it acquired and perhaps, *Ad Age* reported, to offer "a free, ad-supported complement to its Prime Streaming service." Amazon was expected to offer something Les Moonves and his fellow broadcasters could not. Quoting an executive familiar with the plans, *Ad Age* reported: "Amazon is talking about giving content creators their own channels and sharing ad revenue in exchange for a set number of hours of content each week."* In addition, Rishad Tobaccowala warned, "Amazon can damage us by hurting our clients' business by dictating terms," or producing competing Amazon products at a lower price. Amazon, like Facebook and Google, has another asset agencies lack: for clients anxious about tomorrow, they offer reassurance. "They can tell the client, 'We can take you to the future.'"

Fortified by more data and software-enabled smartphones, Tim Armstrong of AOL and his corporate parent, Verizon, aspire to become a digital rival. They have invested heavily in programmatic advertising, hoping to use machines to deliver individualized marketing messages: the software massages the data, targets the desired audience for the advertiser, and the machine automates data-driven decisions. "Technology," Kassan observes, "allows for a more direct relationship between a buyer and a seller, with less need for intermediaries," meaning agencies. Today, advertisers pay premium prices for ads on Thursday nights, the eve of the weekend, when viewers are prepared to make weekend movie and shopping decisions. But, Kassan continues, the programmatic machine turns the world upside down. "You're not watching *Friends* or *Seinfeld* on Thursday nights anymore. You may be watching them on Tuesday morning. Or on an airplane." Because of data, you can know that members of your target audience "watch soap operas at two o'clock, therefore it's going to be cheaper to reach you than on Thursday night. The sellers would like you to think the only way to reach premium viewers is with premium programming." The networks fear, understandably, he says, that if "you can reach that same person

---

* Garett Sloane, "Amazon's Prime Ad Play," *Ad Age*, November 13, 2017.

on reruns of *The Dukes of Hazzard*," paying a two-dollar CPM versus a five-dollar CPM, then their revenues will take a hit. They benefit from "the mystery," just as more information tips the leverage in the negotiation from the seller to the buyer.

Because of network resistance, and because they are not digitized, programmatic advertising has not yet made a big dent in network sales. But it has already begun to make a dent in digital sales. According to a joint study by the ANA and several organizations, of the $178 billion spent globally on digital ads in 2016, $19 billion was done programmatically; in the United States, programmatic sales accounted for $10 billion of the approximately $70 billion spent on digital ads. But GroupM's Rob Norman says that since "Facebook and Google's ads are machine driven," they should be included under programmatic. Since machine buying is thought to be as inevitable as algorithmic computer trading on Wall Street, agencies and Google and Facebook and a variety of companies, including an estimated one quarter of major brands, vie to build their own programmatic machines.

Martin Sorrell has aggressively sought to expand WPP's programmatic efforts, combining several companies it acquired into Xaxis and placing it under Irwin Gotlieb's GroupM. "It is the fastest growing asset of WPP," Xaxis chairman David Moore says. Programmatic machines transform the way ads are targeted and bought. Humans are no match for what the machine can do. Five steps are involved in serving up machine ads, Brian Lesser, then the global CEO of Xaxis before becoming the North American CEO of GroupM, says: "First, I need to recognize you, or some anonymous version of you. Second, I need to understand what I know about you. Third, I need to match that to an advertiser that's trying to reach you. Fourth, I need to value [price] that. And fifth, I need the systems to be able to get you the right ad within two hundred milliseconds." Agencies have to change, he says, and will have to recruit more "software developers and data scientists and analysts. . . . Tech people are going to take over."

Like colleagues at other agencies, Xaxis executives obsess about Facebook. On any given day, a Xaxis vice president confides, they see 130 billion Internet pages that carry an ad. Facebook and Google see trillions. With its walled garden, he says Facebook tries to "curtail people from understanding what's happening in their environments. If you look at what Facebook is doing, they're making it impossible for anybody but themselves to understand what's happening in their environment . . . The reason we like having an open ecosphere is we get to be the people who grade other people's homework and insure that the brands' money is being spent in the most effective manner. That's kind of our job as an agency." But Facebook does not share the granular information clients get from other platforms, he says.

Since Facebook was not transparent, in 2016 anxiety and mistrust escalated. Complaints were lodged against digital platforms for charging advertisers for ads that tricked other machines to believe an ad message was seen by humans when it was not, or the algorithms placed many friendly ads on unfriendly platforms. "What hasn't been reported on," 21st Century Fox CEO James Murdoch said over breakfast in January 2016, "is how much fraud there is in the industry. It has famously been said of advertising, 'I know I'm wasting half my money, but I don't know which half.' Digital advertising was supposed to solve that. But, actually, questions of viewability, questions of bots, of creating false impressions, the leakage—the amount of fraud is staggering." A report written two years earlier by Pivotal Research Group analyst Brian Wieser warned: "Perpetrators of fraud and sellers of wasteful inventory in general become increasingly clever as they look for new ways to produce the appearance of traffic. . . . This is all the greater an issue as programmatic buying of media takes root," and buyers increasingly focus on "less expensive long-tail inventory," not premium platforms. By the end of 2016, one study said ad fraud cost advertisers $12.5 billion.*

※ ※ ※

Programmatic advertising's ability to organize and crunch data and target individuals in two tenths of a second relies—as do digital assistants like Alexa or Viv—on AI, also known as machine learning. Since AI first gained serious attention in the 1950s, a debate has raged: Is AI really intelligence or is it a machine programmed to memorize data? And are AI robots potentially uncontrollable Frankenstein monsters? There is real fear about how to sell the advantages of AI without scaring people with such images.

This was a key subject at another General Electric monthly marketing meeting at their Madison Avenue offices in late 2016. Opening a discussion about their marketing strategy for the coming year, CMO Linda Boff said to the half dozen agency representatives gathered around a large table, "The value of a digital company is much higher than an industrial company." GE needed a defining message and a market. "Amazon and Facebook did that. When we think of our story, what makes us different than IBM? They've done well selling artificial intelligence and Watson. But AI is kind of creepy. What do we do to make GE more efficient that is not creepy?"

"We want to harness machines, not let machines harness us," chimed her deputy, Andy Goldberg.

"How do we talk about that?" Boff asked. "Do we in 2017 take six cases and every month tell a different story?"

"This is the focus," Goldberg said, drilling down. "One thing we

---

* Ad Fraud Report by The&Partnership's media agency, m/SIX and Adloox, March 2017.

all need in storytelling is the human element. Our humor is important. We're human." We're not machines.

"We need fresh ways to tell the GE story of moving from an industrial to a digital company," Boff said. How "do we tell stories of outcomes in human terms?"

"As Linda often says, 'We need people to fall in love with us,'" Goldberg said.

"One advantage we have," said one of several representatives from the Giant Spoon agency, "is that we can tell stories from factory floors, and IBM can't."

They would not reach a consensus in this meeting. Boff ended the discussion by asking the six agency reps to come up with ideas to humanize AI and GE. They would reconvene for an all-day meeting she would schedule.

At a minimum, there is an AI consensus, as one of Microsoft's Distinguished Engineers, James Whittaker, has written: AI relies on three things, "It is, first, a vast amount of data which is, second, organized so well a computer can understand its structure and relevance and then, third, crunched at blazingly fast speeds. The reason that progress in AI has seemed so pronounced in the past few years is that technological advances in all three areas have accelerated."* The race to dominate AI reveals companies with deep pockets—Google, Facebook, Amazon, IBM, Oracle, Apple, Salesforce.com, among others—vying to hire engineers and data scientists.

"The bulk of Fox advertising will be sold by machines," predicts James Murdoch, who goes on to say this will threaten the existence of the advertising holding companies. "The bulk of their business, the buying of media and the analysis of how to generate reach at a low incremental cost, it's hard to see what their role is twenty years from

---

* James Whittaker, "Rise of the Machines," Medium.com, June 24, 2015.

now. Once you have an investment in machines, it's just a math problem." Brian Lesser agrees that machines will perform functions many of GroupM employees now perform, but he believes those machines will be employed by GroupM.

■ ■ ■

Whittaker has argued that traditional advertising will become less relevant because when data is assembled the machines will "determine someone's intent, not their interest," as a search merely does. Airbnb's CMO Jonathan Mildenhall thinks agencies will be further disrupted because AI will allow "customization." He then offers a sweeping generalization that marginalizes human creativity: As the "algorithms anticipate profiles of individuals, brands can engineer without the need for human creativity." The machines will craft the ads. Few question that as advertisers know more about individuals and their actual desires, precise marketing messages can be pushed to them. The pushed messages from Viv's personal assistant could disrupt advertising, Dag Kittlaus said after his TechCrunch presentation. "Priceline is the largest travel company in the world," he explained. "They spend over one billion dollars a year on Google's AdWords. But imagine if we have tools for Priceline to build a transformative travel agent. Imagine that you say, 'I want to take my kids away in the third week of March. Find a place in the Caribbean to take my kids. Your personal assistant looks at your last five trips so it has a general idea of the budget parameters. It knows what the weather's going to be there." The personal assistant works it out with Priceline. Instead of expensive ads, Priceline would pay a fee to Viv only when a sale is registered. Thus Kittlaus believes: "People will migrate away from what I call the discovery economy on the Internet to a consumption economy."

In this consumption economy, plays or restaurants or car services would also pay a service fee for Viv-referred business. Imagine, he said, that you arranged a date on Match.com. Your digital assistant knows you and your date both like the theater, and asks, "Would you like me to get tickets to this show? Would you like me to have a car pick you up? Make a reservation at this restaurant?" Of course, if Viv only recommended the restaurants or vendors who paid them the steepest fees or who were owned by a corporate parent, it might lose the confidence of consumers. Or run afoul of government regulators, as has happened to Google and Facebook in Europe.

Viv threatened to be a classic start-up in a garage menace to Google, Facebook, Amazon, and Watson, but to succeed Kittlaus knew he needed scale. He needed a large, existing base of mobile phones as a partner in order to have Viv installed on millions of smartphones. In the fall of 2016, Viv was acquired by Samsung. But when Samsung introduced its new Galaxy smartphone in 2017, the Viv digital assistant was not included.

Andrew Robertson, CEO of BBDO, and a *Mad Men* look-alike in a grey pin-striped suit, white suspenders, and polka-dot tie, disagrees that machines will cripple creative agencies. Nor does he believe the desire for creative ads will disappear. He agrees that machines will target individuals with precision, altering the traditional way agencies operate and threatening agencies that fail to change. He agrees that traditional ad formats have to change. But he disagrees that machines can create compelling ads. Because there are so many more platforms on which ads appear, "the need for creativity goes up every single day because you are seeing more ads than you ever saw before." And with video becoming the principal way for advertisers to reach consumers on mobile devices, and with just the first two to three seconds of that video to win the consumers attention, he concludes, "Creativity becomes more important. So Math Men and Mad Men are joined."

The other potentially disruptive technology is what's come to be called the Internet of things, or IoT, "smart devices" with Bluetooth connections—refrigerators, light bulbs, watches, thermostats, washing machines, coffeepots, cars, baby pacifiers, and so on. In 2016, Gartner, Inc., a technology research firm, estimated that there were 6.4 billion connected "things," and this number would jump to 20.8 billion in four years. These smart devices will yield a cornucopia of data. Devices monitor and can alert your store when the milk or ketchup in your refrigerator needs replenishment, when your washing machine needs more soap, when a device on top of your TV monitoring your facial expressions communicates whether you watch a commercial. There are, of course, a plethora of unanswered questions: Will these devices be welcoming to marketing messages? Why can't simple marketing messages—your light bulb will soon expire—be crafted by AI without input from an agency? Will devices that give brands a direct relationship with consumers reduce ad spending because, for instance, Heinz ketchup is in touch with your refrigerator? Will another device, virtual reality glasses, be conducive to native or product placement ads as you're transported to a U2 performance or the surface of Mars? With devices in homes connected to marketers, will consumers recoil, feeling spied upon?

What is unassailable is that the combination of rich data and technology fundamentally transforms marketing. Some of the guessing as to who saw a marketing message and whether they needed or wanted a product dwindles. Ads sprayed to demographic groups can be aimed at individuals. With online sales, geography becomes less important. And with customers having more information about merchandise, coupled with a growing unwillingness to be interrupted by ad pitches, many products will become commodities. This will lead, inevitably, to brands seeking to develop direct consumer relationships, as when Bevel, a grooming product for men of color, inaugurated Bevel Code, a site providing information and a community for its customers. Agencies, Rishad Tobaccowala says, "have to increasingly think less about advertising and more about how to deliver utilities and services." He cited Walgreens' enticing app, hailing it as "the best form of utilities and services in the United States." Every time he enters a Walgreens he gets points, which he need not record because they are automatically added to his app. He receives alerts that his prescriptions are ready, and he gets five hundred Balance Rewards points for every refill. He can send photos for Walgreens to print. It offers ways to save money. "This is a utility and a service. We have to stop just creating ads and start creating experiences." By creating experiences, Tobaccowala predicts clients will shift and "spend more on marketing than on advertising," thus increasing the spending disparity that exists today.

■ ■ ■

Central to this shift is technology, which has an underside, as Facebook has painfully learned. On the eve of Advertising Week in September 2016, it was revealed that the Math Men at Facebook overestimated the average time viewers spent watching video by up to 80 percent. The mistake was made because for two years their engineers only counted videos that were watched for three or more seconds, when large numbers of viewers only watch for a second or two. Facebook did its measurement based on two numbers: the number who viewed the video for more than three seconds, and the average time spent on the video. The math mistake was that Facebook calculated the average time spent by totaling all the video watch time, including those who watched for less than three seconds. In arriving at the average time watched, Facebook divided by the number of those who watched more than three seconds, inflating the average view time. When this surfaced, client and agency confidence was shaken. This proved, Martin Sorrell and Keith Weed independently said, the need for Facebook to open its walled garden and allow an independent measurement of its results. Bob Liodice chimed his agreement.

Days later, at an Advertising Week panel, Carolyn Everson addressed their "video metric error," and said that while it understandably shook advertiser confidence, it did not cost advertisers a single dollar extra or impact their return on investment measurement, a conclusion seemingly shared by most of the advertising community. She said the mistake was "a lesson learned." The lesson? They should have made the disclosure when they learned of the mistake a month earlier, she said. She also said Facebook does believe in "third-party verification" of its data, a claim hotly disputed by the ad community.

Unfortunately for the otherwise popular Everson, Facebook would punch itself in the nose again just two months later. An internal audit, the company disclosed, revealed that Facebook miscounted views on four of its products, including time spent with publications on its Instant Articles program. Facebook's machines inadvertently counted repeat visitors more than once when reporting its visitor total. Once again, although the ad community was unhappy, they agreed: the mistakes did not penalize them financially. Once again, the ad community complained loudly about Facebook's failure to have its data independently monitored.

Then it happened again. Over the next several months and into the start of 2017, Facebook would admit a total of ten measurement mistakes. Google also reluctantly admitted measurement errors, the most egregious being programmatic buying by Facebook and YouTube that placed friendly ads on unfriendly sites, including racist, extremist, and pornography sites. None were done venally. They were ads targeted by keywords, like the Confederacy or race. But they undermined trust and strengthened the ad community's claim that a referee was needed so Facebook and Google no longer graded their own homework.

By early 2017, the advertising community was less forgiving. Walmart and PepsiCo and others pulled ads from YouTube. Bob Liodice assailed digital platforms for harming brands and called for an audit of their spending. Appearing in January before the Annual Leadership Meeting of the organization that represents digital companies, the Interactive Advertising Bureau, Procter & Gamble's Marc Pritchard declared, "The days of giving digital a pass are over." He stipulated a 5-point program that the world's largest advertiser expected digital companies to comply with—or else. Citing "brand safety" concerns, Havas pulled its ads off Google in London. Martin Sorrell slammed Google for failing "to step up and take responsibility."

Google and Facebook sought to assuage advertisers, offering contrite promises to fix their mistakes, to welcome more independent measurement. But these were not mistakes that could be so easily fixed. The limitations of Math Men were parading across the runway. "We've gone from the era of *Mad Men* to mad metrics," News Corp's CEO Robert Thomson declared at a UBS Global Media and Communications Conference. An overreliance on machines and a belief that they were engaged in mistake-proof science produced an opaque mathematical model. Although engineers are fallible humans, they often assume their algorithms are infallible. When told that Facebook's mechanized defenses had failed to screen out "fake" news planted on the social network to sabotage Hillary Clinton's presidential campaign, Mark Zuckerberg publicly dismissed the assertion as "crazy." His computers—his science—wouldn't allow it. Or as Eric Schmidt, the executive chairman of Alphabet, the parent company of Google, said at their 2017 annual shareholder meeting, "We start from the principles of science at Google and Alphabet." By relying on programmatic machines to use algorithms to make ad buys, and attaching ads to certain words, the computer might target a consumer who spends time doing history-themed searches on Google. However, the machine is capable of dumbly placing the ad on a white-supremacy site that cites history, or its version of history, offering one clear limitation of AI.

The University of Michigan's Christian Sandvig demonstrates how a reliance on tools like search algorithms can be faulty guides. He offers an example of an insurance company that purchased data and might blackball an insurance applicant because he spent a lot of time searching Alcoholics Anonymous. "A lot of judgments the insurance company may make are unreliable. Maybe you were Googling Alcoholics Anonymous for a friend. Maybe a lot of people in the house use your computer." The weaknesses of an overreliance on algorithms was exposed by a *ProPublica* reporting team that examined computerized "risk scores" that are used across the country to determine if those arrested are high or low risks to commit future crimes. They obtained the risk scores of seven thousand of those arrested in Broward County, Florida, and found that the risk-factor algorithm "proved remarkably unreliable" because only 20 percent of those "predicted to commit violent crimes actually went on to do so." White defendants with multiple arrests "were mislabeled as low risk more often than black defendants" with scant rap sheets. If you had a job and committed crimes and had a criminal record, the algorithm likely ranked you as a lower crime risk than a homeless black man.*

Cathy O'Neil, a data scientist, explored the biases of the algorithms that increasingly rule our lives in her 2016 book, *Weapons of Math Destruction: How Big Data Increases Inequality and Threatens Democracy.* For people with bad credit scores who live in high-crime precincts, she writes, algorithms shower "them with predatory ads for

---

* Julia Angwin, Jeff Larson, Surya Mattu, and Lauren Kirchner, "Machine Bias: There's Software Used Across the Country to Predict Future Criminals. And It's Biased Against Blacks," *ProPublica*, May 23, 2016.

subprime loans," and the same data is used to "block them from jobs" and drive their credit rating down.

Mathematical algorithms and AI tools are important, but limited, says Wendy Clark of DDB. It offers science but not art. "Play it out in your life," she continues. "You go to a neighbor's cocktail party. You have a conversation with someone that is quite generic—'What did you do today? How was work? How many kids do you have?'" That is her version of an algorithmic conversation. On the other hand, if at the same cocktail party you meet someone and say, "'Oh wow! You're a nurse! My mother was a nurse! Gosh, tell me about where you work?'" The first conversation is generic, the second, engaging. What humans have that machines lack is empathy. If consumers are swayed by emotion, then the copywriter has some advantages over the algorithm.

Michael Kassan adds marketing and serendipity to the mix in his own favorite anecdote about Math Men's limitations: "When my birthday was approaching, I told Ronnie I didn't want a watch. But I picked up a magazine and saw a picture of a watch and said, 'Maybe, on the other hand, I do want a watch.' There's nothing math about that. It's serendipity. It's marketing. The picture of the watch caught my eye." The same thing happened to him when he saw a picture of the new Tesla. He wasn't thinking of getting a new car. But he bought a Tesla. "Math Men can't anticipate moments of serendipity," he says.

Because she works with advertisers and agencies and publishers and not in the bowels of Facebook's machines, Carolyn Everson straddles the worlds of Mad Men and Math Men. "A machine can't come up with a strategy," she says. "A machine can't come up with a creative idea. A machine can execute. Machines can help us organize. But this business is still a relationship business." She acknowledged that she has had her share of battles with Facebook engineers, who can have "black-and-white answers, ones and zeros." In her early days at Facebook she would use the word "magic" to describe the power of a creative ad, and "the engineering folks here said, 'We don't use the word magic here.'" Over the years, she continues, "I have been very vocal internally that marketing is an art as well as a science." With mobile, the science improves. The data collected improves. "But the art I would argue becomes more important because in a mobile world consumers have more choices. Marketers have to earn the attention of consumers."

Her argument, and those of irate advertisers, obviously carried some weight, for in May 2017 Facebook acknowledged a limitation of machines and algorithms when it announced that it was hiring three thousand humans to monitor and take down inappropriate content and to better protect both consumers and advertisers. And Google in the summer of 2017 announced it was granting refunds to hundreds of advertisers because its programmatic purchasing arm, DoubleClick, ran their ads on Web sites inflated by fake traffic. And when it was revealed that Facebook's algorithms inadvertently enabled advertisers to target consumers with cringe-worthy keywords like "Jew hater," and a Russian troll farm secretly purchased $100 million of ads to spread "fake news" to further polarize Americans during the 2016 presidential contest, founder Mark Zuckerberg acknowledged the limitations of his managers to control the algorithms. "I wish I could tell you we're going to be able to catch all bad content in our system," he announced in September 2017. "I wish I could tell you we're going to be able to stop all interference, but that wouldn't be realistic." This prompted Kevin Roose of the *New York Times* to label this Facebook's "Frankenstein moment," likening this to Mary Shelley's book, when the scientist— Dr. Frankenstein—realizes his robot creature "has gone rogue."

In October 2017, Mark Zuckerberg sheepishly admitted he should not have been so quick to defend the ability of Facebook's machines to block "fake" news pushed by Russian hackers to subvert the Clinton presidential campaign. "Calling that 'crazy' was dismissive and I regret it," he declared, announcing that Facebook would hire an additional thousand curators to screen news accounts and ads. To prevent ads from appearing in offensive videos, YouTube announced in January 2018 that it would hire "human reviewers" to screen its premium content.

A subtle but meaningful meditation on the consequences of the labors of blinkered engineers, whether at Facebook or Google, was penned by Silicon Valley venture capitalist Roger McNamee,* cofounder of Elevation Partners and an early investor in both companies. While he praised the many advances technology has made possible, McNamee lamented the "addictive behaviors" they create, compelling "consumers to check for new messages, respond to notifications, and seek validation from technologies whose only goal is to generate [advertising] profits for their owners. . . . Like gambling, nicotine, alcohol or heroin, Facebook and Google—most importantly through its YouTube subsidiary—produce short-term happiness with serious negative consequences in the long term." Many people check their smartphones 150 times daily, and spend 50 minutes a day on Facebook. For advertisers, a Facebook executive in Australia promised, they could "target teens who were sad or depressed," and the ads could make them happier. Facebook and Google have to stop "brain hacking," McNamee concluded, or government must intervene.

---

* Roger McNamee, "I Invested Early in Google and Facebook. Now They Terrify Me," *USA Today*, August 8, 2017.

17.

DINOSAURS OR COCKROACHES?

"People say agencies are dinosaurs. We are not dino-
saurs. We are cockroaches. Everybody hates us. Nobody
likes to see us. But cockroaches have outlived everyone."

—Rishad Tobaccowala

Michael Kassan kept popping up from his seat like a jack-in-the-box. He was at the Hearst dinner for 75 advertisers and media notables on the sunny terrace of the Hotel du Cap during the 2016 Cannes Lions Festival. Nervously, he kept glancing over at a table 150 feet away on the balcony perched above the Mediterranean. He had arranged dinner between AT&T's senior executive vice president and global CMO, Lori Lee, her deputy, Fiona Carter, a former BBDO executive, and Omnicom CEO John Wren and BBDO CEO Andrew Robertson. He wanted them to have a relaxed discussion about AT&T's decision to put out for bid its annual $3.8 billion marketing account. In the United States alone, AT&T ad spending trailed only General Motors, Comcast, and Procter & Gamble. Kassan had organized a second dinner for the AT&T marketing team the following night at Tetou in Antibes with the competitive bidder, WPP's Martin Sorrell and Irwin Gotlieb. Yet with his mouth agape, Kassan saw Sorrell, hovering over the AT&T table when he walked in, boisterously trading friendly jabs with Wren and Robertson and seemingly ignoring the AT&T executives, while his wife, Cristiana, waited at a table about five feet away. Sorrell seemed to be smiling; Wren and Robertson looked puzzled. Each time Kassan jumped up, he saw Sorrell languidly dining within earshot of the AT&T table.

"It was an accident" with no devilish purpose, Sorrell would say later, noting that he was staying at the hotel and had a dinner reservation. Whether it had an impact on AT&T's final decision is hard to affirm. In any event, what AT&T was setting out to do that summer was consequential. The company announced in early June that it would no longer rely on separate agencies like BBDO to handle creative while WPP's MEC did media planning for its AT&T brand, or WPP's Grey did creative and MEC did media planning for its DirecTV. Instead, they wanted one holding company to do all of their marketing and advertising, and only invited Omnicom and WPP to bid. Instead of a media agency to mine data and shape strategy, and a separate creative agency, or confederacies of agencies, in the same room representing the client—as practiced by GE, Bank of America, and Unilever—AT&T went in another direction. Lori Lee says they sought a "holistic" approach, by which she meant a new agency formed to service just AT&T at a separate location and "to come to the table and understand the marketplace and understand our customer base." There would be no internal competition among agencies. And the client would not, Lee says, "be responsible for stitching together" all the ideas. With the wealth of data now available, AT&T envisioned the media agency ascendant over the creative in a world where ads will increasingly be targeted at individuals. "We want decisions based on data," not guesses, she says. The creative ideas would flow from the data. And a single entity would coordinate data, creative, media, and analytics.

A single dedicated agency for one client is not unique. Before holding companies came to dominate the agency business, this was the universal agency model. Today, WPP has long dedicated a single entity ("One Ford") to service Ford and another ("Red Fuse") to service Colgate; later this summer, McDonald's designated Wendy Clark's DDB to replace Publicis's Leo Burnett and to form an agency with its own odd name—We Are Unlimited—to offer one-stop marketing services. What was unusual at the time is that the dedicated AT&T agency would be headquartered near AT&T's offices in Dallas, be under the command of the media agency, and commencing in June 2016 the decision cycle was brutally compressed. Michael Kassan and MediaLink were tasked with organizing an unusually rapid sixty-day competition. The process started with AT&T briefings with MediaLink, followed by a request for proposal sent to the two holding companies, followed by AT&T briefings with two agencies, then meetings to answer agency questions, then meetings for the agencies to make initial and then final strategy and creative pitches, followed by meetings to present the proposed agency structure and the team assigned to the client, and, finally, contract negotiation meetings between the lawyers. AT&T wanted to make a decision in August. "MediaLink project-managed this for us," Fiona Carter says. They parsed the agency submissions, offered questions for AT&T to ask, and suggested clauses to include in the contract. "They were sort of an objective third party."

In the end, AT&T chose Omnicom and a dedicated team of nearly five hundred staffers, placing Omnicon's media agency, Hearts & Science, in the driver's seat. "It was the first time a media agency and a creative agency were merged into one agency," Kassan says. "AT&T's clear intention was to have a truly integrated model where data sits at the center and informs creative and media." For Sorrell's WPP, losing the AT&T account subtracted some $100 million from its annual revenues.

The jury is still out on whether the single agency approach of AT&T, or McDonald's, represents the future model for agencies. But there is a growing belief that giant companies have to rid themselves of competitive, noncooperative silos. The impediment is often cultural, the sharp elbows of ambitious people, Martin Sorrell says. "The more successful someone is, the more difficult it is to manage them. Getting people to share knowledge and information is not easy. The biggest issue in our industry is how to get people to share."

Another impediment, as Linda Boff of GE says, is that "big can be slow." Acknowledging that "big" has buying clout, Boff adds, "But what disrupts big? Speed. Scrappiness. Flexibility." There is a financial incentive to one agency. Instead of paying fees to multiple agencies, as GE does, a single agency means AT&T pays "lower fees," says Andrew Goldberg. Perhaps the only thing that is clear, Bank of America's Lou Paskalis half-jokingly says, is that AT&T now "has only one neck to choke."

Whatever the changes in the agency model, Rishad Tobaccowala is a believer in the resiliency of agencies, big or small, led by media or by creative agencies. "People say we are dinosaurs," he says. "We are not dinosaurs. We are cockroaches. Everybody hates us. Nobody likes to see us. But cockroaches have outlived everyone. We scurry out of corners. We soldier on and hire people with different skill sets. When I started at Publicis we got two percent of our revenue from digital. Now it is fifty-two percent."

Among the new agency models is the one being fashioned by Bob Greenberg of R/GA, who regularly says that his is no longer an ad agency. "I built a company around the concept of building a home and next generation replacement for ad agencies that were designed in the *Mad Men* model," Greenberg says. He doesn't believe ad agencies are resilient cockroaches. Or as he put it in an e-mail:

> The Agency Model is dead. It's 70 years old and they're
> still holding on to "the Art of Persuasion," as everything is
> deconstructing around them.
>
> Film is dead, the 30-second spot is dead, outbound
> creative is dead, the writer/art director model of
> Bernbach is dead. The DDB model is dead. Magazines
> are dead. The consulting model is dead. . . . No vision,
> no investment, no restructuring, no risk, no collaboration,
> no innovation. . . . Everything is run by accountants and
> bean counters.
>
> Like deer in the headlights.

A visit to R/GA's loft office space on the eleventh and twelfth floors of a newly constructed building in the burgeoning Hudson Yards neighborhood celebrates the future, not the past. Their 230,000-square-foot space that Greenberg conceived feels more Silicon Valley than New York ad agency. The ceilings soar like an airplane hangar, a rubber carpet mutes the sound, employees share glassed offices, meals are subsidized, snacks are free, employees collaborate in open spaces while gathered around low couches and white Formica tables, everything is digitally connected, including giant overhead screens flashing information from social networks, and there is a fully equipped gym and yoga classes. Few look up from their Formica tables when the white-bearded sixty-nine-year-old Greenberg ambles by in his round, frameless, Ben Franklin–style eyeglasses and descends a giant staircase to the eleventh floor. He has on his accustomed uniform: black jeans, a black, long-sleeved T-shirt, and a black beret; a heap of curly grey Brillo-like hair falls onto his shoulders. He is on his way to a conference room to be joined by members of his executive team: Nick Law, vice chairman and global chief creative officer; Barry Wacksman, executive vice president, global chief strategy office; Stephen

Plumlee, executive vice president, global chief operating officer; and Daniel Diez, executive vice president, global chief marketing officer.

"We don't call ourselves an agency," Wacksman begins. "We call ourselves a company for the connected age. We don't just make ads. We help clients solve problems." To identify as an ad agency "puts you in a box." A more accurate description of R/GA would be to call it a new kind of marketing enterprise.

Starting in the 1990s, four new technologies—first the Internet, then the smartphone and social media, and now AI—have transformed all businesses, requiring innovation. Apple was among the first to connect its products, continues Wacksman, who has written articles and books on disruption. Apple became "a retailer of music" when it originated the iPod and a content platform with iTunes and its App Store. R/GA's vision is to follow the model of Apple, Google, and Amazon, three companies that define their business broadly and abandon old, familiar ways. Apple can't be defined narrowly as a computer company, any more than Google can be defined as a search company, or Amazon as an online store. Yes, Wacksman says, the railroads would have done better if they had acted as if they were in the transportation business and not just the railroad business. But they would not have leapt into unrelated businesses.

R/GA leapt, says Law, when it helped invent a business product for Nike in 2003, the NikeiD, allowing its consumers to utilize a Nike Web site R/GA fashioned to individually design their Nike products. Nike online sales shot up by one third, says Wacksman. In 2006, when Nike's prime advertising agency, Wieden+Kennedy, was winning awards for its various campaigns, R/GA helped invent Nike+. They designed and placed software in Nike shoes to allow users to collect data on their performance. Forty million Nike customers signed up for Nike membership, Greenberg says, granting Nike a bounty of data and an ability to communicate with its customers directly. Four years later, R/GA produced the software for the Nike+ FuelBand, a wearable device that allows customers to gauge their performance but also allowed Nike to gather data to improve its products and communicate with its consumers. With a one-on-one relationship with customers, Law says, "Over time, Nike did fewer ads." And while Greenberg insists that R/GA is not an agency, he does boast that R/GA has nudged aside Crispin Porter as "the biggest agency on their roster."

The Nike membership community R/GA boosted is today imitated by many brands. Unilever, for example, purchased the Dollar Shave Club for $1 billion not just to compete with Gillette, but to capture its membership community of customers who communicate directly with the company.

Technology and digital is at the core of R/GA's DNA. "It's not enough for Martin Sorrell to say he is willing to eat his own children or to acquire companies," Greenberg says. "He's not a disrupter, an innovator." On another visit, Greenberg would say of Sorrell, "At the end of the day, Martin is a forensic accountant. He's truly brilliant. But he has too much control for innovation. I would never work for Martin. He's too controlling." He does work for Michael Roth, CEO of IPG, his parent company, who he praises for granting R/GA operating freedom. Roth says of Greenberg, "Bob is a visionary. . . . Everyone thinks he's this technology genius. He is that. But he's also a very good businessman. I don't think he gets enough credit for that." With R/GA profit margins of 20 percent, Roth has reason to be content. (So does Sorrell, whose 2016 WPP revenues of almost $20 billion were fifty times greater than R/GA's $406 million, and more than twice IPG's, and though its profit margin of just over 17 percent was slightly below R/GA's, it certainly did not reflect a company in decline.)

In the conference room, Wacksman swaggered that R/GA won more Cannes Lions awards than any agency in 2015 and a raft of awards in 2016. R/GA now had six revenue spigots. Its two thousand employees in eighteen worldwide offices harvest revenues first from what it labels its Agency work, creating advertising and marketing campaigns, including the design and development of products and services for Nike. Among R/GA's many unusual ad ventures, perhaps none is more celebrated than the campaign Nick Law supervised and the agency donated to the Ad Council, "Love Has No Labels." Meant to show how love can knock down barriers, we see a succession of couples who appear as skeletons behind a giant X-ray screen. They kiss, embrace, dance, and when each steps out from behind the screen we see, holding hands, same-sex couples, mixed-race couples, couples of different religions and ethnicities.

The revenue from the software and products they create for clients like Nike is grouped under a second revenue stream, its Intellectual Property arm.

A third revenue source is their in-house Studios, which produce polished commercials and podcasts and social media messages for current clients such as Samsung, Google, Nike, Lego, Apple's Beats, Pepsi, and Mercedes. They crafted, for example, the "Hear What You Want" ads for Apple's Beats by Dr. Dre, featuring controversial athletes like Kevin Garnett and Colin Kaepernick tuning out the noise from mobs of haters by putting on their Beats earphones and listening to music that puts them in another state of mind. R/GA's Agency, Intellectual Property, and Studio arms collectively produce about 60 percent of its revenues, and the products R/GA creates produce about 20 percent.

Another 5 percent of its revenues comes from a fourth revenue source, Ventures, which is what R/GA calls its Accelerator program, providing venture capital to start-ups and, as Andreessen Horowitz does in Silicon Valley, offering mentoring services to these baby companies. Absent the mentoring services, investing in start-ups, including brands, is what Gary Vaynerchuk does. But R/GA's Ventures, started in 2013, is much broader. Out of 1,370 worldwide applicants and counting, R/GA selected 66 companies, a number that was expected to swell to 100 by the end of 2017. In return for their money and services, Greenberg says R/GA receives between 1 to 6 percent ownership, and when these companies go public or are acquired, R/GA will profit. R/GA makes money from this program in another way as well. They invite clients like Snapchat and the Dodgers and Verizon to help select start-ups that might offer "knowledge capital" to these established companies. Between R/GA and the established companies, they offer mentoring to the start-ups. R/GA provides the office space and assigns staff members to work with them, and in return R/GA charges them fees that produce, Greenberg says, "eleven to fifteen percent margins" for R/GA.

One such incubated company is Alvio. It is a mobile game controller that allows children with asthma to breathe into a plastic handheld wireless device that controls games, allowing kids to strengthen their breathing and parents to monitor whether their child's breathing is improving through data sent to the company's cloud. At first, Alvio designed their wireless device for athletes. R/GA's market research, Stephen Plumlee says, convinced them to focus on kids with asthma— the third largest cause of hospitalization for children under fifteen. R/GA also designed the children's games. Additionally, R/GA works with other connected companies, including Snaptivity, which captures and analyzes fan reactions at live events to decide who to photograph, and Owlet, a baby's sock with embedded chips that forwards an infant's vital signs to parents on their smartphone app.

A fifth revenue source is Consulting, generating 10 percent of R/GA's revenues. Greenberg says they consult directly with C-suite executives, just as the major consulting companies do. Walmart was a consulting client; its CEO hired R/GA to boost innovation and to help design an app and systems to better compete online against Amazon. The Campbell Soup Company was another client. Unlike the consultant companies, who he says leave after their PowerPoint presentations, R/GA stays and tries to offer the kind of creative input they tender Nike.

A final source of revenue—about 5 percent—comes from what R/GA calls Architecture, a group of engineers and designers that devise companies' working environments. The group designs offices that replicate what Greenberg has done, not just in his office but his glassed weekend home perched on 200 acres overlooking the Hudson River in Ghent, New York, modeled on Mies van der Rohe's Farnsworth House. "I have the world's most connected house," Greenberg says, lifting an iPad and pressing to open the front gate, showing how from this device he can learn the temperature outside, control the lights, shades, heat, solar panels, and the cameras in Ghent or in his 8,000-square-foot Chelsea loft. "When people talk about connected space, I am really doing it." Greenberg says this growing business generates $25 million, and includes the connected hotel rooms they designed for Loews, and offices for Walmart, Nike, and Du, Dubai's telephone company. The office design, consulting, and ventures are expanding faster than marketing and advertising, Greenberg says. And he asserts that if R/GA pulled out the actual revenues its IP, Ventures and Consulting, and Architecture generated, it would total close to one third of R/GA's revenues.

Greenberg's demeanor is modest, his voice is faint, and he speaks excruciatingly slowly. He does not tout the awards he has personally won. But he is immodest about R/GA's goals. "We could disrupt the holding companies," he declares. "We could disrupt the consulting business. We can disrupt architectural firms. We can disrupt the production studios. We can disrupt the venture business. And we're doing all that." One thing he is not disrupting is advertising's lack of diversity. Although he often invokes the word "diversity" to describe a necessary ingredient of future agencies, only six of the thirty-six top executives pictured on R/GA's Web site are female, and none appear to be black.

Greenberg calls to mind a famous description of Samuel Johnson: "temperamentally . . . always in revolt." He looks it, driving to work attired completely in black, including a black leather jacket and black scarf in colder months, zooming between lanes on his powerful Ducati 1199 Panigale S motorcycle. His business hero was the late Steve Jobs, whom he describes as a fellow "rebel," a "person I look to. He had no patience—neither do I—with people who get in the way of progress." Like Jobs did, Greenberg has a passion for simple, beautiful artistic design; he is said to be the world's largest individual collector of Chinese Buddhist art from the Qi and Wei dynasties.

Greenberg grew up in a working-class Chicago home. He was a terrible student. "I struggled with academics because I was really dyslexic," he says. He enrolled in Parsons College in Iowa, and later transferred to Arizona State, where he majored in communications and advertising. After graduation, his uncle, who had sold his business to Royal Crown Cola and served as an executive there, offered him a bottom-rung sales job in Chicago. He sold mirrors, and was pretty good at it. By this point however, his marriage was collapsing. He got divorced, and to escape he moved to Toronto, where his uncle helped him get a job managing a Royal Crown plant.

"I gained confidence because of my uncle, who mentored me," he says, so much confidence that he and his brother Richard, who was doing motion graphics and title designs for movies, decided to team up in 1977 and create a special-effects company in New York, R/Greenberg Associates. They created the first integrated computer-assisted production process. Dyslexia imposes many burdens, he believes, but brings with it "pattern recognition," or the ability to glimpse the new world technologies will introduce. With Richard as the designer and Robert as the cameraman and producer, their computer-assisted film-making company soon employed two hundred people. They created the opening title sequence for *Superman* in 1978 and the title designs for many movies and trailers, as well as special effects for many others. In 1986, their work won them a technical Academy Award.

Bob saw another pattern: technology was fundamentally changing the advertising business. He had a leg up because he and his brother were immersed early in the digital revolution. "I wanted to reinvent the agency business," he says. "You couldn't say that because it's very arrogant. Yet the more I got into it the more I saw it was possible." Bob wanted to create an interactive ad agency; Richard wanted to go to Hollywood to produce and direct movies. Bob's first client was IBM, which retained R/GA to redesign its Web site, and it soon became the digital agency for clients like Nike, Verizon, and Nokia. R/GA received an infusion of capital when it was acquired by True North Communications in 1995, and again when True North was acquired by IPG in 2001.

"What I'm interested in is to have a new model to replace the traditional agency model," Greenberg says. He rejects AT&T's new model. The work R/GA did for Nike illustrates what he believes will be the hub of a future model that relies more on marketing than advertising: "People want to interact with brands and avoid annoying advertising." Either on Facebook, its Web site, e-mail, or IM, innovations like Nike's FuelBand and its membership clubs create a one-to-one relationship between customer and brand, giving Nike a loyal customer base to share new products with and a vehicle to provide two-way communication between customer and brand. "When I come to New York, I ask to see him," says marketing consultant and former Procter & Gamble

CMO Jim Stengel. "I think he has the most forward-looking operation of anyone. I wanted to hire his agency when I was at P&G, but my clients would not agree."

Like his business heroes, Steve Jobs and Jeff Bezos, Bob Greenberg does not lack for confidence. Unlike Jobs, he does not glare at or scream at underlings. Unlike Bezos, he does not have a high-pitched laugh. Unlike both, he does not treat his work as if it were a national security secret. However, like them, his self-confidence borders on messianic. Near the close of a long conversation in his conference room, Greenberg was asked, "What do you worry about?"

"We don't worry about anyone displacing us." Turning to Barry Wacksman, he says, "Do we worry about anyone?"

"We don't," Wacksman says.

"Personally, I'm Jewish. You can't stop worrying," says Greenberg. But his worry is more personal, centered on nearing seventy. "I'm worried that I'm going to run out of runway, which is time."

18.

GOOD-BYE OLD ADVERTISING AXIOMS

The thought many marketers try to banish is whether for consumers—spoiled by Netflix and YouTube, by ad-skipping DVRs and ad blockers, by personal devices we hold in our hands—the interruptive ad message may be a relic. Are consumers irrevocably alienated by sales pitches? Has the consumer, on whom marketing relies, become a frenemy?

An eternal verity of the advertising and marketing business is that no one can be certain about what advertising will work. Longtime advertising sage Jeremy Bullmore recalls meeting an old friend for lunch outside London. When they stepped from the restaurant, the friend pointed to his shiny new Aston Martin.

"Well done," Bullmore said.

"I bought it because of an advertisement," the friend said.

"Good to know that what we do works," Bullmore said.

"I saw the advertisement when I was fourteen!" the friend responded.

"How," Bullmore asks, "do you attribute that seventy-five-thousand-pound purchase to an ad that ran fifty-two years earlier?" Even with digital ads, whose clicks are more easily measured, if his friend had clicked on the Astin Martin Web site, Bullmore says, "The click would get the credit for the purchase. But nobody would know and could possibly calculate what led to the click in the first place." He believes the mysteries of what shapes a purchase are largely impenetrable.

The mysteries of marketing were underscored by the election of Donald Trump. A month after the 2016 presidential election, Michael Kassan moderated a panel at the Paley Center for Media in Midtown Manhattan. The panel's topic was the anticipated big advertising trends ahead in 2017 and beyond. Introducing the topic, Kassan re-cited some stark facts:

— 62 percent of Americans get their news from Facebook.
— 90 percent of Americans consult a second screen while watch-ing TV.
— The attention span of a goldfish (nine seconds), according to a Microsoft study, exceeds that of a human (eight seconds).

An initial advertising prediction was offered by Arpita Chowdhuri, a digital marketing vice president at Hewlett Packard Enterprise, who said: 2017 and beyond "is going to be the year for data. . . . Data is going to be the new oil."

With the surprising election of Donald Trump in mind, Kassan wondered whether there were some lessons to be learned from the contest, especially about data. "People are going to question data more," he said, "because the projections said there was a ninety-one percent chance on the morning of the election that Hillary Clinton would be president." Data from the polls and the predictions of prog-nosticators were dead wrong.

Donald Trump's success in winning the Republican nomination, and his election as president, challenged not just conventional political wisdom but some cherished precepts of advertising and marketing, starting with the assumption that there is a meaningful relationship between vast expenditures on advertising and the electoral outcome. Jeb Bush spent $80.2 million on ads—nearly five times Trump's expenditures. Trump and his independent and Republican Party PAC raised over $500 million less than Clinton and Clinton reportedly spent more than two times what Trump spent on advertising. In an era when advertising is increasingly perceived as an interruption, more ad dollars appeared to equal fewer votes. Trump's campaign shrewdly spent more money on targeted digital messages to pull his supporters to the polls.

A second axiom—that public relations usually belongs in the back of the advertising caravan because it can't be counted on—did not fare well. Traditionally, marketers want to spend more for "paid" media, worrying that the "free" media generated by news stories can't be relied upon the way a thirty-second ad can. Historically, unpredictable "free media" does not deliver for most candidates; it did for Trump. His campaign relied on media coverage, and the *what's-he-going-to-say-next* fascination with Trump boosted TV ratings and newspaper circulation.

When Donald Trump was attracting television audiences in 2016, Les Moonves told a reporter after Trump won the New Hampshire primary that the campaign was "a circus." But he was pleased nevertheless. "Man, who would have expected the ride we're all having right now? The money's rolling in and this is fun. . . . This is going to be very good for us. Sorry, it's a terrible thing to say. But bring it on, Donald. Keep going." Critics howled at Moonves for cheering on the "circus" because it was good for CBS.

Months later, I asked Moonves, who was a Hillary Clinton supporter, to explain his crude words. "It was a joke," he answered. "It was said in front of three hundred bankers. I got them to laugh." It may have been a wisecrack, but for CBS and much of the press that slavishly devoted airtime and front-page treatment to Trump in 2015 and 2016, it was true. Trump was good for ratings and circulation; his coverage harmed journalistic credibility because it revealed journalists were not always chasing what was news or important but rather what was good for business.

MediaQuant, a firm that computes the financial value of media coverage pegged to advertising rates, concluded that by the spring of 2016 Trump earned close to $2 billion in free press attention, far eclipsing his Republican or Democratic adversaries. Studies of the general election revealed he received more press attention than Clinton, and even though much of it was negative it did not deter his hard-core supporters who blamed the "fake news" press.

A third marketing axiom—that celebrity endorsements are valuable—backfired on Hillary Clinton. Clinton's rallies in the final days were headlined by Jay-Z and Beyoncé, by Bruce Springsteen and Katy Perry. Without dissent from his panel, Kassan asserted, "Celebrity endorsements turned out to be a negative." They served to reinforce the impression that Clinton was an "elitist" and Trump was the outsider.

The Trump campaign did buttress an emerging marketing axiom: targeting works. It is one adopted by Nike and by every modern president who used technology to communicate directly with citizens. While polling data failed Clinton, targeting data assisted Trump. Relying on the sophisticated targeting work of Cambridge Analytica, a privately held data-mining firm that assembled what it said were three thousand to five thousand pieces of data on each potential Trump supporter, the campaign pumped money into Facebook and social network messages. In an interview with *60 Minutes* days after the election, Trump bragged of his success at circumventing the press on Facebook and Twitter: "I think that social media has more power than the money they spent, and I think maybe to a certain extent I proved that." Martin Sorrell believes the digital targeting and messaging undertaken by the Trump campaign was "vindication, in a way, of all the stuff we're doing with programmatic advertising and the use of technology." The reliance on data, he continued, is "highly supportive of the way we see the business going. It's not good news for Don Draper."

Bank of America's Anne Finucane, a dejected Clinton supporter, was impressed with how Trump communicated directly with his customers. This is what brands like Nike do with Nike+ and its FuelBand and the creation of a Nike membership community. It's what Unilever is doing with the members of its Dollar Shave Club. And it's what Finucane aims to do with her bank and Merrill Lynch's fifty million customers. Trump's success in building a community, she said, "makes me think of going directly to our customers more often."

There was at least one other parallel between the Trump effort and many advertising campaigns: Trump's well-documented use of hyperbole and untrue claims—what Stephen Colbert has labeled "truthiness"—replicates the exaggerated, emotionally manipulative claims of too much advertising. In this sense, Trump was at least partially copying, not innovating (though a president's falsehoods are far more consequential).

Trump's victory injected more uncertainty into the marketing and media industry, especially since he is not anchored to a predictable ideology or core Republican/conservative convictions. With media consolidation accelerating, right after the election media and tech executives were asking: Would the Trump administration approve the announced acquisition of Time Warner by AT&T? Outraged by what he gratuitously labels as its "fake news," would he hold AT&T hostage and demand it shed, or punish, CNN? Would the new administration and the Congress alter the tax code to end "the immediate write-off of all advertising expenses," as the Republican chairman of the House Ways and Means Committee advocates? (Days after the election, the ANA wrote its members and cautioned that if Trump and the Congress did this it would cost advertisers and agencies up to $200 billion.) Might Trump punish media and advertisers by having the FTC crack down on native advertising? Would Trump and the Congress rescind the privacy protections imposed by Obama's FCC? Might the Trump administration restrict immigration, including of the qualified engineers digital efforts require? Might his Justice Department assert that digital giants—Google, Amazon, Facebook, Apple—had monopoly power? What would Trump do with the net neutrality rules promulgated by the Obama administration, which are opposed by telephone and cable broadband providers and embraced by media and tech companies who stream their content via the Internet?

The net neutrality rules were seen as especially significant by outgoing FCC chairman Tom Wheeler, who somberly said in a conversation we had weeks before he departed that equal broadband access was vital to advertisers. "Martin Sorrell ought to care about the ability of folks advertising on IP-based services being able to freely reach consumers in a fast, fair, and open net." Consumers, he continued, want access to advertiser-supported content "without somebody setting the terms of how you can get there or, worst of all," do what DirecTV once did, which was to learn of an attractive business and jump into that business themselves and give it away for free. This monopolist behavior is why federal courts ruled against Microsoft when it crippled the Netscape browser by giving away its own Internet Explorer browser for free. Within weeks of taking office, the new Trump administration and the Republican Congress did roll back the privacy strictures of the Obama administration. And, in November 2017, FCC chair Ajit Pai proposed to scrap the Obama administration's net neutrality rules.

He did this on the same day Trump's Justice Department announced it would block the merger of AT&T and Time Warner as a violation of antitrust laws.

■ ■ ■

The changing rules of the game in Washington only heightened the advertising and marketing world's sense of turmoil. Yes, agencies were increasingly troubled that clients were treating them as extraneous middlemen by performing more agency functions in-house. Yes, they were not happy that their customers, media platforms, now vied to become ad agencies. Yes, they worried about competition from consulting companies. And yes, they obsessed about the growing power of procurement officers and the escalating mistrust between agency and client fanned by Jon Mandel's accusations and the resulting ANA report.

But these could all be categorized as competitive challenges, not existential threats. The digital giants, however, particularly Facebook and Google, might pose an existential threat. By their nature, these companies are disrupters. They want to eradicate extraneous middlemen. They may begin in one industry, but when they spot new opportunities, they seize them: Google's tentacles spread from search to television to mobile phones to driverless cars to the Internet of things to cloud computing. Facebook went from social networking to IM to Instagram to the work of Carolyn Everson's growing armies of marketing teams. Imagine the advantages Facebook will reap if, as Carolyn Everson predicts, it adds a Buy button to facilitate e-commerce for its advertisers. Digital frenemies follow the immortal words of George Washington Plunkitt, "I seen my opportunities and I took 'em."

Asked what Facebook and Google's real designs on advertising were, a central player in the digital world with deep ties to both companies says he would honestly answer if he could speak anonymously.

The answer, he says, begins with the fact that executives below the top in the ad world who perform much of the copywriting and art and account work are poorly paid and no match for the talent at companies like Facebook and Google. "I think what Facebook and Google see is, 'Oh my God, this is The Gang That Couldn't Shoot Straight and they've been given the keys to the U.S. Treasury! If we could just get our shit together marginally better than these jokers, we'd be rolling in dough.' There's an arrogance there. But a valid arrogance." He was dubious that digital companies would try to compete by creating ads, because "that business doesn't scale" since it's not reliant on machines and algorithms. But he had no doubt they would come after media agencies like Irwin Gotlieb's GroupM: "No question they're competitors. Frenemies was Martin's word. I think he was just trying to be polite. The digital companies try to be equally polite because they still have to go through the gatekeeping of a GroupM or a WPP. But in the end, it's a battle of two cultures: Math Men versus Mad Men."

Martin Sorrell was not polite when he said worries about a third digital giant, Amazon, sometimes kept him awake nights. With almost half of all online retail sales and a wealth of the most valuable consumer data, "Amazon knows what sells and what doesn't. They provide 25 percent of all cloud computing," Sorrell says. They don't share their data. Increasingly, they enter WPP's client businesses— making products that compete with what Unilever and P&G sell, taking on Walmart, buying TV shows, selling food and produce. "If I ask my clients what they worry about most," Sorrell says, "they say Amazon." With the data they have, he frets that Amazon will slide into the advertising business, offering to help target and place the ads of his clients, supplanting GroupM.

Mobile phones pose another existential threat. They have already fundamentally transformed the ad and marketing business, and when 5G replaces 4G and 3G speeds for mobile devices sometime in the next several years, nearly matching the broadband speeds of cable or telephone fiber, the impact should be profound. A movie can be downloaded in an eyeblink. Annoying download waits will disappear, providing a boost to all video, including video ads and virtual reality. Driverless cars, which must ping other cars on the road many times each second to avoid crashes, will receive a boost, as will robotics. The varied devices that make up the Internet of things will seamlessly communicate. A decade ago, most digital content was text. By 2016, half was video and photos. Advertisers know that the most effective mobile ads engage the consumer with video. This experience can only be enhanced with 5G.

Once, when information about products was scarce, consumers learned about products from advertising. The consumer was hungry for information and traded their time for it. Today, as marketing consultant Gord Hotchkiss wrote for online publication *MediaPost*, "The basic premise of advertising has changed. Information is no longer scarce. In fact, through digitization we have the opposite problem. We have too much information and too little attention to allocate to it. We now need to filter information." Advertising that attempts to sell feels false, intrusive. Available ad-free options—Netflix, HBO, Showtime, YouTube—reinforce the desire to watch television the way we watch movies, without interruption. This desire is further reinforced by social networks, which accustom citizens to two-way communication. The new "central verb for us in marketing is: listen," Hannah Grove, the executive vice president and CMO for asset manager State Street, said at a *Financial Times* marketing conference. "We're all humans and we don't want to be marketed to. We've gone from a cathedral to a marketplace."

What we definitely do know is that sending ad messages to our very personal mobile phones, whether over 5G or 4G, is fraught with both danger and opportunity for advertisers. Terry Kawaja of Luma

Partners holds up his iPhone and says, "This thing fundamentally changes everything. We have never had a media channel like this one. We've never had a media channel that's personal, that's gone with us. The ubiquity—everyone has a phone. And the persistence—it's always with you. And the functionality—I can buy something online, I can get to a Web site, I can make a phone call." He is optimistic that in the long run advertisers will figure out how to better market their products. But he concedes the peril when he adds, "Advertising was constructed on the notion of interruption." In an era of mobile phones and social networks, word of mouth becomes the killer marketing tool. Power has dramatically shifted to the consumer. Or as NBC Entertainment chairman Bob Greenblatt declared at a late November 2017 forum sponsored by his network, "Consumers hate advertising. People are running away from advertising in droves, and so that, to me, is the crux of the problem. How do we stop that from happening?"

Artificial intelligence poses another existential threat to advertising. Rishad Tobaccowala thinks of AI as the third disruptive era, a "seismic shift" as profound as the introduction of the Internet browser in the 1990s, followed by the iPhone in 2007 and what it meant for social networks. All the data AI collects in the cloud from search and social networks and stores allows "the machine to figure out who to talk to" and all these ingredients "write software with the ability to create an ad." Or an individualized message. Tobaccowala's prognostigations are supported by a late 2016 global marketing survey that reported that more than half of CMOs expected AI's impact on marketing and communications to exceed the impact of social media.* Just the increased use of virtual assistants like Amazon's Alexa or

---

* "Toolkit 2017," a joint study by the marketing company Warc and Deloitte Digital, released December 14, 2016.

Microsoft's Cortana will translate to what they call "programmatic consumption." Instead of a consumer spending time selecting a product and placing an order, these will be automated—"in other words, purchase decisions will increasingly be made by computers, rather than by consumers standing in shops."

Joe Schoendorf, a veteran venture capitalist at Accel Partners in Silicon Valley, imagines a time when AI installs software in your refrigerator. With bar codes on the bottles and containers, the sensors in the refrigerator will send replacement orders to your store when the milk is low. Or will tell you "of a generic product that can save you eighteen percent. How is an agency going to market to machines? And when AI is fully developed and you have machines talking to machines and machines can produce ads, what's the agency's value now?" More ominous for the agencies, he adds, "I think Amazon has already figured this out and the Amazon Dot"—a voice-controlled device connected to Alexa—"is the first incarnation of this strategy."

James Whittaker at Microsoft says, "In a world of data, you may not need ads." Machines will determine the cheapest prices and take the guessing out of deciphering what the consumer wants. "Once you know the consumer's intent, why do you need a creative ad?" Or an agency, since, he says, the store or the brand can communicate directly with the consumer, ushering in what marketers hail as one-to-one marketing.

This brave new world is not imminent, concedes Whittaker. Figuring out a consumer's intent "is revolutionary," he says, but change usually occurs "incrementally." And maybe machines will be unable to decode a person's intent. Or unable to create marketing messages that move consumers emotionally. Or to supply the human judgment we call wisdom.

Enter programmatic advertising, which relies on AI. While programmatic has grown more slowly than some predicted, and has been successfully resisted by Les Moonves and TV network sales forces, today a majority of digital display ads are automated, and a 2016 study by Zenith Programmatic Marketing Forecasts predicted it would swell from $5 billion in the United States in 2012 to $64 billion in 2018, although its growth lags in the rest of the world.

"Our Manhattan Project is programmatic advertising," says Bob Pittman, CEO of iHeartMedia. "If we invented radio today we would call it digital. Yet we still sell advertising the same old way." To automate sales is quick and easy and reliant on a wealth of data, he says. Unlike TV, whose big audience is at night when viewers are home, his radio audience is all day, so he believes he has a shot at locating consumers when they are about to shop, thus demonstrating to advertisers the effectiveness of his radio ads. If programmatic buying spreads to all platforms, including television, many questions arise, led by: Since the machines buy audiences, not space on Web sites or TV channels, how do marketers prevent their friendly ads from appearing on unfriendly sites, as happened in 2016?

*　*　*

A central future question for marketers becomes: How to reach consumers with messages that don't feel like an annoying and interruptive sales pitch? Too slowly, the industry has begun to address this question. Think how slow the ad world has been to stop relying on annoying banner and pop-up ads. Think of those TV ads that hog about twenty minutes of each cable or broadcast hour. Think of the products you just purchased online that appeared constantly in ads on your Gmail screen. Why did it take Google until June 2017 to announce it would terminate these?

Designing the Apple Store as a tourist attraction as well as a service center has been a brilliant marketing tool for Apple. Starbucks stores attracted more traffic by creating a community spirit with free Wi-Fi.

Elon Musk's Tesla does no advertising, yet news of this innovative and stylish electric car has propelled Tesla's stock above that of most other auto companies. Advertisers have begun to recycle the "Brought to you by" approach once so popular that in 1950 three of the top-rated shows on television were NBC's *Texaco Star Theater*, the *Philco Television Playhouse*, and *The Colgate Comedy Hour*. The impediment to a sponsor paying for a half or full hour of programming is, of course, financial. The cost of each episode of a one-hour drama would be north of $5 million, and a lot more for a hit, whereas the cost of producing and placing a thirty-second ad would be about $300,000.

Today, as we've seen, instead of the *General Electric Theater*, General Electric offers *Breakthrough*, a series it codeveloped with the National Geographic Channel directed by such renowned storytellers as Peter Berg and Ron Howard. The cost is not extravagant. Instead of a "Brought to you by GE" banner announcement at the beginning of an episode, it weaves GE scientists into the script. This form of product placement has enjoyed a comeback. Fox's *Empire* took it further: Pepsi didn't just pay for the sight of a Pepsi bottle; Pepsi was integrated into the story line when an actor competed for a Pepsi Performer contract. More blatant sales pitches were adopted by former ad man Donny Deutsch. On his USA Network show *Donny*, his character faces the camera and rhapsodizes about Hak's BBQ Sauce and Purity Vodka, two sponsors. Deutsch's pitch is bolder than the Jack Benny show when Benny extolled Lucky Strike cigarettes or Jell-O.

In the future, Les Moonves predicts, there will be more sponsored shows on CBS, more product placement, and more experimentation with shorter interruptive ads, with six-second pop-up ads replacing thirty-second commercials. But he did not plan to follow the lead of NBC, Fox, and Turner Broadcasting, who vowed to reduce the number of commercial minutes and charge a premium for what they assumed was more exclusivity. "I think our ad load works," he says, stressing that 65 percent of CBS's viewers watch their programs in real time. However, Fox did produce some contrary evidence: by reducing its ad loads by 20 percent for the Teen Choice Awards in August 2017, advertiser prices went up and the show produced one third more revenue than it did in 2016.

Inevitably, other marketing moves will substitute for interruptive ads. Witness popular Red Bull concerts, or brand names on the shirts of professional sports teams or their stadiums and arenas. Still another surging form of marketing, IPG's Michael Roth thinks, will be rewarding consumers with discounts, as long as they're "relevant" to the particular consumer. Advertisers will know more about individual consumers—for example, what they search for—allowing car manufacturers to target potential car buyers. "Artificial intelligence will say, 'This guy buys a car every two years.' Six months before the two years come up, they inundate him with messages: 'We know it's time for you to be looking for a new car. Here's two thousand dollars off if you come in next week to buy a car.' That's relevant." Digitally connected cars will have smart windshields that flash to the driver who is low on gas where the nearest gas station is located, along with an offer of a free coffee. Or a food order can be placed and picked up at a nearby fast food restaurant. Of course, exchanging intrusively annoying ads for intrusively annoying marketing messages may be no less irritating to consumers.

At the same time, native ads are becoming ever more craftily camouflaged. Gary Vaynerchuk writes, "Eventually ads won't look like ads anymore; they will all be natively woven into the platforms, and we'll consume them without even knowing it."* The ANA estimated in mid-2016 that spending on native ads would grow from $13.9 billion in

---

* Gary Vaynerchuk, *#AskGaryVee: One Entrepreneur's Take on Leadership, Social Media & Self-Awareness* (New York: HarperCollins, 2016).

2016 to $21 billion in 2018. "To a significant extent, native is the future of advertising for us," *New York Times* CEO Mark Thompson says. "Adjacent advertising, which is more than a century old in newspapers and is when someone is looking at content and their eye can be drawn to an advertising message which is adjacent to the content, that is a model of limited value in the world we're heading into. There is no sort of white space on a smartphone screen. And so our expectation is advertising will be part of the content stream people consume." He predicts that both the interruptive ad and the adjacent ad model will fade.

Although Thompson believes the *Times* has hired the journalistic storytellers and has advertiser relationships that allow it to build and sustain native advertising, critics raise red flags. They chorus: like advertorials, these can compromise the integrity of both the media and the brand. Another enormous impediment, says Rob Fishman of Niche, a software company that recruited influencers to market native ads and was sold to Twitter, is scale. Because native ads have to be shaped differently for each platform, targeted to various audience segments, are not as repeatable, and each has to endure a laborious storytelling process, he says, "Native is the enemy of scale. The monolithic ad model breaks down."

As we've also seen, more and more, brands latch on to the idea of championing a larger movement or cause, extolling the good they do. This is not entirely new. Volvo in the 1980s chose not to compete with sleek car designs but to promote car safety; Ikea democratized stylish furniture for those with modest incomes; Patagonia flourished by conveying to consumers that it had a social purpose, using recycled bottles to make fleece jackets, employing solar power for their headquarters, donating a portion of their revenue to improve the environment. But the growing unpopularity of big business has prompted brands to dress differently. Every year Edelman issues what it calls its Trust Barometer, a global survey contrasting the level of trust toward business (and other institutions) of the "informed public" versus the "mass population." In 2016, they reported a "significant divide," with nearly two thirds of the "informed public" trusting business and other institutions and under half of the "mass population" sharing that trust, with the divide widening as the income gap spread. Brands that promote the good they do—as Unilever and P&G and Colgate did—seek to demonstrate that they value more than just making money. There's a money reason for this as well. Vaseline or detergents or toothpaste are commodity products, with little to distinguish them.

Scott Goodson founded his fifty-person advertising and marketing agency, StrawberryFrog, and chose the name as a way to differentiate his company. They decided a frog was more agile, and research told them that the strawberry frog from the Amazon has a red body and blue legs "so it looked like a rebel with jeans," a perfect symbol for an agency designed to create movements to sell what he deems to be worthwhile products. He wrote a book about how marketers can help companies build brands and help change the world.* He rejects Rosser Reeves's "unique selling proposition" because, he says, there are today too many unique platforms and most products are commodities with competitors constantly subverting them by offering lower prices. What companies must do is "differentiate on values. You differentiate on your point of view in the world. That's the only way you differentiate." So he sells Nature's Variety, a nutritious dog food, the way he says he would use "a wedge issue" in a political campaign: the company has mounted a movement to save the nine thousand sheltered pets killed daily in the United States.

Goodson acknowledges the corrosive "values" marketing sometimes promotes. "I admit marketing can be evil," he says, "and can be manipulative and make people spend their money when they shouldn't, and

---

* Scott Goodson, *Uprising: How to Build a Brand—and Change the World—by Sparking Cultural Movements* (New York: McGraw-Hill, 2012).

sometimes on things that are bad for them—and maybe more often than not. But I also think companies have tremendous power, and when power is wielded in the right way they can tackle some of the big issues that we face in society. . . . It's in the interests of these companies that they solve some of these big issues. The environment is falling apart? Yes, they should fix it; otherwise they will have fewer consumers."

Straining to convey their goodness can backfire on brands, as Pepsi learned in the spring of 2017. Pepsi made a two-minute thirty-nine-second video of a millennial protest march while reality TV star Kendall Jenner posed for a modeling assignment. It is not clear what they're protesting but the march slowly seduces Jenner, who keeps looking over at the marchers before receiving a beckoning nod from a nice-looking male protester and finally joins the march, to cheers. She grabs a cold can of Pepsi, strides to a wall of policemen in riot gear, and hands the Pepsi to a cop, who takes a swig, to more cheers. The screen fills with these bold white letters: JOIN THE CONVERSATION. Viewers are left with the impression that protest marches would be more effective if protesters shared a Pepsi. The Twitter and Facebook jury did not take long to rage. Martin Luther King, Jr.'s daughter, Bernice King, tweeted: "If only Daddy would have known about the power of #Pepsi." Pepsi quickly yanked the online ad before it graduated to TV. Animating Pepsi was the same quest it shares with other brands who are convinced they must "build relationships" with consumers, become "brand stewards," and demonstrate their "authenticity."

On the other hand, there are marketing campaigns that do good while doing well for the corporation. One such campaign was designed by the McCann New York agency for the financial firm State Street Global Advisors. It contains a fifty-inch-tall statue, *Fearless Girl*, planted on the sidewalk glaring at Wall Street's charging bull. It is a proud, bronzed girl, her fists jammed into her hips, her chest out, her implicit message that more women belong in leadership positions. The company designed the statue to promote its SHE fund, which invests in companies that recruit women for top jobs. When *Fearless Girl* won three Grand Prix awards on the first day of the 2017 Cannes Lions Festival, jury president Wendy Clark announced that the SHE fund was up 374 percent since *Fearless Girl* struck her pose on a Wall Street sidewalk.*

Another compelling example of a fresh form of advertising and marketing is Citi Bike, New York City's bike-sharing program. Launched in May 2013 by Citibank for zero tax dollars and at a cost to the bank of $41 million, by the summer of 2017 it had ten thousand bikes in use in fifty-five city neighborhoods. As Andrew Essex observes in his 2017 book, *The End of Advertising*, Citibank, by choosing not to spend this sum on TV commercials or "squandering that eight-figure investment on useless pollution, built something additive that actually reduces our carbon footprint." The benefit to Citibank in New York and New Jersey where Citi Bike has been introduced, was equally clear, Essex shows: by 2015 the bank's internal data revealed that "favorable impressions of Citibank" rose twenty-eight points to 72 percent, and people who said they would consider acquiring a product from Citibank climbed forty-three points. But since Citibank is a worldwide business, to impact its overall "favorable impression" by extending Citi Bike globally would be as costly as a massive thirty-second TV ad campaign.

■ ■ ■

Whatever form advertising and marketing takes in coming years, a certainty is that data-fed targeting will be a pillar. Irwin Gotlieb believes that in the future, agencies will have to guarantee results to clients, and better results will boost agency compensation.

---

* The firm sponsoring the statue received a black eye in the fall of 2017 when it paid $5 million to the federal government to settle claims that it paid female employees less than men.

We can also be certain that privacy will remain a third rail to marketers, always worried that governments will grow alarmed and impose regulations. The European Union, for example, passed legislation scheduled to go into effect in May 2018 restricting the ability of companies to collect personal information without the user's consent.

Some, like Andrew Robertson of BBDO, believe that the blizzard of different platforms and better targeting will place a premium on creative advertising that captures people's attention and will invite advertisers to spend more to lure those identified as potential customers, as advertising spending becomes more cost effective. Others, like Michael Kassan, offer a bleaker view. "My biggest fear is that the inextricable link that existed historically between serving up content financed by commercial messages, that link is broken because consumers can get their content without commercials now. Think what it would have cost you to get *Life* magazine if there were no ads in it. It was subsidized by advertising." But today too many people "just won't watch commercials."

So what replaces the commercials?

"We will live in a subscription world," he boldly, and I believe wrongly, answers.

Tim Wu is among the most prominent advocates for replacing ads with subscriptions. Harking back to 1833 and the first ad-subsidized newspaper, the *New York Sun*, he calls this "the original sin." In his provocative book *The Attention Merchants*, Wu argues that in advertiser-supported media the reader or viewer is not the customer; the advertiser is. Thus, letting advertisers into the tent inevitably means a diminution of quality, because advertisers pressure the platform to deliver a bigger audience. More news about Kim Kardashian magnetizes an audience. The way to improve media is to pay for it, he says, preferably with subscriptions and micropayments. Wu is not alone. In February 2017, Twitter cofounder Evan Williams, who had raised $134 million to improve journalism by forming Medium, an ad-supported blogging and publishing site, announced that he was laying off one third of his staff and ending its reliance on ads. Echoing Wu, he told *Business Insider* that ad-driven media was "broken" because corporations fund it "in order to advance their goals. . . . We believe people who write and share ideas should be rewarded on their ability to enlighten and inform, not simply their ability to attract a few seconds of attention." When Jim VandeHei left as CEO of Politico in 2016 to start a provocative online publication, *Axios*, he assailed the "crap trap" of "trashy clickbait" designed to attract more page views and thus to satisfy advertisers. The "trap" was set by a reliance on ads. For *Axios* to produce quality journalism, he said, "readers will have to pay up and if they need and love the product, they will, and gladly so."*

The thoughts are noble, the analysis of what often ails advertising-supported content is correct. But the economics don't support the noble idea. The economics of Axios certainly doesn't support Vande-Hei's bold words, for roughly 90 percent of Axios's revenues, one of their principal investors says, comes from corporate sponsorships, or advertisers who are granted a sandwiched paragraph and often a picture introduced with headlines like this: "A MESSAGE FROM BANK OF AMERICA." Hillary Clinton and Donald Trump didn't agree on much in the 2016 presidential contest, but they did agree that most Americans in the middle were being squeezed, their incomes frozen. Although median income did rise between 2014 and 2015, it was little changed from the pre-recession year 2007. The Census reports that median household income in 2009 was $54,988; by 2015 it had inched up to only $56,516. And those just below median income but above the poverty line saw their income drop. The Brookings's

---

* Jim VandeHei, The Information.com, April 19, 2016.

Hamilton Project found that, after adjusting for inflation, wages in the U.S. rose just 0.2 percent over the past forty years.

Think about the subscription toll today, including mobile phone, broadband, cable or satellite TV, newspaper and magazine subscriptions, Netflix, HBO or Showtime, Amazon Prime, apps, music. Jeffrey Cole, who teaches at USC, says the average household pays monthly subscription charges of $267 per month, which does not include electricity, gas, and other unavoidable monthly bills.

How do most overstretched consumers pay more? They probably don't. There are, of course, successful efforts to reduce dependence on advertising. Hulu is growing its subscriber base. The Apple App Store rang up $2.7 billion in subscriptions in 2016. Spotify's subscriber base swelled from thirty million to fifty million in 2016. Amazon's Prime membership, for a modest annual fee of $99, offers an estimated sixty million subscribers free delivery, free streamed movies and television shows, free music, and other enticements. The *New York Times*'s reliance on advertising revenue has been cut from 80 percent to about 40 percent. (But unlike most newspapers, the *Times*— like the *Wall Street Journal* and the *Financial Times*—could pull off this feat because they successfully raised the subscription price and their affluent readers were willing to pay.)

Some novel experiments to lessen reliance on advertising have also been tried. Rather than impose a paywall to deny free online access to news stories, a practice followed by most newspapers, the *Guardian* provides open access. But at the bottom of each story they append this:

> **Since you're here . . .**
> . . . we have a small favour to ask. . . . If everyone who reads our reporting, who likes it, helps fund it, our future would be much more secure. For as little as $1, you can support the *Guardian*. . . .

Readers can then click on a credit card or PayPal link. A total of 300,000 readers volunteered a contribution, the NiemanLab reported in November 2017. Another 500,000, they reported, either joined various membership programs for a monthly fee granting them access to various events and newly published books, or were print or digital subscribers. These monies now eclipse the *Guardian*'s ad revenues.*

For those not wanting to see ads, YouTube offers Red for $9.99 per month. Many other platforms charge extra to be free of commercials. It is not uncommon to hear the argument advanced by entrepreneur Kevin Ryan, a founder of DoubleClick and *Business Insider*: many could afford new subscriptions because they "are going to Starbucks and paying five dollars a day for a coffee."

Maybe. But let's return to the economics. The *New York Times*'s subscriber base is expanding nicely, up by 46 percent between 2015 and 2016. They, like the *Washington Post,* have done a spectacular job puncturing the untruths and disarray of the Trump administration, and they've been rewarded with a burst of new digital subscribers. These subscribers have made the *Times* less reliant on ad dollars. This is great news. But, and here's the rub: the *Times* makes most of its profits from the print newspaper, including 62 percent of its advertising revenues. And it's not clear how a much-cheaper-to-produce digital newspaper could generate comparable ad revenues.

Why? The average reader of the print edition of the *Times* spends about thirty-five minutes a day with it. But the average online *Times* reader spends about thirty-five minutes *a month*. Because advertisers know readers spend much less time looking at their ads, they pay

---

* Nevertheless, the *Guardian* is still bathed in red ink losing $61 million in fiscal 2016–2017.

about 10 to 20 percent for the same online ad as appears in the news-paper.

Despite the growth in digital subscribers, and the rise of circulation revenues of 3.4 percent, and the growth of digital ad revenue of 5.9 percent, the overall revenues and profits of the paper fell in 2016. This left the *Times* to caution about its future in its 2016 annual financial report, "We may experience further downward pressure on our adver-tising revenue margins."

By the end of the third quarter in November 2017, the *Times* re-ported that despite the further erosion in print newspaper revenues, overall revenues rose by 6 percent. Obviously, if the *Times* could one day abandon its print edition, the cost savings in paper, printing, and distribution might offset the disproportionate profits the print paper generates. Or if the *Times* can increase its subscription revenues from 60 to 70 percent, as it hopes it can, analyst Ken Doctor has written that the *Times* could escape from its struggle to maintain slim profits to "generate actual, lasting growth, ahead of inflation." Alas, *Times* prof-its in the years ahead will be slim. And like other smart analysts, Doctor knows that if the *Times* succeeds in maintaining slim profits, it will be an aberration, not a trend for other newspapers. The dominant trend was defined by Gannett's *USA Today* and its 109 regional newspapers, and chains like McClatchy and A. H. Belo, which saw their 2017 print advertising and circulation losses exceed their digital advertising and subscription gains.

No question: consumers can reconfigure their cable bundles and can make choices among various subscription models. But to believe that the bulk of consumers who live on tight budgets can afford sub-scriptions as a substitute for the ad dollars that subsidize most of our "free" media and Internet activity is to ignore the math.

Yet the conundrum is that the advertising ATM subsidy may also be unreliable. The thought many marketers try to banish is whether for consumers—spoiled by Netflix and YouTube, by ad-skipping DVRs and ad blockers, by personal devices we hold in our hands—the interruptive ad message may be a relic. Are consumers irrevocably alienated by sales pitches? Has the consumer, on whom marketing relies, become a frenemy?

19.

"NO REARVIEW MIRROR"

"Two weeks ago I skied down the mountain in Deer Valley and it's the first time I didn't have a rearview mirror in a long time."

—Michael Kassan

Disruption has not always been kind these last several years to marketers, but it has been kind to Michael Kassan and Media-Link. By mid-2016, Kassan was ready to make some real money. He was soon to turn sixty-six, and his sole other shareholder, Wenda Millard, was sixty-three. LionTree's Aryeh Bourkoff's exploration of a possible sale was heating up. By summer, Kassan confided that he had four bidders. He guessed that in any deal he would agree to sign up for another five years, and his company would command a sales price in the $150 million range, with performance rewards driving the price up from there.

Bourkoff explored a range of possible suitors, including the talent agencies in Hollywood who had branched out as marketers, the advertising holding companies, the consulting companies, digital giants like Facebook or Google that were encroaching on the ad business, and perhaps a company in the events business that was eager to expand. "Someone asked me if I would be interested in buying it," Martin

Sorrell says. He was not interested. He believed the natural home for MediaLink "would be one of the consultancies." Kassan did have personal discussions with his friend Maurice Levy about being acquired by Publicis's consulting arm, Sapient. That idea was attractive to Kassan, for he was especially fond of Levy and Sapient was competing with McKinsey and Accenture to offer strategic marketing advice to the C-suite. "In pure strategy," Kassan said, "we do make a difference."

The problem working for an agency holding company or a Facebook or a consulting company with a roster of clients was that MediaLink would have to shed its neutrality. How to conduct agency reviews of your parent company as a neutral? Financially, he might be willing to consider abandoning his agency review business because "reviews are not a big percentage of my business. Single digits." But they were a big part of his power.

More than a few members of the advertising community thought Kassan's "neutrality" claims were a salesman's contrivance. "I choose sides," Rishad Tobaccowala of Publicis says of Kassan, whom he has known for years. He was uncomfortable that Kassan did not choose sides. "There are two forms of Switzerland 'neutrality.' You are neutral. Or you sell out to everyone equally, and everyone pays."

Although he does not assail Kassan publicly, Martin Sorrell knows how to inflict pain. When Kassan attended WPP's afternoon Stream conference during the 2016 Cannes festival, Sorrell came over to Kassan's table at an outdoor picnic lunch and loud enough for others to hear exclaimed, "I hear you're selling your company!" Kassan was horrified, and enraged, but laughed it off. Late that night, he huddled with Bourkoff. By August, Kassan said he had an offer from an unnamed consulting company that he would not accept.

Looking ahead, Kassan and Bourkoff scanned the field of possible suitors, assessing their pluses and minuses. With his friend Maurice Levy soon to step down as CEO of Publicis, and with the uncertainty as to who would succeed Sorrell, John Wren, and Michael Roth, all north of the customary retirement age, their stocks might be impacted. Viselike cost pressures on the holding companies were tightening, driven by C-suite demands to slash spending, by fears of corporate raiders mounting hostile takeovers, and by poisonous and spreading mistrust between clients and agencies. Procter & Gamble would announce that over the next five years it would slash its $10.5 billion marketing budget by $2 billion. Keith Weed's Unilever, which fended off a Kraft Heinz takeover assault in February 2017, would cut its agency fees by nearly 20 percent and the number of ads it produces by 30 percent, especially impacting its foremost supplier, WPP.

Clearly, Jon Mandel's 2015 speech to the ANA, and the K2 transparency report that followed, had injured the agencies. When the ANA's annual report on agency compensation was published in May 2017, it revealed that advertisers were "aggressively addressing transparency concerns and streamlining and simplifying agency compensation practices." Senior management involvement in negotiations with agencies, the ANA reported, more than doubled from 33 percent three years earlier to 73 percent, and agency fees were shrinking. In an offshoot of Mandel's "kickback" claims, by the summer of 2017, five of the six giant holding companies, it was reported, were also in the crosshairs of the Department of Justice, being investigated for cheating clients, though by the spring of 2018, no legal action had been instituted. The Justice probe allegedly centered on whether agencies, to fatten their wallets, engaged in bid rigging of production contracts by leaning on independent production houses they did business with to submit inflated bids for production work, allowing the in-house production arm of the agency to submit a lower bid and win the contract. (By the spring of 2018, this alleged probe remained a mere rumor.)

By contrast, turmoil remained MediaLink's friend. The K2 report "forced the agencies not to make money the way they used to," Michael Kassan says. He doesn't believe they were doing anything criminal. They were doing what their contracts allowed. However, motivated clients questioned their agencies more severely and amended their agency contracts. "We're in more agency reviews now than we were in 2015 and 2016," Kassan says. In the summer and fall of 2017, MediaLink would conduct agency reviews for Anheuser-Busch, Intuit, Lego, Mattel, and Subway, among others. At the same time, troubled agencies sought Kassan's counsel, as did newspaper and magazine companies, consulting firms, Facebook, Google, and many digital aspirants.

■ ■ ■

Few companies escaped the turmoil. Although Les Moonves's CBS seemed in particularly good shape—its revenue sources swelled, its profits exceeded those of two decades ago, by the end of the 2016–17 season CBS had been number one in prime time fourteen of the last fifteen seasons, and its stock price had soared. But there was no ducking the fact that it confronted existential threats. Live viewing is dropping, and one day the networks would not be able to charge advertisers more for less. "The joke's going to be over at some point," Kassan, among others, flatly predicts. A hit show like *American Idol* on Fox in 2002 attracted a prime-time audience of nearly forty million viewers. A hit show like *Empire* on Fox in 2016 attracted one quarter as many. Even if delayed viewing and a swelling American population yielded comparable audiences for hit shows over the course of a month, advertisers knew that many fewer commercials were watched. "What is declining is people watching the ads," Kassan says. "Brands need to find another way to communicate their brand message." Plus, the young viewers advertisers craved were fleeing, many to shorter videos watched on smart phones where 30-second ads are a no-no. Prime-time viewing among those under the age of thirty-four, Nielsen reports, plunged by 34 percent over the past five years. And unlike digital television streamed over the Internet, which scooped up data on its viewers, broadcast television could only tell advertisers the broad demographics of who watched but not supply deeper data on individuals who actually watched. By the end of 2017, Michael Nathanson of MoffettNathanson projected that total TV advertising would drop by 5 percent, which would include network as well as cable and station declines.

Long term, Irwin Gotlieb believed the networks were making a potentially fatal mistake by selling their programs to video on demand competitors like Netflix, and that this would pose a future risk to advertisers. "There are two fundamentals that are impacting the television business today," he says. "The first is we are gradually training people to consume less linear content—you watch it when a network schedules it— and to consume more nonlinear content—you decide when you want to watch it. That's a problem because television as a medium was initially built around the concept that you create a schedule and a promotion strategy that relies on people seeing the promotion at the right time." Nonlinear watching means networks need "new ways to think about scheduling, and it will weaken their ability to promote their schedule," inevitably shrinking their audience. "Second, viewing is moving from advertiser-supported content to subscriber-supported content. We have already passed the tipping point where subscriber-supported content can outbid the advertiser-supported channels anytime they choose to. This trend will have long-term implications. This is a huge problem, because supply will go down because there are no commercials. That's a huge problem for advertisers. And it's a huge problem for legacy media."

Mindful that content platforms like CBS and Disney were, in the short term, corralling huge profits by selling movies and TV programs to Netflix while in the long term building up a muscular frenemy, Disney announced in August 2017 that it would cease selling movies to Netflix in 2019. In another potentially disruptive move, CEO Bob Iger also announced that it would begin streaming sports (including ESPN) and movies and TV programs directly to consumers—as Les Moonves had earlier promised for CBS's own streaming services, highlighted by the exclusive offering of a popular *Star Trek* series. Both were implicitly proclaiming that they were competing with Netflix. They were also, in effect, admitting they were competing against their cable distribution partners, allowing more consumers to potentially drop their expensive cable subscriptions and substitute cheaper "skinny bundles" of Disney and CBS and other content. Whether cable distributors would continue to pay hefty retransmission consent fees to networks for "exclusive" content that was not exclusive invited a potentially massive and destructive future clash.

Another possible short-term enticement for the network entered the mix in the summer of 2017, when Apple said it planned to spend $1 billion annually on TV shows and movies to compete against Netflix and Amazon, and both Facebook and Google also announced they would expand their original program offerings, aiming to siphon some of the $70 billion advertising dollars now earmarked for traditional television. If these digital giants seek to buy network shows, once again Les Moonves and his network brethren must decide whether to take the easy money but risk strengthening a frenemy. If Apple, Google, and Facebook aim simply to launch their own original programs targeted at younger audiences, it will take them years to amp up.

This battle awaits another day, perhaps after Les Moonves is gone. In the meantime, Moonves is not following Disney's lead in yanking content from Netflix. He has received deserved plaudits for his skill at diversifying CBS's revenue streams, which were projected to rise over the next several years. Standing on the Carnegie Hall stage for CBS's Upfront presentation in the spring of 2017, Moonves glowed as brightly as his purple tie. Despite the speed of change and the many challenges, he told the audience, "In this fragmented world, the social and economic value of any medium with the power to bring people together is more important than ever, and that's what we do here. . . . Great content is always king."

❊ ❊ ❊

Carolyn Everson was equally bullish as 2016 came to a close. She had just turned forty-six and was entering her seventh year at Facebook, a year that would see Facebook reach two billion monthly users. Google and Facebook were gobbling up 77 percent of every new global advertising dollar.* Everson believed the measurement travails of the fall were history. In the year-end diary she privately composes each year she wrote:

> Our business has exceeded all expectations and we are trusted by the industry as to "who has your best interests at heart?" When I speak to our closest C-level marketers, they believe that "Facebook delivers more than they take," that we are a culture of givers, and we simply care more about growing their business than any other partner. We led the industry to develop standards for measurement that could be used across media and we have set ourselves apart from the "noise" about digital not being transparent.

By January 2017, her optimism would resemble Voltaire's Dr. Pangloss—this is "the best of all possible worlds"—as an avalanche of embarrassing Facebook and YouTube headlines stirred a massive backlash. Exposed was their reliance on automated machines to place ads on sites deemed offensive to advertisers, their platforms' role in transporting unverified "fake" news, a cascade of new measurement

---

* Rob Norman, "Interaction," GroupM preview, February 2017.

mistakes, and stories about how their data might threaten user privacy. Advertisers cried foul and began to pull some of their ads. Onstage at the June 2017 Cannes Lions Festival, Keith Weed complained that 60 percent of advertising online is directed to bots. "We want to buy eyeballs of viewers, not bots," he said. Procter & Gamble's Marc Pritchard warned that his ad dollars would not be funneled to digital companies unless their advertising and brand safety was verified by independent measurement firms. Then in the fall of 2017, Facebook embarrassingly disclosed that it had unknowingly accepted ads aimed at dividing Americans during the 2016 presidential campaign, ads that were paid for by a shady Russian company with Kremlin ties.

The trust issue, which has hobbled relations between agencies and clients, now subverted Facebook and Google's relations with advertisers. Carolyn Everson and her Google counterparts made efforts to assuage advertisers. But it was a "serious" setback for Facebook and Google, Kassan said as he looked back later in 2017. "Last year at Cannes if you stood on the Croisette and looked at duopoly beach"—Facebook and Google's popular cabanas on the beach—"you would have thought they were impregnable. What we found out in this last cycle was that they were penetrable. Facebook has all the issues around measurement and YouTube has all the issues around brand safety. In the Upfronts this week, everybody's story was 'Brand Safety, Brand Safety.'"

Why did Facebook and Google screw up?

"It happens online because they don't have a filter," Kassan said. He went on to say of his mentee, Carolyn Everson, "She was affected profoundly. Carolyn is somebody who has a high standard. This impugns her integrity, and she's not comfortable with it. Nor should she be." She knew advertisers and agencies were less trusting, more suspicious of Facebook.

To gauge and defang the level of mistrust toward Facebook, Everson retained Kassan and MediaLink. She did lean on Kassan for advice, she says. And she goes out of her way to praise Marc Pritchard, a forceful critic of digital practices, who she says, "called on us to lead the way to clean up what he would call 'the digital swamp.'" Everson retains the humility to be a really good listener, which helps explain her ability to win over critics. Of Pritchard she says, "He's been advising me. He's been a mentor to me."

Yet by the fall of 2017, advertising clients still grumbled. In a presentation he made to an Advertising Week audience in September 2017, Keith Weed offered a report card to Facebook and digital companies. He gave them a mere C for Ad Fraud, and an even harsher F for Cross Platform transparency, insisting, "We've got to see over the walled gardens" and allow measurement companies to monitor and measure their claims.

Everson knew another big challenge for Facebook in coming years was what she calls the "regulatory environment globally." Beginning in the winter and spring of 2017, a chorus of critics weighed in against the digital giants, warning that governments must police companies like Facebook, Google, Apple, Microsoft, and Amazon because they threatened both competition and privacy. Data was "the oil of the digital era," *The Economist* editorialized in May 2017. "Old ways of thinking about competition, devised in the era of oil, look outdated in what has come to be called the 'data economy.'" Abundant data, they continued, alters the nature of competition, and companies with this data benefit from network effects. The data empowers Google to "see what people search for, Facebook what they share, Amazon what they buy." They have the resources to erect "barriers" to entry by absorbing potential competitors. And their abundant data allows a peek into private lives, employing this information as a marketing tool.

Apple raised its voice against Facebook and Google. With little reliance on advertising, in September 2017 Apple wielded privacy as a weapon against its digital competitors. For its upgraded Safari browser,

Apple said it would limit how advertisers and websites could use cookies to track and target users. Apple was, once again, portraying itself as a company on the side of consumers and their privacy. Arrayed against Apple were the trade groups of the entire advertising universe—the Interactive Advertising Bureau, the ANA, and the 4A's. In an open letter, they accused Apple of "sabotage," insisting that the blocking of cookies could murder the advertising business.

Governments were awakened. The European Union was questioning Facebook's privacy protections. The British government announced that it was weighing whether to demand that Facebook and Google delete personal information from their data banks. The attorney general of Missouri announced an antitrust investigation of Google, and nearly forty State Attorney Generals joined in a demand to learn how Facebook guards privacy. The *Australian*, the Murdoch-owned national newspaper, revealed a twenty-three-page Facebook presentation that offered advertisers the ability to target over six million Facebook users, some as young as fourteen, who have said in their posts that they felt "worthless," "insecure," "defeated," and needed a boost. (Facebook denied that it offered tools to advertisers to target emotionally vulnerable people. But *Wired* magazine exposed their misleading response when it noted that Facebook did not "explain how the research on minors ended up in a presentation to potential advertisers.") The Federal Trade Commission was investigating Facebook's massaging of user data, and was urged to investigate Google's privacy policies. Convinced that Google was violating its antitrust laws by favoring sites it owned in its search results, the European Union wanted to inspect Google's crown jewel, its search algorithm, which was fiercely resisted as Google claimed it was an attempt to protect and strengthen European business competitors. By the summer of 2017, the EU announced it would impose a huge $2.7 billion fine on Google. In May 2018, the 28 countries of the EU imposed a General

Data Protection Regulation, requiring companies to obey strictures limiting what personal information they could collect – or face severe fines. Mark Zuckerberg was summoned to testify before Congress in April 2018. Concerned with maintaining their political control, China and authoritarian governments on various continents had already sealed their borders to Facebook and Google.

░ ░ ░

By early 2017, Aryeh Bourkoff had unearthed a surprise buyer and was close to completing the sale of MediaLink. His pitch, he says, was simple: "Michael Kassan sits at the epicenter of all that is going on in the advertising landscape. In an information- and events-driven business, you want to drive more connectivity and brand awareness. Michael is a rare figure whose relationship acumen can really help to blow up awareness and help businesses and brands everywhere."

"It's a big day for us. It's a big day for everybody," Kassan said on February 7 while standing in the open workspace at MediaLink, his staff arrayed in front of him, with the CEO of the company he would now report to, Duncan Painter of Ascential, standing to his side. Ascential is a public company in the UK that owns the Cannes Lions Festival, operates out of offices in sixteen countries, and offers nineteen different services and subscription products to businesses, including festivals and exhibitions and publications. With his booming voice amplified by a handheld wireless microphone, Kassan strode across the space in front of the windows overlooking the Avenue of the Americas. Casually attired in a blue zippered sweater over an open-necked pale-blue dress shirt and grey slacks, he came back to the center of the room to perch on a marble stool. Painter stood to his side in a charcoal-grey suit, white shirt, and plain grey tie. This was an 8:30 A.M. staff announcement; the media would be served a press release and invited to speak to Kassan and Painter by phone afterward.

"We want to help you expand globally," Painter affably said, speaking in a reassuring way. He was amazed, he said, to learn of "the high regard clients had for you. We see ourselves as enablers, and we're proud to make you our twentieth brand." MediaLink served about two-hundred-plus companies around the world, Painter said in the press release. "We serve 24,000, so we want to get MediaLink in with their business model through all the applicable businesses and clients that we work with."

"What this means for everybody," Kassan said, "is that we'll expand our global footprint. We will open London and Hong Kong offices this year." Otherwise, "things will stay the same." He said that he had signed a four-year contract and that Wenda Millard had also signed a long-term contract. "The name on the door will still be MediaLink. There will just be more doors." He stressed their shared approach: "Neutrality is a key focus of both businesses."

Kassan and Painter later shared with the press for the first time that MediaLink's revenues reached $56 million in 2016, generating a profit of $14 million. The purchase price entailed a cash payment of $69 million—less than half the $150 million Kassan had guessed in June, but the purchase price would climb to $207 million over three years if MediaLink hit its targets. In truth, MediaLink was a relatively small company, as was Ascential, its revenues just topping $300 million.

Although Kassan told his staff MediaLink would "still be an arms-length partner with Cannes Lions," he expected we "will expand what we do in Cannes." Just as they started an Entertainment vertical in Cannes in 2016, inviting entertainment figures to speak, which was highlighted by an interview Kassan conducted with Les Moonves. Perhaps a sports vertical was next, he said. What Kassan didn't say that morning was that each of the 120 MediaLink employees would receive sizable bonuses, which came out of his and Wenda Millard's pocket from their 100 percent ownership of MediaLink. He also didn't announce this day that Wenda Millard would step aside as president, become vice chair, and move to London to open their office there and begin MediaLink's global expansion.

The night before the announcement, Kassan took care to phone and alert five holding company CEOs: Maurice Levy of Publicis, John Wren of Omnicom, Michael Roth of IPG, Yannick Bolloré of Havas, and Martin Sorrell of WPP. He told friends that four of the five "were effusive in their congratulations and kudos. Martin just said, 'Thank you for the call.'"

    ■ ■ ■

With Kassan and Sorrell seemingly secure in their roles, there promised to be lots of opportunities for these frenemies to interact over the next several years. Seventy-two and still robust, Sorrell was unlikely to step down anytime soon. Lazard vice chairman Jeffrey Rosen, who was WPP's lead independent director and served on the board for almost eleven years until June 2015 and is an ardent admirer of Sorrell's, says the board's independent directors "always thought about and discussed succession. Martin always hated discussing it because it was like discussing his own mortality. The board became much more systematic about it in 2010, and Martin started talking with us about succession formally once a year and informally more often." The chair of the WPP board, Roberto Quarta, publicly addressed the succession question in April 2016: "Whether, in Sir Martin's case, that happens tomorrow, in one, two, three, four, or five years, or even over a longer period, we have already begun to identify internal and external candidates who should be considered."

Could she imagine, Cristiana Falcone was asked, her husband retired?

"No!" she exclaimed, laughing hysterically. "Can you imagine him in my kitchen putting knives and forks in order? I would have to out-source to a call center in India to call him all the time!"

Sorrell offered another version of his wife's response when asked in 2017 about his future at WPP: "I will stay here until they shoot me!"

Of course, the deft Sorrell might choose another way to exit. Several years ago he did negotiate to sell WPP to Warren Buffett, but they did not see eye to eye on the price and the discussions amicably collapsed. It is not inconceivable that consulting or software companies who are rumbling into the marketing space and have deep pockets could seek to acquire WPP. "I'm making this up. I have no knowledge," Michael Kassan says. "But if I'm Accenture or Adobe or Oracle, and I'm mov-ing into that business and I have the market cap, why not buy it?"

One reason not to buy it was delivered in a July 2017 report by Brian Wieser of Pivotal. He was one of several analysts to downgrade the stocks of the advertising holding companies from "Buy" to "Hold." He wrote, "It's a difficult time for the agency holding companies." He cited "slowing underlying business growth for core clients, zero-based bud-geting at many of them, more aggressive" procurement officers, client mistrust, new competitive threats, increasing reliance on automated ma-chines, and evidence that the engines of their economic growth, the media agencies, were sputtering. In a fall 2017 analysis of the agency business, Wieser concluded, "Negative narratives toward agencies in general and WPP in particular are likely to continue for some time."

Sorrell and his holding company compatriots were anxious. Wor-ried about costs and unconvinced that advertising dollars equaled growth, clients, particularly consumer goods clients who accounted for one third of WPP's revenues, hacked away at their agency spend-ing. Spurred by the ANA-sponsored investigation, mistrustful clients reopened agency contracts searching for loopholes. With rising politi-cal and economic volatility, most companies, including agencies, grew cautious. The holding companies altered their future public financial projections, from 2 percent or slightly higher overall growth to flat or barely above that in 2017 and maybe 2018. WPP's stock price, like that of the other holding companies, plunged. It's a mistake to curb advertising spending because it assures growth, Sorrell warned. "Our industry may be in danger of losing the plot."

Whether slowed growth is temporary or not, agencies are destined to change. There is no way to know today if AT&T and McDonald's insistence on having a single large agency provide one-stop shopping will be the future model. Or if David Droga is correct that a small agency like Droga5 is less afraid of losing business and will thrive because he offers clients fearless independence: "Our starting point is that clients pay us for our opinion, not to take dictation."

But what if Bob Greenberg is right and the agency model is really a dinosaur? During WPP's earnings call with analysts in August 2017, when Sorrell was asked about a drop-off in business, he said his company's "first critical priority" was to get its employees to work "horizontally," offering integrated teams to better serve clients. Ben Thompson, who writes the acute *Stratechery* business blog, dismissed Sorrell's response as "feeble" because it assumed the main competitive threat was from rival agencies. But as advertising and marketing shifts to a plethora of digital platforms, Thompson wrote, the idea of agencies as the essential middleman, "a one-stop shop for advertisers," fades into history. The Internet ends the limited ad space of old media as online stores like Amazon offer unlimited shelf space. Distribution and transaction costs become "zero," and "the critical competency is discovery"—where to find and target desired customers. At the same time, discovery on digital is monopolized by two companies, Facebook and Google. (He overlooked emerging rival Amazon.) Assuming that all media, old or new, will in the future be delivered digitally, the problem agencies haven't confronted, he concluded, is that "their business model is obsolete." Since "there are only two places an advertiser might want to buy ads, the fees paid to agencies . . . become a lot harder to justify." Clients, he believes, will turn to Google and Facebook to serve as their media agency.*

Whether this analysis is correct or not, few question that the infrastructures of giant holding companies will have to be slimmed, Kassan says. "I do not think it is deck chairs on the *Titanic* for the holding companies. But they have to end up with a smaller ship." Martin Sorrell, who is never passive, has begun to aggressively combine some of his agencies together, wringing costs out via consolidation.

Further consolidation among the six holding companies is an expectation expressed by more than a few senior marketing executives. They expect there will be at least one marriage among the six, as there almost was when Omnicom and Publicis announced they would marry but broke up before the wedding. Speculation today usually centers on Dentsu, a company that lacks creative agencies, making a bid for, say, IPG. Or for Bill Koenigsberg's Horizon, an independent agency whose revenues eclipse those of Dentsu and Havas. Or perhaps a deep-pocketed consultant company will make an offer one of the agencies can't refuse.

Unquestionably, the importance of data to target consumers assures that media agencies will become more vital and that clients will insist that creative and media work more closely. And as media agencies become more central, as he nears seventy the advertising career of the Yoda of the media agency business, Kassan's closest friend, Irwin Gotlieb, is coming to a close. He has a daughter and grandchildren in California, and he's not happy with the poisonous mistrust enveloping the business. While relaxed in his Seventh Avenue office sipping an espresso in the summer of 2017, he said, "I was brought up in a business where you put your clients' interests first, your company's interests second, and your own personal interests third. Today's environment makes that kind of thinking naïve." Told he sounded like he had one

---

* Ben Thompson, *Stratechery*, September 6, 2017.

foot out the door, he declined to confirm or deny this. (In April 2018, Gotlieb announced he was stepping down as Global Chairman of GroupM.)

Further muddying the succession questions at WPP was the surprise departure in August 2017 of Brian Lesser, the North American CEO of GroupM. The well-regarded Lesser, who assumed that role in 2016, was thought to be a potential successor to Gotlieb and maybe one day to Sorrell. "He was very much on a fast track," Gotlieb says sadly. But he chose to become CEO of a new advertising and analytics division at AT&T reporting directly to CEO Randall Stephenson.

Why did Lesser leave? A senior WPP executive who asked not to be named traced the cause back to Jon Mandel's speech and the ANA investigation. "Many agency people are dispirited. They call us crooks. They say our people will go to jail. Yet no one has produced evidence to fault us on. It's really hard to come to work and put your clients' interests first. The long-term consequence is you lose good people. Brian is just the tip of the iceberg."

Unexpectedly, Martin Sorrell became part of the iceberg. On April 14th 2018, the WPP board announced that, after thirty-three years as CEO, Sorrell had resigned, prior to receiving a report from an outside law firm hired by the board to investigate his alleged "personal misconduct." Sorrell vehemently denied the allegation. We don't know for certain the cause; the board and Sorrell agreed to sign, in the words of someone close to the board, "strict NDAs," meaning that they would not share the results of the investigation. This lack of transparency has provoked a hurricane of rumors among WPP executives and the advertising community.

It seems unlikely the board would have ordered an investigation unless they had reason to believe there were serious infractions. However, the board had said earlier that the "allegations" against Sorrell "do not involve amounts which are material to WPP." And, after he resigned, the board treated his departure as a retirement rather than a termination, allowing him to continue to enjoy stock grants and inviting him to be "available to assist with the transition." Gracious? Perhaps. Transparent? About as transparent as Facebook.

What is clear, a securities expert I spoke to shortly after Sorrell's resignation said, is that the true reasons for Sorrell's departure will eventually get out, despite the NDAs. His prediction was, "the SEC will be announcing an investigation, as will the Financial Conduct Authority, in England." Shareholder lawsuits will demand that the company define what "material" amounts are. For a company with almost twenty-one billion dollars of revenue, and with Sorrell earning sixty-eight million dollars last year, is a hundred thousand dollars material? Is five million? Is twenty?

Looking back, what is also clear is that Martin Sorrell's unexpected departure from WPP blemishes an unusually successful business legacy. A senior WPP executive, saddened by Sorrell's departure, is reminded of famed wrestler Dan Gable: "He had a stellar career, and yet a blemish unfairly marred it. Gable was one of the great wrestlers in college and the Olympics. He was undefeated—until he lost his last match."

■ ■ ■

Les Moonves's future at CBS seemed clearer. In May 2017, his CBS contract was extended another two years, to mid-2021, when he will be approaching his seventy-second birthday. "I have not come up with anything I like better than what I'm doing now," he says when asked what else he might like to do. He loves going to the Super Bowl, "but if I never go to another I'm fine. I've done twenty-five Super Bowls, twenty-five Grammy Awards, twenty Kennedy Center Honors. I've seen most places in the world. No matter what happens, they can't take what I've accomplished away from me. I think my legacy's been established."

What wasn't as clear was CBS's future. Believing content is king, Moonves had wanted to find a way to acquire the much larger Time Warner, but AT&T swooped in. "They would have been a good fit for us," he admits. He had always wanted to own a movie studio under the CBS umbrella, but now says, "Owning a studio is not as glamorous." His eyes were fixed on owning a more profitable television production studio, which was the allure of Time Warner. This helps explain his ambivalence to heed the wishes of Shari Redstone, whose family's National Amusements owns 80 percent of the voting shares of both Viacom and CBS. Shari Redstone wanted the two companies to merge with Moonves as CEO. Viacom's Paramount studio had faltered, as had MTV and many of its cable channels, and she believed Moonves might remedy this.

Publicly, in 2016 Moonves professed his reluctance and said he was not in a standoff with Redstone over whether he or she would control the board of the combined companies. "Control was not a very large issue," he says. However, privately, through his attorney, Martin Lipton of Wachtell, Lipton, Rosen & Katz, Moonves did in fact demand control. A three-page September 30, 2016, letter from Lipton to Redstone's attorney, Christopher E. Austin of Cleary Gottlieb Steen & Hamilton, declared, "an appropriate governance framework" was "critical" if the two companies were to be united. Assurances were needed that the new "management team will have complete and irrevocable authority to manage the combined businesses." The form of these assurances were contained in nine demands Lipton attached to the last page. Instead of board control residing in the hands of Redstone, it specified that control would reside in the hands of independent directors, three quarters of them truly "independents," including the addition of all the current CBS directors; Redstone would appoint only two of the board members. And to remove Moonves, who would serve as both chairman and CEO, would require "approval by two-thirds of the independent directors."

Despite her eagerness to combine the companies and lure Moonves as CEO, Shari Redstone was not about to cede her voting control of the company, and the secret negotiations ended.

With media consolidation a fact of life—AT&T buys first DirecTV and then makes a bid for Time Warner; Charter buys Time Warner cable; Verizon buys AOL and then Yahoo, which it renames Oath; Time, Inc. sought and found a buyer, as did MediaLink. And even Rupert Murdoch announced the sale of much of 21st Century Fox to Disney. Moonves acknowledged that tech and telephone companies were sniffing around content companies like CBS. In an interview with *Bloomberg News* in the spring of 2017, Verizon CEO Lowell Mc-Adam publicly proclaimed that AT&T's "buying into content has made people reevaluate their portfolio." He said he would be interested in a merger with CBS, Disney, or Comcast. But Moonves said he liked the hand he was holding. In a conference call with analysts, Moonves declared, "We've always said we are self-contained and we like our position."

But Les Moonves has an ultimate boss, Shari Redstone, and she doesn't like his position. She is clearly convinced, as are members of the Viacom board, that Viacom lacks the resources to make bold acquisitions. Like others, they were stunned when Rupert Murdoch announced the sale in December 2017 of most of his film and TV studio and other assets to Disney, claiming that Fox lacked scale. More troubling, they believe Viacom's financial growth has plateaued. Redstone believes a marriage between the weaker Viacom and the more robust CBS offers potential financial salvation. And she wanted Moonves to be in charge. But Redstone has told associates she would never give up her ownership control to Moonves or anyone else.

Into the spring of 2018, Redstone and Moonves negotiated. They differed over the price CBS was willing to pay to acquire Viacom. They differed over whether Moonves or Redstone would choose the COO of the combined companies. Perhaps most of all, they differed over whether Moonves or Redstone would control the combined companies.

With Shari Redstone unbending, it appeared that the most successful television executive of the modern era might be outed, just as the most successful advertising executive was.

◼ ◼ ◼

It has long been a goal of Carolyn Everson's to one day be a CEO. Asked about this with a Facebook PR person in the room, she answers, "It's not a goal I think about now. I literally love what I'm doing. . . . Maybe in five years." Asked the same question in the summer of 2017 without a Facebook colleague present, Everson candidly says, "I have a mixed answer to that question. Part of me feels as though I have the best job in the world working for a life-changing company and running revenue larger than many Fortune 500 companies. Another part of me says, 'Is there another chapter for Carolyn Everson?' I don't know."

"If she wants to get on the CEO track, then she has to step off the track she's on," her mentor, Michael Kassan, says. "Sometimes she has to take a step back to take a step forward," meaning it is likely that before a CEO job would be offered she would want to step out of her revenue-generating role and take another executive position. He cites the example of another mentee, Wendy Clark, who was once CMO of Coca-Cola: "If she does well as CEO of DDB, she can be CEO of Coca-Cola."

◼ ◼ ◼

Michael Kassan confronts many looming questions. Is MediaLink a one-man shop, a company too dependent on his remarkable skills and relationships? "Michael is unique," Maurice Levy says. "The biggest challenge Michael will have is how to scale. MediaLink is a boutique of artisans, of craftsmen and craftswomen, and I don't know how many Michaels there are on earth." Kassan demurs. Ascential would not have spent so much money "just for Kassan," he says. "They saw a real team. We built an extraordinary team. We have over a hundred clients today." (As we've seen, the press release announcing the sale said two hundred.) "You think I could alone keep a hundred clients happy?"

One of the individuals Kassan is banking on to play a huge future role in the growth of MediaLink is his first chief of stuff, Grant Gittlin. Gittlin believes the resources of their new parent company will provide MediaLink with the scale it needs. "There's a really good reason we should have been sold," he says. "A service company our size lacks infrastructure. When purchased by a large company, we will benefit."

Six months after MediaLink announced its sale, Michael Kassan said of his corporate parent, "It's working out well. We have tremendous momentum. They're great partners and they are letting us run our own business."

MediaLink's parent company hit some turbulence during the June 2017 Cannes Lions Festival. Offended by the steep costs and sometimes Babylonian excesses, Martin Sorrell slashed the number of WPP executives attending by half, to five hundred. He again claimed people feel "ripped off" by the Festival, and said that in 2018 they would reevaluate coming to Cannes. Irwin Gotlieb chose not to attend in 2017. His room at the Carlton cost $2,500 a night and he said he was required to pay for ten nights even though he stayed fewer. This and what he said was the total cost for room, food, travel, and entertainment—about $75,000—annoyed him. What outraged him was the inefficiency of what he called a "a boondoggle. The crowding is not conducive to getting business conducted. You can't get in or out of the lobby of the Carlton." What was once a celebration of creativity, he believed, had warped into a party. And he was upset that the $63 million the Lions hauled in this year and the money they generated from the 41,170 award entries made "the largest awards ceremony in our business"—and the most prestigious—"a for-profit event. I think as an industry we deserve a nonprofit award," as is true of the Academy Awards, the Tonys, Grammys, or Emmys. Interestingly, he and Sorrell are not on the same page on the awards, for Sorrell says the primary value of Cannes for WPP is in the awards. "Winning the awards is our number-one objective," he declared (before WPP won Holding Company of the Year in 2017 for the seventh straight year).

Maurice Levy's successor at Publicis, CEO Arthur Sadoun, also took a shot at the Cannes Lions. On the eve of the 2017 gathering, Sadoun announced that in 2018 none of his employees would attend Cannes or submit entries in any awards programs, and would engage in no other promotional events. Instead, he said, Publicis would invest the savings in Marcel, an internal tech platform connecting and sharing information and talent among Publicis's eighty thousand employees; it would, he hoped, transform their ability to collaborate.

While many Publicis employees were surprised and upset by Sadoun's seemingly impulsive announcement, they weren't as concerned as Ascential's team was. The stock market sent Ascential's stock tumbling on the news. To prevent a fire from spreading, the Festival hurriedly assembled a prestigious advisory committee that included Keith Weed and Marc Pritchard. "There have been a lot of discussions this week about the structure of the Festival, and we want to create the right Cannes Lions experience for all participants," said Philip Thomas, who had been promoted to CEO of Ascential Events. Despite the criticism, Festival revenues rose 7 percent in 2017. Nevertheless, this growth fell short of the 18 percent spurt for the Festival in 2016.

Michael Kassan stoutly defended his new corporate parent and the Festival. In an op-ed commentary in *Campaign US*, an online advertising news publication, he implicitly rebuked his friend Irwin Gotlieb, not to mention Sorrell and Sedoun. The Cannes Lions, he wrote, was not "a giant, rosé-infused party. . . . If you can't extract value from Cannes Lions, you aren't approaching it properly. And if you lost your compass because Cannes looks so different than it used to, that's because our industry is in the midst of transformation." The Cannes Lions "has been reinvented the same way the industry is being reinvented."

ALL GOOD.

It wasn't "ALL GOOD" to Martin Sorrell. In the fall of 2017, he escalated his attack on the Cannes Lions. An enterprising *Adweek* reporter got hold of internal WPP e-mails from Sorrell demanding that they withdraw from Eurobest, an advertising conference put on by Ascential. Sorrell also threatened: unless the Cannes Lions streamlined the Cannes conference and reduced costs, WPP might withdraw entirely. A decision would await a summit meeting between Sorrell and Ascential's Duncan Painter.*

With agencies being squeezed by clients and competitors, Ascential eased their financial burden by announcing major changes for the 2018 Cannes Festival. Instead of eight days, the festival would conclude after five; the number of rewards and thus submission costs would be reduced; delegate passes, which had cost more than 4,000 euros, would be slashed to 900 euros; working with the city of Cannes, hotel prices would be frozen and more than fifty restaurants would offer delegates less expensive fixed-price menus. A smiling Arthur Sadoun said Publicis would be happy to return in 2019. And Martin Sorrell said he was pleased Ascential had agreed to reduce some of what he considered bloated costs, but wanted to see additional changes he chose not to specify.

And what about Michael Kassan's future?

His attitude toward retirement was similar to Martin Sorrell's. "It will never happen," says his wife, Ronnie. "He can't sit home. He needs to be doing something."

In truth, Kassan was even more ebullient than normal; the sale of

---

* Patrick Coffee, "WPP Tightens the Screws on Cannes Lions Owner amid Threats to Skip Next Year's Festival," Adweek.com, September 27, 2017.

MediaLink lifted a giant burden from his shoulders. I caught a glimpse of that burden the first time I tried to quiz Kassan about his legal travails in California. He insisted he did not want me to record or take notes at this session. It was late in the fall of 2016, months before the 2017 sale of MediaLink. We were in his glassed office with the doors closed and no staff present. He asked that there be no phone call interruptions. Salads waited on the small round table in his office, but he did not eat. As he started recounting the events of three decades ago, he started to sob. He was speechless. With the ALL GOOD sign above his head, he confessed to being terribly self-conscious, not certain if people knew of his past and fearful that they did. Not having spoken of this in many years, this buoyant man found it hard to open up. We agreed to confront the subject on the record at a later date. If I wanted to raise it in an e-mail, he asked that I send any communication on the matter to his personal Gmail so it would be private.

In the course of interviews over the next few months, he relived what happened to him in California and its courts, his conviction for embezzlement, his suspension from the practice of law, and the California State Supreme Court's acknowledgment that he made a mistake but did not take money from investors to enrich himself, and his vindication in his battle with the State Bar of California. But always he wondered: Did people know? Did they think he had been an embezzler? Did they whisper about his past?

Some did. "Michael Kassan embodies the contradictions of advertising," one senior marketing executive who knows him well confides after being promised anonymity. "Those in the business have no definable expertise. We're an insecure profession. Unlike lawyers or those in finance or journalism, we don't have advertising degrees. You make commercials and you're a star. Here we are in the middle of a kickback controversy, with complaints about a lack of transparency, with the ANA hiring a detective agency to investigate, yet the industry is advised by a man who was once drummed out of business, disbarred, for similar crimes." This executive did not know the specifics of Kassan's past, and much of what he thought he knew was dead wrong. But the whispers were exactly what aroused Michael Kassan's paranoia.

Weeks after the February sale of MediaLink, Kassan sat at a corner table at Scalinatella and opened up about why he now felt relief: "Two weeks ago I skied down the mountain in Deer Valley and it's the first time I didn't have a rearview mirror in a long time. Ascential looked at the record and said, 'OK.'"

Kassan felt comfortable. He believed that Ascential did their due diligence and concluded that MediaLink was not a one-man operation, that he had built a sturdy company. Humbly he said, "It's easier to have this conversation today because of the sale. I needed the validation. It's emotional. OK, take a breath."

He took a sip from his dry martini and said he was fortified by the four thousand supportive e-mails he received after the sale announcement. Before, whenever he thought of writing a book the title he had in mind was *"Confessions of a Jewish Prince.* Now it's *No Rearview Mirror."* He smiled broadly.

ACKNOWLEDGMENTS

Given that I've written about the media and communications for *The New Yorker* since 1992 and before that as an author, some friends wondered why I was drawn to write a book about advertising and marketing. The idea, *pace* Watergate, was to "follow the money." Without ad dollars, most old or new media would starve.

When I began reporting the book in the late spring of 2015, I had no fixed ideas or sweeping conclusions. And three years later, while I offer no sweeping bromides I do offer a picture of an industry convulsed by profound change. The reporting encompassed approximately 450 interviews, all recorded. These interviews are woven throughout this book, though readers will find few Trumpian personal pronouns, à la *Reacting to my brilliant question, he/she said . . .*

The introduction to this book is, however, written in the first person. I blame my editor, Scott Moyers, for this. Scott said it was important for me to draw a link between my subject and the larger context, offering a sense of the reporting I have pursued for the past three decades. Scott is special. One hears constant complaints about editors at publishing houses who don't do more than a cursory edit, overwhelmed as they often are by a steady rush of new titles. I don't know where Scott finds the time to so fully engage, but he does. I signed on with him when my longtime editor at Random House, Jason Epstein, retired. And I left with Scott and Ann Godoff when they departed for Penguin. I am happy to say we are all back together after Penguin merged with Random House.

While I'm at it, I'd also like to thank, in addition to conductor Ann Godoff, the other members of her orchestra who helped harmonize this effort, including Ann's immediate boss, Madeline McIntosh, president of Penguin Publishing Group; fastidious copy editor Jane Cavolina and her supervisor, Victoria Klose. In the preproduction phase, Christopher Richards and Beena Kamlani, assisted by Mia Council, are the capable editors who were entrusted to help make the publication trains run on time. Their allies in the marketing department were Matt Boyd and Caitlin O'Shaughnessy. As we neared the June 2018 publication date, publicity director Sarah Hutson sprang into action. I had worked with Sarah starting several books ago when she joined Penguin. Her rise to the top of her department is no surprise. She is ably fortified by Colleen Boyle.

I brought this book to HarperCollins in London in order to work with my long-time editor, Ed Faulkner. Although Ed has his name adorned with the title Publisher, this distinction has not intruded on his ability to focus on serving as a first-class editor. Assisting Ed were editor Zoe Berville and the publicity and marketing team of Polly Osborn, Rosie Margesson, and Jasmine Gordon.

My agent and friend, Sloan Harris of ICM, weighed in with invaluable editorial advice. Representing the foreign rights for this book, Gordon Wise of Curtis Brown UK, once again served me well. A salute to my friend Terry McDonell, a member of the American Magazine Hall of Fame, who volunteered his deft editing eye to an early draft of this book. All the people who had a hand in making this book better, I thank. Any mistakes are, of course, mine.

A word about the people in the industry: I would have written a very different book without the array of individuals who generously made themselves available for multiple interviews and allowed me to view some of their sausage making. A special hat tip to Michael Kassan, who dared open his life and also kept me both informed and laughing. His team at MediaLink, especially Wenda Millard, were always helpful, including Martin Rothman and Vilna Joven. I am grateful for the time and brainpower offered by four of the smartest people in the advertising/marketing business: Martin Sorrell and Irwin Gotlieb at WPP, Rishad Tobaccowala at Publicis, and Randall Rothenberg of the Interactive Advertising Bureau. Carolyn Everson and members of her Facebook team like Adam Isserlis defied the emerging, and often accurate, Facebook stereotype: they were not opaque. Les Moonves was generous with his time, as were his colleagues at CBS. So, too, were Beth Comstock and Linda Boff and their GE colleagues, and Anne Finucane and her compatriots at Bank of America. Ditto Bob Greenberg of R/GA, Keith Weed of Univision, and Gary Vaynerchuk of VaynerMedia, among others whose many names would swell this brief acknowledgment into a tome. The stream of news from a couple of dozen daily posts from *MediaPost* and its indefatigable editor in chief, Joe Mandese, and from industry bibles such as the online *Ad Age* and its print parent, *Advertising Age*, offered valuable daily updates on the industry they cover.

Several reader alerts: Although this book most often uses the shorthand "advertising" rather than joining together advertising and marketing, I do so because advertising is a more familiar term and uttering both terms together is a mouthful. Advertising and marketing, in fact, are two sides of the same coin. They take different forms—an IM alert or a supermarket product coupon versus a TV ad—but each vies to sell something to the consumer.

Unless a publication, study, or book is cited in the text and footnoted, the quotes were given to the author. Thus, I saw no need to include page-by-page author's notes, since it would have repetitiously reported, *This was told to the author on such and such a date.* And with Google search at our fingertips, if a report or news story is not footnoted I saw no need to add thick pages of notes when the study or news source is cited in the text.

A reader might also ask: Why does this book spend so much more time on digital giant Facebook rather than that even larger giant, Google? Blame me. Because I extensively reported on Google for a 2009 book, *Googled: The End of the World as We Know It.* I wanted to mix it up.

Unless otherwise explained, the ages of those described in these pages match the year when they first appear in this book.

Finally, the idea for this book was sparked by my wife, Amanda "Binky" Urban. If she needed another career after literary agent, she would be a brilliant editor.

BIBLIOGRAPHY

Barnouw, Erik. *The Sponsor*. New York: Oxford University Press, 1978.

Barnouw, Erik. *A Tower of Babel: A History of Broadcasting in the United States to 1933*, vol. 1. New York: Oxford University Press, 1966.

Barnouw, Erik. *Tube of Plenty: The Evolution of American Television*. New York: Oxford University Press, 1990.

Beers, Charlotte. *I'd Rather Be in Charge: A Legendary Business Leader's Roadmap for Achieving Pride, Power, and Joy at Work*. New York: Vanguard Press, 2012.

Bell, Daniel. *The Cultural Contradictions of Capitalism*. New York: Basic Books, 1976.

Berger, Jonah. *Contagious: Why Things Catch On*. New York: Simon and Schuster, 2013.

Bernays, Edward. *Biography of an Idea: Memoirs of Public Relations Counsel Edward L. Bernays*. New York: Simon and Schuster, 1965.

Bernays, Edward. *Propaganda*. New York: Routledge, 1928.

Bogart, Leo. *Strategy in Advertising: Matching Media and Messages to Markets and Motivations*. Lincolnwood, IL: NTC Business Books, 1990.

Boorstin, Daniel. *The Americans: The Democratic Experience*. New York: Random House, 1973.

Brinkley, Alan. *The Publisher*. New York: Alfred A. Knopf, 2010.

Carr, Nicholas. *The Shallows: What the Internet Is Doing to Our Brains*. New York: W. W. Norton, 2010.

Chandler, Alfred D. *The Visible Hand: The Managerial Revolution in American Business*. Cambridge, MA: Harvard University Press, 1977.

Cracknell, Andrew. *The Real Mad Men: The Renegades of Madison Avenue and the Golden Age of Advertising*. Philadelphia: Running Press, 2011.

Della Femina, Jerry. *From Those Wonderful Folks Who Gave You Pearl Harbor*. New York: Simon and Schuster, 1970.

Dreiser, Theodore. *Sister Carrie*. New York: Doubleday, 1900.

Dwyer, Jim. *More Awesome Than Money: Four Boys and Their Heroic Quest to Save Your Privacy from Facebook*. New York: Viking, 2014.

Einstein, Mara. *Black Ops Advertising: Native Ads, Content Marketing, and the Covert World of the Digital Sell*. New York: OR Books, 2016.

Essex, Andrew. *The End of Advertising: Why It Had to Die, and the Creative Resurrection to Come*. New York: Spiegel & Grau, 2017.

Farmer, Michael. *Madison Avenue Manslaughter: An Inside View of Fee-Cutting Clients, Profit-Hungry Owners and Declining Ad Agencies*. London: LID Publishing, 2015.

Fox, Stephen. *Mirror Makers: A History of American Advertising and Its Creators*. William Morrow, 1984.

Galbraith, John Kenneth. *The Affluent Society*. Boston: Houghton Mifflin, 1958.

Galloway, Scott. *The Four: The Hidden DNA of Amazon, Apple, Facebook, and Google*. New York: Portfolio|Penguin, 2017.

Gates, Bill. *Business @ the Speed of Thought: Using a Digital Nervous System*. New York: Warner Books, 1999.

Gates, Bill. *The Road Ahead*. New York: Viking, 1995.

Gleick, James. *Genius: The Life and Science of Richard Feynman*. New York: Vintage Books, 1993.

Goodrum, Charles, and Helen Dalrymple. *Advertising in America: The First 200 Years*. New York: Harry N. Abrams, 1990.

Goodson, Scott. *Uprising: How to Build a Brand—and Change the World—by Sparking Cultural Movements*. New York: McGraw-Hill, 2011.

Greenberg, David. *Republic of Spin: An Inside History of the American Presidency*. W. W. Norton, 2016.

Halberstam, David. *The Powers That Be*. New York: Alfred A. Knopf, 1979.

Higgins, Denis. *The Art of Writing Advertising: Conversations with Masters of the Craft*. Lincolnwood, IL: NTC Business Books, 1986.

Hower, Ralph. *The History of an Advertising Agency: N. W. Ayer & Son at Work, 1869–1949*. Revised edition. Cambridge, MA: Harvard University Press, 1949.

Hurman, James. *The Case for Creativity: The Link Between Imaginative Marketing & Commercial Success*. London: AUT Media, 2011.

Isaacson, Walter. *The Innovators: How a Group of Hackers, Geniuses, and Geeks Created the Digital Revolution*. New York: Simon and Schuster, 2014.

Isaacson, Walter. *Steve Jobs*. New York: Simon and Schuster, 2011.

Kirkpatrick, David. *The Facebook Effect: The Inside Story of the Company That Is Connecting the World.* New York: Simon and Schuster, 2010.

Klein, Naomi. *NO LOGO.* New York: Picador, 2000.

Kluger, Richard. *Ashes to Ashes: America's Hundred-Year Cigarette War, the Public Health, and the Unabashed Triumph of Philip Morris.* New York: Alfred A. Knopf, 1996.

Kluger, Richard. *The Paper: The Life and Death of the New York Herald Tribune.* New York: Alfred A. Knopf, 1986.

Lasch, Christopher. *The Culture of Narcissism.* New York: W. W. Norton, 1978.

Lawrence, Mary Wells. *A Big Life (in advertising).* New York: Alfred A. Knopf, 2002.

Levenson, Bob. *Bill Bernbach's Book: A History of the Advertising That Changed the History of Advertising.* New York: Villard Books, 1987.

Lessig, Lawrence. *Code and Other Laws of Cyberspace.* New York: Basic Books, 1999.

Lessig, Lawrence. *The Future of Ideas: The Fate of the Commons in a Connected World.* New York: Random House, 2001.

Lippman, Walter. *Public Opinion.* New York: Macmillan, 1922.

Lois, George. *What's the Big Idea?: How to Win with Outrageous Ideas (That Sell).* New York: Doubleday Currency, 1991.

Maas, Jane. *Mad Women: The Other Side of Life on Madison Avenue in the '60s and Beyond.* New York: St. Martin's Press, 2012.

Mayer, Martin. *Madison Avenue U.S.A.: The Extraordinary Business of Advertising and the People Who Run It.* Lincolnwood, IL: NTC Business Books, 1992.

Mayer, Martin. *Whatever Happened to Madison Avenue? Advertising in the '90s.* Boston: Little, Brown, 1991.

McLuhan, Marshall. *Understanding Media: The Extensions of Man.* New York: McGraw-Hill, 1964.

Ogilvy, David. *Blood, Brains & Beer: The Autobiography of David Ogilvy.* New York: Atheneum, 1978.

Ogilvy, David. *Confessions of an Advertising Man.* New York: Atheneum, 1986.

Ogilvy, David. *Ogilvy on Advertising.* New York: Vintage, 1985.

O'Neil, Cathy. *Weapons of Math Destruction: How Big Data Increases Inequality and Threatens Democracy.* New York: Crown, 2016.

Packard, Vance. *The Hidden Persuaders.* New York: Simon and Schuster, 1957.

Pertschuk, Michael. *Revolt Against Regulation: The Rise and Pause of the Consumer Movement.* Berkeley: University of California Press, 1983.

Pope, Daniel. *The Making of Modern Advertising.* New York: Basic Books, 1983.

Postman, Neil. *Technopoly: The Surrender of Culture to Technology.* New York: Alfred A. Knopf, 1992.

Presbrey, Frank. *The History and Development of Advertising.* New York: Doubleday, 1929.

Reeves, Rosser. *Reality in Advertising.* New York: Alfred A. Knopf, 1961.

Riesman, David, with Nathan Glazer and Reuel Denney. *The Lonely Crowd.* New Haven, CT: Yale University Press, 1950.

Roman, Kenneth. *The King of Madison Avenue: David Ogilvy and the Making of Modern Advertising.* New York: St. Martin's Press, 2009.

Rothenberg, Randall. *Where the Suckers Moon: An Advertising Story.* New York: Alfred A. Knopf, 1994.

Schmidt, Eric, and Jared Cohen. *The New Digital Age: Reshaping the Future of People, Nations and Business.* New York: Alfred A. Knopf, 2013.

Schudson, Michael. *Advertising, The Uneasy Persuasion: Its Dubious Impact on American Society.* New York: Basic Books, 1986.

Smith, Sally Bedell. *In All His Glory: The Life of William S. Paley.* New York: Simon and Schuster, 1990.

Starr, Paul. *The Creation of the Media: The Political Origins of Modern Communications.* New York: Basic Books, 2004.

Stengel, Jim. *Grow: How Ideals Power Growth and Profit at the World's Greatest Companies.* New York: Crown, 2011.

Steyer, James P. *Talking Back to Facebook: The Common Sense Guide to Raising Kids in the Digital Age.* New York: Scribner, 2012.

Taplin, Jonathan. *Move Fast and Break Things: How Facebook, Google, and Amazon Cornered Culture and Undermined Democracy.* Boston: Little, Brown and Company, 2017.

Tungate, Mark. *Adland: A Global History of Advertising.* London: Kogan Page Limited, 2007.

Wakeman, Frederic. *The Hucksters.* New York: Rinehart & Company, 1946.

Wind, Yoram (Jerry), and Catharine Findiesen Hays. *Beyond Advertising: Creating Value Through All Customer Touchpoints.* Hoboken, NJ: John Wiley, 2016.

Wu, Tim. *The Attention Merchants: The Epic Scramble to Get Inside Our Heads.* New York: Alfred A. Knopf, 2016.

Wu, Tim. *The Master Switch: The Rise and Fall of Information Empires.* New York: Alfred A. Knopf, 2010.

Wunderman, Lester. *Being Direct: Making Advertising Pay.* New York: Random House, 1996.

Vaynerchuk, Gary. *#AskGaryVee: One Entrepreneur's Take on Leadership, Social Media & Self-Awareness.* New York: HarperCollins, 2016.

Veblen, Thorstein. *The Theory of the Leisure Class.* New York: Macmillan, 1899.

INDEX